PROPHECY FULFILLED

The Old Testament Realized in the New

PROPHECY FULFILLED
The Old Testament Realized in the New

by
René Aigrain and Omer Englebert

Translated by
LANCELOT C. SHEPPARD

With a Preface by JOHN M. OESTERREICHER

DAVID McKAY COMPANY, INC.
New York

The texts of the Holy Bible from the books of Genesis, Exodus, Leviticus, Numbers, Deuteronomy, Josue, Judges, Ruth, Job, Psalms, Proverbs, Ecclesiastes, Wisdom, and Sirach contained in this book are reproduced by license of Confraternity of Christian Doctrine, Washington, D.C., the owner of the copyright of the translation quoted. Used with its permission. All rights reserved.

Preface

WHEN God wished to disclose His will and way, He made history a means of His communication. Events were His voice, and so was the speech of inspired men. At the beginning the voice sounded only in one small corner of the earth, in one brief period of the world's existence, that later it would be heard wherever there are human ears. It was in the land of Israel, in the days of her patriarchs, prophets, and sages, that God spoke to the people of His choice and through them to all mankind; it was there and then that He prepared the coming of Him who is His first and final Utterance, the Word-made-flesh. Thus the history of ancient Israel is sacred history, history truly universal, and the books that relate it are not merely the chronicle of one people, they are also the story of the Church in the making, the record of the youth of all men redeemed.

But of what use is the story of the Old Covenant to the heirs of the New, now that the former has given way to the latter, more perfect and full of grace? Is it not the sign of maturity to cast away the things of the child? Yes and no. Some things must be discarded, others retained. The fully integrated man has the wisdom of age and the firmness of manhood, but for all that holds fast to the vigor and enthusiasm of youth, to the confidence and openness of childhood. Some institutions of the Ancient Dispensation have lost their binding power. Having been fulfilled in Christ, the laws of diet, the rites of purification, the rules of sacrifice no longer obligate Christians. Still, if we listen, they speak to us of the luster that was theirs: to keep the children of Israel apart, free from pagan contamination; to mortify their bodies and souls that they may learn submission to the divine will; to keep alive in them the need, the desire, the cry for redemption. But there are many other marvels of the Advent that, far from being dead, live on in the Church. The fruit of Christ's love —of the Heart opened with a spear so that blood and water flowed from it—she is also the fruit of the wonders God wrought in the days of old and of the wisdom the Holy Spirit gave to the seed of Abraham.

The ringing of bells, for instance, reminds the Church of the gentle melodies of David's harp and of the thunder that dispersed Israel's foes. In the music of the organ she sees a continuation of the song with which the chosen people praised God to the sound of trumpets and cymbals. At the consecration of a bishop, one of the prayers recalls the instructions God gave to Aaron, the high priest. When an abbess is consecrated, she is likened to Miriam, Moses' sister, who led the women of Israel with tambourine and dance safely through threatening sea. Again, the Church hopes that every bride be clothed with the glory of Sarah, Rebekah, and Rachel; that she be as dear to her husband, as prudent and faithful as they were. And, most significant of all, heaven the Church calls Abraham's bosom.

Heaven is called Abraham's embrace because the patriarch is the father of all the faithful. When told to leave his ancestral home and go to a new land, he obeyed. Offspring was promised him, numerous as the stars of the sky, and he believed, though no heir was born to him, year after year. When finally the birth of Isaac was announced, Abraham did not doubt that Sarah's withered womb would blossom. Years later, he was called to sacrifice the son of promise, still he was ready. Clearly, Abraham's way is a pattern; he is alive in all who truly believe in the living God.

And so are Isaac and Jacob. While one was an instrument in the hands of God from first to last, the other wrestled with Him. We, too, are the work of His hands and at the same time His co-workers: sons of His love and conquerors of His heart. A similar relevance to our spiritual life could be shown with regard to all the chosen men and women of the Ancient Dispensation. To follow Christ is to be of their company, too.

There would be no Church today, no divine covenant with all mankind, had there not been the covenant with what the liturgy calls the one people. Never could we have heard Christ's gospel of redemption, had not Israel first received the good news of creation, of Love that made and moves the world; had not the prophets preached the terror of sin and the wonder of forgiveness; had not the Old Testament taught justice and hope. Such is the interpenetration of the Old and the New, the unbroken economy of salvation. Hence a bishop about to be consecrated affirms that One is the Author of the Law, the Prophets, and the Apostolic Writings: God, the almighty Lord.

Here the bishop speaks for the whole Church. This Oneness is the belief of every Catholic. But to make this belief more than lip profession, we must know and love the whole of Scripture. If we do and walk again and again the road divine truth traveled through the centuries of preparation, we learn to marvel at the pains God took in bringing about our redemption; we learn to marvel at His patience and unfailing providence.

To this end, toward a deeper knowledge of the essential unity of the two covenants, the present book should be a valuable aid. Abbé Aigrain and Abbé Englebert have stored a great deal of basic information in *Prophecy Fulfilled* and will therefore win many friends among those seeking an orientation in a field both vast and rich. Though my approach differs from theirs, I welcome their work.

Christ, the Light of the world, has come; yet the goal of history will not be reached till the final manifestation of God's kingdom, when God will be all in all. Thus the Christian, like the Israelite of the exodus, is a pilgrim, a man en route, one marching through the desert toward the land of promise, toward an indescribable goal.

JOHN M. OESTERREICHER

The Institute of Judaeo-Christian Studies
Seton Hall University

Translator's Note

IN THE original French work the numerous quotations from the Bible are taken from an authorized French translation made from the original languages in which the books of the Bible have come down to us. In producing an English rendering of this work, the translator was faced with the by no means easy problem of deciding what authorized English version of the Bible to use for these quotations. The Douay version is a translation from the Vulgate (itself a translation from the original languages into Latin) which is not always based on so accurate a text of the originals as we nowadays possess. The translation by Msgr. R. A. Knox (which has much to recommend it as a translation into English) suffers from the same drawback: it is a translation from the Vulgate. The Confraternity Bible, now in course of publication, is unfortunately not yet complete, but that part of the Old Testament which is published, since it is translated from the original tongues, in every way, both in point of English and of accuracy, fulfills the needs of this book. It was therefore decided to use it for those books of the Bible in which it is available.

In consequence, all quotations from the books of Genesis, Exodus, Leviticus, Numbers, Deuteronomy, Josue, Judges, Ruth, Job, Psalms, Proverbs, Ecclesiastes, Canticle of Canticles, Wisdom, and Sirach (Ecclesiasticus) are taken from

"*The Holy Bible*, translated from the original languages with critical use of all the ancient sources by members of the Catholic Biblical Association of America, sponsored by the Episcopal Committee of the Confraternity of Christian Doctrine," Volumes I (Genesis to Ruth) and III (the sapiential books, Job to Sirach)—published by the St. Anthony Guild Press, Paterson, New Jersey, 1952 and 1955.

All other books of the Bible are quoted from the Douay version.

Whenever the Douay translation offered a notably different version from that given in the French original of this book, the sense of the passage has been given between square brackets [   ]; occasionally the sense of the French has been given in the main text in order not to spoil the continuity of the sense, and in this case the Douay rendering has been given within square brackets immediately afterward, or else an explanation has been added in a footnote. On one or two rare occasions it has been necessary to follow the same practice with the quotations from the Confraternity version.

Readers are referred to the important footnote on page 10 which lists the books of the Bible in their categories with their names and, in cases where it applies, their alternative names, and explains the numbering of the Psalms.

The names of the books of the Bible are the same in all versions except for the following, which correspond:

1 Samuel	1 **Kings**
2 Samuel	2 Kings
3 Kings (1 Kings)	3 Kings
4 Kings (2 Kings)	4 Kings
1 Paralipomenon	1 Chronicles
2 Paralipomenon	2 Chronicles
Nehemias	2 Esdras
Sirach	Ecclesiasticus

This book uses the names as given in the first column.

By referring to this table, no difficulty should be encountered in finding at once in the Bible the passages quoted or referred to in this book.

L.C.S.

Contents

xi

Maps

PROPHECY FULFILLED

The Old Testament Realized in the New

Introduction

THE BIBLE, as the origin of the word (from the Greek *biblos*) signifies, is for all Christians *the* Book above all others, since in their view it contains the word of God. Yet, in practice, for many the Bible consists of the New Testament. If they are aware that the Bible contains also the Old Testament, they know it only in theory, so little are they acquainted with this part of Scripture. Some are almost hostile to it; others are inclined to regard it only as forming a part of the history of religions; those who seek in it sustenance for their spiritual life are rare indeed.

Of course the New Testament contains the principal truths of our faith, but not everything that God has revealed to man can be found in it. He spoke, according to the Epistle to the Hebrews, "at sundry times . . . in times past to the fathers by the prophets . . . in these days [he] hath spoken to us by his Son." (1:1-2). It is in the books of the Old Testament that the first revelations made by God are to be found.

If it is true that the word of God is a "living word"—since it comes from Him who lives eternally and its purpose is to obtain life for us—is it not offending God and doing great injury to ourselves to regard the Old Testament as a dead letter?

In this book we hope to help bring about a better understanding by portraying the riches that are contained in the Old Testament and by showing those who are unacquainted with them the way in which they may be discovered.

As we shall see presently, Jesus himself teaches us to regard the Old Testament as an enduring message, with universal application (Chapter 1).

Proof that He considers it as the word of God in regard to himself is found in the fact that He continually refers to it as the sanction for His mission and the confirmation of His teaching.

But He also desires that we regard it as the word of God in application to ourselves. If it were otherwise, He would have warned us. He would not have failed to declare that the revelations made to Moses and the Prophets were reserved to the Jews, that they belonged to a past now gone, and that, in consequence, we need no longer concern ourselves with them. Yet He asserts precisely the contrary: "Do not think," He says, "that I am come to destroy the law, or the prophets. I am not come to destroy, but to fulfil. For amen I say unto you, till heaven and earth pass, one jot, or one tittle shall not pass of the law, till all be fulfilled" (Matt. 5:17-18).

Isaias had already contrasted the eternal nature of the divine word with the perishable nature of earthly things:

All flesh is grass,
    and all the glory thereof as the flower of the field. . . .
The grass is withered, and the flower is fallen;
    but the word of the Lord endureth for ever.
(Isa. 40:6, 8)

What Jesus teaches amounts then to this:

I have come not to destroy the foundations laid by my Father, but to consolidate them and build on them my house and yours. I have come not to abolish the maxims and precepts that He revealed, but to restore to them their original purity and to add to them this second part of the Revelation, which will complete it and facilitate entry into the kingdom of heaven.

The Apostles, faithful interpreters of the teachings of our Saviour, gave the same credence to God speaking in the Old Testament as to God speaking in the Gospels.

Similarly, the Church never considered them separately. To her own New Testament she added the sacred books of the Jews and pronounced anathemas on those Christians who tried to exclude them from the Scriptures. Polycarp, bishop of Smyrna and Saint John's disciple, said to Marcion, who dared to do this: "I regard you as Satan's first-born." And not long ago Pius XI, condemning certain protagonists of racial purity who out of hatred for the Jews desired to exclude the Old Testament from the Bible, stated the orthodox Christian teaching on the subject in the following terms:

> The sacred books of the Old Testament are all God's Word, an organic part of His revelation. . . . He who wants to see the biblical history and wisdom of the Old Testament banished from the Church and school, blasphemes the Word of God, blasphemes the Almighty's plan of salvation, makes the narrow and limited mind of man judge over the divine plan of history. He denies belief in the real Christ, who appeared in the flesh. . . . He stands uncomprehendingly before the world-drama of the Son of God . . . who brought the Old Testament to its fulfilment and completion in the New.[1]

As Pius XI stated, the books of the Old Testament contain both history and doctrine; and it is this twofold theme that we shall study in the pages that follow.

The history is that of the relations of God with humanity from Adam to the time of Christ; after Abraham, it is fused with the history of the Jewish people.

To the Jews, God gave the responsibility of transmitting to

[1] From the encyclical of Pope Pius XI to the Bishops of Germany: *On the Condition of the Church in Germany*, March 14, 1937.

humanity the promise of its redemption; to them He entrusted
the deposit of faith in Him, the one true God, and the Decalogue; from among them He raised up the Redeemer. The
Covenant that He made with them lasted until the coming of
Christ and the foundation of the Church.

In the Bible this history is set out at great length and sometimes with a lack of clarity. We have summarized it so as to
help the reader follow and remember it (Chapters 2, 3,
and 4).

For the same reason we have grouped together the teach-
ings scattered throughout the Old Testament. They concern
the nature of God (Chapter 5), the person of the Messias
(Chapter 6), the universal character of revealed religion
(Chapter 7), the future life (Chapter 8), the moral law
(Chapter 9), and the manner of worshiping and praying to
God (Chapter 10).

The benefits to be gained from careful reading of the Old
Testament are too many to enumerate here, and they will
appear clearly in the course of the book. Let us mention only
a few.

Some of them derive from the lessons of history, when
history is read as narrated under the inspiration of the Holy
Spirit; others, from the teachings of the Holy Spirit which
are found throughout the Old Testament.

It is clear that for effects to be known adequately, they
must be traced back to their causes; that to understand an
institution, its origins and evolution must be studied; that love
is sustained in large part by memories, and that gratitude for
gifts received is measured by the price that was paid for them.

The Old Testament will remind those Christians who have
forgotten it that their religion is as old as the world; that they
are the spiritual sons of Adam, Abraham, and the Prophets,
to whom the Redemption was revealed; that they are the heirs

of the Old Covenant, of which the New is both the continuation and fulfillment; that to them, as to the faithful Jews, are addressed the promises made, and kept, by Yahweh.

How patient and persevering were His efforts! How many the saints and great men He raised up! What miracles and successive revelations and interventions of all kinds were required, under the Old Covenant, to prepare the New, that is, the coming of the Messias!

For it is Christ that the Old Testament shows as the final cause of creation. He is the Alpha and Omega, the purpose and explanation of the divine plan.

Joys and sufferings, fidelity and betrayal, success and failure, the shedding of blood, the rise and fall of empires, the labors of the lowly, the virtues of the righteous, man's inventions and man's unrest—all, from the first year of the world to the first year of our era, occurred in order to lead to the Crib, the Sermon on the Mount, Calvary, and the Resurrection.

It all occurred for the incarnate Christ, and consequently for us, for whom the Incarnation took place—for us, the members of His Mystical Body, called to share His destiny and His glory.

When we remind ourselves of this, we are grateful. Once we understand this as the Holy Spirit has revealed it, we know the essential and the mind can be at peace. For the rest—the temporary triumphs of the evil spirit; the detours, enigmas, and seeming fantasies of the divine plan; a civilization falling in ruins; a hair that falls from one's head; in a word, all the ups and downs in the history of the world and in our own history—our understanding of it can await the time of its revelation to us.

The doctrines of the Old Testament are those which are indispensable to man and which, once they are understood, enable him to do without all others except, of course, the teaching of Christ. They concern God's nature and our own.

God is shown in the Old Testament as infinitely distant and at the same time understanding and near, as justice and sanctity itself, pursuing His ends by disconcerting but infallible means, seeming to have no other concern than man and his happiness, relentless against pride, touched by repentance, and, above all, merciful.

Man is shown with the dual tendencies of his nature, to which he has been reduced by original sin: good, yet wayward; above all, weak; often the plaything of his passions, of circumstances, and of the devil. His sole duty here below is to accomplish humbly the will of God. The Old Testament reveals it to him, whatever his age, his state, the means of transportation and the tools at his disposal, the civilization or the country in which he lives, the internal or external conditions under which he finds himself.

All this is taught us by the sages, and the saints as well; but God, man's creator and the only one who knows him in truth, shows it to us in a more useful and efficacious way, in tones that directly touch our hearts and melt away our resistance, in words that light up the path and give us the strength to make our way along it.

Since for man all depends upon the help he receives from God, we shall consider the prayers of the Old Testament.

The Psalms, especially, contain prayers to be said in joy and sorrow, in anxiety, when abandoned by men and apparently deserted by God, in prosperity, in poverty, in temptation, sin, disease, and death—in all circumstances that make up the web of human life and destiny. Written under the inspiration of the Holy Spirit, they have a beauty of expression, a lyrical quality, a power to touch man's heart that is beyond compare. In them, the soul finds full expression and has the impression that it is heard. And God does indeed hear these prayers and grant them, since no prayer of repentance, petition, and love will find a better road to His heart than those in words that He himself formulated.

These are only some of the "good things, old and new," *nova et vetera*, to be found in the Old Testament. Aside from the reading of the Gospels, there is no other reading that will help us as much to gain the greatest of all benefits within our grasp here on earth, the peace of heart which Jesus bequeathed to us on His ascension, desiring that it should remain with us until His return (John 14:27).

O.E.

CHAPTER 1

What the New Testament Says of the Old

By his human nature Jesus, the Son of Mary, of the line of David, was a Jew. Like him, all the authors of the New Testament except Saint Luke, Jews by birth and education, were steeped in the Scriptures. Although, except for Saint Paul, they did not frequent the rabbinical schools, the knowledge of the Scriptures which they acquired at the synagogue was completed in two ways: through the teaching given them by Jesus and the inspiration they received from the Holy Spirit on the day of Pentecost. As for the Master himself, who had not studied with the teachers of Israel, we know that the scribes were astonished to find him so well versed in the Scriptures; it is true, of course, that he knew all things by a knowledge that was not human.

THE OLD TESTAMENT IN THE WORDS OF JESUS

Of all those who in the New Testament bear witness to the Old, Jesus is the first to be heard.

In his day the thirty-nine books of the Bible were divided into three sections: the Law, the Prophets, and the Psalms. The Law corresponded with what we now call the Pentateuch; [1] the Prophets included the actual prophetical books

---

[1] The forty-five books of the Old Testament can be divided as follows: The books of the Law, the Torah, also called the Pentateuch, the five books of Moses: Genesis, Exodus, Leviticus, Numbers, and Deuteronomy.

and the historical books down to the end of the books of Kings; the Psalms comprised the Psalter and all the remaining writings. Our Lord used this division when he quoted the Old Testament. Let us note briefly what he said about it.

The substance of the Law, that is, the fundamental principles of religion and morality, Jesus declared to be sacred. Within this category fall especially the great precepts of Deuteronomy and Leviticus concerning love of God and of our neighbor:

> One of the scribes . . . asked him which was the first commandment of all. And Jesus answered him: The first

---

The historical books: Josue, Judges, Ruth, 1 and 2 Samuel (or 1 and 2 Kings), 1 and 2 Kings (or 3 and 4 Kings), 1 and 2 Paralipomenon (or 1 and 2 Chronicles), Esdras, Nehemias (or 2 Esdras), Tobias, Judith, Esther, and 1 and 2 Machabees.

The prophetical books: Isaias, Jeremias and the Lamentations, Baruch, Ezechiel, Daniel, Osee, Joel, Amos, Abdias, Jonas, Micheas, Nahum, Habacuc, Sophonias, Aggeus, Zacharias, and Malachias.

The sapiential books: Job, Psalms, Proverbs, Ecclesiastes, Canticle of Canticles, Wisdom, and Sirach (or Ecclesiasticus).

Six of these forty-five books (Tobias, Judith, 2 Machabees, Baruch, Wisdom, and Sirach) were not recognized by our Lord's Jewish contemporaries in Palestine, but they were admitted by the Jews of Alexandria. The Latin Church included them in the canon in the fifth century and the Greek Church followed her example. These six books are termed "deuterocanonical" (belonging to a second, or later, canon), while the thirty-nine others are known as "protocanonical" (belonging to the first canon).

Most of the books of the Old Testament were written in Hebrew, a Semitic language that in Palestine took the place of Canaanite; but from the fifth century onward Aramaic increasingly replaced Hebrew as the language in ordinary use, and Tobias and Judith, as well as parts of Esdras and Daniel, were writen in Aramaic. Wisdom and 2 Machabees were written in Greek.

The present division of the Bible into chapters dates from 1226; the division of chapters into verses was introduced in 1551, by the French printer, Robert Estienne.

It should be noted that the numbering of the Psalms is not the same in the Hebrew, in the Greek translation of the Septuagint, and in the Latin version of the Vulgate. After Psalm 9 the Hebrew version is one ahead of the Septuagint and Vulgate, because of this psalm it makes two, 9 and 10. The numbering corresponds again after Psalm 147, because the Septuagint and Vulgate divide this psalm in two. (For the origin of the Septuagint, see page 110.)

commandment of all is, Hear, O Israel: the Lord thy God
is one God. And thou shalt love the Lord thy God with
thy whole heart, and with thy whole soul, and with thy
whole mind, and with thy whole strength. This is the first
commandment. And the second is like to it: Thou shalt
love thy neighbour as thyself. There is no other commandment greater than these. And the scribe said to him: Well,
Master, thou hast said in truth, that there is one God, and
there is no other besides him. And that he should be loved
with the whole heart, and with the whole understanding,
and with the whole soul, and with the whole strength; and
to love one's neighbour as one's self, is a greater thing than
all holocausts and sacrifices. And Jesus seeing that he had
answered wisely, said to him: Thou art not far from the
kingdom of God. And no man after that durst ask him
any question (Mark 12:28-34).

The positive precepts of divine origin contained in the Law
were also firmly maintained by Jesus, though he freed them
from the casuistry and additions with which the jurists had
surrounded them. He did so, for example, when he declared
that it was no breach of the Sabbath (Exod. 34:21) to rub a
few ears of corn together in one's hand or to heal a sick man
on that day:

And it came to pass on the second first sabbath, that as
he went through the corn fields, his disciples plucked the
ears, and did eat, rubbing them in their hands. And some
of the Pharisees said to them: Why do you that which is
not lawful on the sabbath days? And Jesus answering
them, said: Have you not read so much as this, what David
did, when himself was hungry, and they that were with
him: How he went into the house of God, and took and
ate the bread of proposition, and gave to them that were
with him, which is not lawful to eat but only for the

priests? And he said to them: The Son of man is Lord also of the sabbath.

And it came to pass also on another sabbath, that he entered into the synagogue, and taught. And there was a man, whose right hand was withered. And the scribes and Pharisees watched if he would heal on the sabbath; that they might find an accusation against him. But he knew their thoughts; and said to the man who had the withered hand: Arise, and stand forth in the midst. And rising he stood forth. Then Jesus said to them: I ask you, if it be lawful on the sabbath days to do good or to do evil; to save life, or to destroy? And looking round about on them all, he said to the man: Stretch forth thy hand. And he stretched it forth: and his hand was restored. And they were filled with madness; and they talked one with another, what they might do to Jesus (Luke 6:1-11).

Particularly noteworthy is the series of contrasts that Jesus enumerated between what "was said to them of old" and what it was his mission to declare:

You have heard that it was said to them of old: Thou shalt not kill. And whosoever shall kill shall be in danger of the judgment. But I say to you, that whosoever is angry with his brother, shall be in danger of the judgment. And whosoever shall say to his brother, Raca, shall be in danger of the council. And whosoever shall say, Thou fool, shall be in danger of hell fire. . . .

You have heard that it was said to them of old: Thou shalt not commit adultery. But I say to you, that whosoever shall look on a woman to lust after her, hath already committed adultery with her in his heart. . . .

You have heard that it hath been said, Thou shalt love thy neighbour, and hate thy enemy. But I say to you,

Love your enemies: do good to them that hate you: and
pray for them that persecute and calumniate you (Matt.
5:21-4).

Jesus' emphasis here is not on the external act so solemnly
condemned by the Torah but on the interior disposition
(anger, impure thought, lack of charity) that leads to it.

The Prophets and the Psalms were frequently used by Jesus
either to endow the quoted texts with a more spiritual, a
broader meaning—this is the case with the text from Osee, "I
desired mercy [love], and not sacrifice" (Osee 6:6), quoted
by him on many occasions—or to correct the false beliefs of
some of his contemporaries, as in the case of the text from
Exodus concerning the God of Abraham, Isaac, and Jacob
(Exod. 3:6):

Now that the dead rise again, Moses also showed, at the
bush, when he called the Lord: The God of Abraham,
and the God of Isaac, and the God of Jacob; For he is not
the God of the dead, but of the living: for all live to him
(Luke 20:37-8).

But the most frequent use that Jesus made of the Prophets
and the Psalms was in quoting passages that foretold the reign
of the Messias, a prophecy fulfilled in his own person. Among
other passages that he used are those referring to the unbelief
of the willful deaf and blind (Isa. 6:9-10; 29:13), which is
contrasted with the praise from the mouths of babes and
sucklings (Ps. 8:3); the rejection by the builders of the stone
that became the cornerstone (Ps. 117:22-3); the coming of the
Son of Man on the clouds (Dan. 7:13); the sufferings of the
Messias prophesied by Isaias and Zacharias, which was to be
followed, according to the sign of Jonas, by the resurrection
on the third day.

Our Lord's statements also contain fundamental observations of more general bearing on the subject of the prophecies. From the beginning of his preaching he applied to himself the famous passage from Isaias (61:1-2) concerning the Lord's anointed who is sent to announce the Good News: "This day is fulfilled this scripture in your ears" (Luke 4:16-21). Later, in Jerusalem, alluding to Deuteronomy (18:15)—"A prophet like me will the Lord, your God, raise up for you among your own kinsmen; to him you shall listen"—he told the incredulous Jews, "Think not that I will accuse you to the Father. There is one that accuseth you, Moses, in whom you trust. For if you did believe Moses, you would perhaps believe me also, for he wrote of me" (John 5:45-6). But after his resurrection Jesus no longer referred to one book or one section of the Scripture in proof of his mission, but put the whole Bible before the pilgrims of Emmaus to reveal to them its Messianic implications: "And beginning at Moses and all the prophets, he expounded to them in all the scriptures, the things that were concerning him" (Luke 24:27). Similarly, to the assembled Apostles he showed that his mission had been foretold in all the writings of the Old Testament: "All things must needs be fulfilled, which are written in the law of Moses, and in the prophets, and in the psalms, concerning me. Then he opened their understanding, that they might understand the scriptures" (Luke 24:44-5).

From all this it may be inferred that when we seek to discover in the Old Testament what the revelation made to Israel has to teach us concerning Christ and his work, we need have no fear of being misled. This fundamental interpretation, this royal road of exegesis enabling us to surpass mere human understanding, is revealed to us by the Master himself, who teaches us to set out upon it in complete faith.

The Evangelists and the Old Testament

It is in this same sense that the Old Testament was understood by the Evangelists; and this is the firm belief that they all expressed (Matt. 3:3; Mark 1:3; Luke 3:4-6; John 1:23) in their application, from the outset, of the following passage from Isaias to Jesus and his mission:

The voice of one crying,
    In the desert [2] prepare ye the way of the Lord,
    make straight in the wilderness the paths of our God.
Every valley shall be exalted,
    and every mountain and hill shall be made low,
    and the crooked shall become straight,
    and the rough ways plain.
And the glory of the Lord shall be revealed,
    and all flesh together shall see,
    that the mouth of the Lord hath spoken.
                       (Isa. 40:3-5)

Saint Matthew and Saint John are the ones who appealed most frequently to the prophecies to show their fulfillment in our Saviour. Indeed, this appeal to the prophecies is a characteristic feature of the first Gospel; "this took place," "this was done," in order that "the prophecy might be fulfilled," are expressions found continually on the pen of Saint Matthew.

He used them particularly to introduce what was clearly a prophecy: that from Isaias foretelling the virginal conception of Emmanuel, the Messianic significance of which the Evangelist confirmed (Isa. 7:14); that of Micheas concerning the birth of the Messias at Bethlehem (5:2); that of the light shining in Galilee, enlightening the people walking in darkness (Isa. 9:1-2); that of the Servant of the Lord who takes

[2] The Douay version, following the Vulgate, has "The voice of one crying in the desert: Prepare ye ..."—Translator's note.

our infirmities and sorrows upon him (Isa. 53-4), or that of this same Servant preaching to the Gentiles and by his gentleness leading the true faith to victory [Vulgate: "shall bring forth judgment unto truth"] (Isa. 42:1-4); or that of the King of Sion coming "riding upon an ass, and upon a colt the foal of an ass" (Zach. 9:9; Isa. 62:11).

In other passages the interpretation appears less convincing and applicable if we do not take into account the strong tradition of spiritual exegesis that existed among the Jews and the charism of inspiration enjoyed by the Evangelist. Instances of this are found in the application of a verse from Osee (11:1) to the return from Egypt of the child Jesus; or of the lamentation of Rachel (Jer. 31:15) to the children of Bethlehem, Herod's victims (Rachel wept over her descendants who were massacred or died in exile). Another instance is the application of a passage from Zacharias (11:12-13) to the thirty pieces of silver which Judas received for his betrayal and which he cast down in the Temple (Zacharias mentions a prophet receiving a paltry wage of thirty shekels and casting them down in the Temple).

More curious is the prophecy, "He shall be called a Nazarene," which, according to Saint Matthew (2:23), Jesus fulfilled by his return to Nazareth. This prophecy, in so many words, is not to be found in the Old Testament. The saying must have reminded the Evangelist of the Nazirite vow (the dedication to the Lord mentioned in Numbers 6) and of the sorry reputation of the people of Nazareth, which aptly corresponded with the Messias' humbled state. He was recalling, therefore, an idea found in various places, and for this reason he referred to no prophet in particular but to "the prophets" in general.

This broad interpretation of the Scriptures shows us how firmly Saint Matthew was convinced that the life of Jesus accomplished them in the widest sense. A last example of his

method is the use he made of the verse of the Psalms, "I will
open my mouth in a parable, I will utter mysteries from of
old" (Ps. 77:2), to explain Jesus' teaching by parables. Here
again there is a slender connection between what is foretold
and what occurred, for in this verse the Psalmist does not
allude to so specific a literary form as the parable.

Saint John's references to the prophecies are remarkable in
that, except in one instance, they do not repeat those given
in the first Gospel; the exception is Zacharias foretelling the
entry into Jerusalem on an ass.

It was natural that the holy anger of Jesus when he drove
the money-changers and the sellers out of the Temple should
have reminded John and the disciples of the passage from the
Psalms: "Zeal for your house consumes me" (Ps. 68:10). The
parallel was the more obvious since this Messianic psalm contains passages that could be applied to the Passion; one was
later referred to by John as a prophecy concerning the
vinegar offered to Christ.

John, unlike Matthew and Mark, did not place the first
verse of Psalm 21 ("My God, my God, why have you forsaken me?") on the lips of Jesus on the Cross, but he quoted
verse 19 ("They divide my garments among them, and for
my vesture they cast lots") in connection with an event that
the other Evangelists simply recorded.

Saint John applied two passages from Isaias to the incredulity and blindness of many of his kinsmen. One is taken
from chapter 53 (verse 1): "Who hath believed our report?";
the other, concerning the vision that the prophet experienced
in the Temple, is taken from chapter 6 (9-10). "These things,"
wrote Saint John, "said Isaias, when he saw his glory [the
glory of Jesus], and spoke of him" (John 12:41).

Lastly, in his account of the Passion, Saint John quoted
from the Old Testament two passages that have a wonderful
spiritual meaning. The first (Exod. 12:46; Num. 9:12) con-

cerns the eating of the paschal lamb: "You shall not break
any of its bones." To the Evangelist this was a prophecy
that on the Cross our Lord's legs would not be broken, and
thus he identified our Saviour as the true Lamb, of whom
that in Exodus was only a type. The second passage, taken
from Zacharias (12:10), concerns the Servant whose death
is mourned like that of an only son: "They shall look upon
me, whom they have pierced." This is a reference to the
wound of the spear in the Heart of Jesus, which, from being
a fruitful subject of meditation among the Fathers, has become one of the most cherished themes of modern devotion.

The Apostles and the Old Testament

Also in the early preaching of the Apostles, as we find it
reflected in the Acts of the Apostles, the Old Testament is
regarded as the word of God—that word which is proof in
itself and sufficient to close all discussion.

All Saint Peter's sermons tend to show that in Jesus the
prophecies were fulfilled. For this Apostle, the Old Testament is a preparation for the Gospels and conceals a spiritual
meaning that was revealed by the Holy Spirit at Pentecost.

In his first speech to the crowds gathered in Jerusalem
(Acts 2:14-36) Saint Peter declared that the gift of tongues
bestowed on the Apostles by the Holy Spirit had been foretold by Joel:

And it shall come to pass after this,
    that I will pour out my spirit upon all flesh:
And your sons and your daughters shall prophesy:
    your old men shall dream dreams,
    and your young men shall see visions.
Moreover upon my servants and handmaids
[Even upon the menservants and maidservants]
    in those days I will pour forth my spirit.

And I will shew wonders in heaven;
> and in earth, blood, and fire, and vapour of smoke.
The sun shall be turned into darkness,
> and the moon into blood:
> > before the great and dreadful day of the Lord doth
> > > come.
And it shall come to pass,
> that every one that shall call upon the name of the Lord
> > shall be saved.
> > > (Joel 2:28-32)

Saint Peter also asserts that Christ, the Lord's anointed, in escaping the corruption of the grave, receiving the inheritance of David, and sitting victoriously at the right hand of the Father, fulfilled the promises of Psalms 131 and 15:

The Lord swore to David
> a firm promise from which he will not withdraw:
"Your own offspring
> I will set upon your throne."
> > (Ps. 131:11)

I set the Lord ever before me;
> with him at my right hand I shall not be disturbed.
Therefore my heart is glad and my soul rejoices,
> my body, too, abides in confidence;
Because you will not abandon my soul to the nether
> > world [Sheol].[3]
> nor will you suffer your faithful one to undergo
> > corruption [see the Pit].
You will show me the path to life,
> fullness of joys in your presence,
> > the delights at your right hand forever.
> > > (Ps. 15:8-11)

[3] See pages 204-9.

In his second sermon Saint Peter declared that Jesus was foretold by all the prophets, not by Moses alone (Deut. 18:15, 18; Lev. 23:29) but also by Samuel and those who came after him. It is necessary to look even before Moses, Saint Peter asserted, as the salvation bestowed on the "children of the testament [covenant]" is none other than the fulfillment of the promise made by the Lord to Abraham: "In your descendants all the nations of the earth shall be blessed." Thus Abraham's posterity will be the first to be called to salvation (Gen. 12:3; 22:18; Acts 3:20-6). And so that nothing of the great themes of apostolic exegesis would be lacking, in the same sermon he formally ascribed to the Prophets the prediction of our Saviour's sufferings and of "the restitution [restoration] of all things," to await which Jesus ascended again to heaven.

In his speeches to the Sanhedrin and in the house of Cornelius, Peter applied to Jesus the verse of the Psalms (117:22) in which is mentioned the stone rejected by the builders which became the cornerstone, and he recalled that Isaias foretold the whole of our Saviour's mission and the coming of the Good News to mankind.

An echo of this same reproach to the bad "builders" is found in Saint Peter's words at the time he and John were apprehended (Acts 4:11), and in the prayers of the Christians on their release (Acts 4:25-6) it is stated that this imprisonment was foretold in Psalm 2 (1-3):

> Why do the nations rage
>   and the peoples utter folly?
> The kings of the earth rise up,
>   and the princes conspire together
>   against the Lord and against his anointed:
> "Let us break their fetters
>   and cast their bonds from us!"

But it is Saint Stephen particularly who, in the speech recorded in the Acts (7:2-53), made a stand against the foolish
"builders." Stephen, a Jew by birth, with a Greek education,
felt less ready than the inhabitants of Jerusalem to humor
the local authorities. He therefore attacked those who had
earlier accused Jesus of changing the observances of the
Law and were now urging the same charge against him. Saint
Stephen did not defend himself, as Saint Paul was to do, by
saying that the yoke of the Law had grown too heavy, but
by making use of the Scriptures, and in terms directly inspired by them, he accused his co-religionists of being themselves violators of the Law and false to its spirit.

In his exhortation to the queen of Ethiopia's eunuch, Philip
the deacon did not choose his own theme; the eunuch asked
him to explain the sufferings of the Servant of the Lord (Isa.
53:7-8).[4] The eunuch did not know of whom Isaias was
speaking. Philip explained to him that Isaias spoke of Christ
crucified, who had brought salvation to the world. The manner
in which Philip interpreted this chapter of the prophet shows
clearly the important place accorded to these verses of Isaias
in the teaching of the early Church.

What Saint James, "the brother of the Lord," emphasized
in his speech to the Council of Jerusalem was the extension to
the Gentiles of the call addressed in the first place to Israel.
In this connection we should note three things. First, that it
is to a passage from Amos ("In that day, I will raise up the
tabernacle of David . . . and I will rebuild it as in the days of
old"—9:11) that the speaker referred to show that this extension had been prophesied and was in accordance with the
intentions of Providence; secondly, that this universalist interpretation is the more remarkable since it came from Saint
James, who was a leading figure in Jerusalem and acknowl-

---

[4] See pages 100, 103, 178-82.

edged as an authority by the Jewish Christian party; thirdly, that it is in agreement with what Saint Peter had allowed at Caesarea and with what was to be one of the central themes of Pauline preaching.

Biblical references occur throughout the Epistle attributed to the same Apostle, Saint James, but since its theme is principally moral exhortation, the author referred in it especially to the sapiential books, and more by allusion than by direct quotation.

In the same way the first Epistle of Saint Peter refers to the Psalms, Proverbs, and Isaias. On the subject of the inspiration of the Scriptures, his second Epistle furnishes one of the most valuable pieces of testimony in the New Testament. This testimony points especially to the Epistles of Saint Paul; it places them on the same footing as the "other scriptures," which, we are told, constitute a "prophecy" coming from God and not from man:

> And we have the more firm prophetical word: whereunto you do well to attend, as to a light that shineth in a dark place, until the day dawn, and the day star arise in your hearts: Understanding this first, that no prophecy of scripture is made by private interpretation. For prophecy came not by the will of man at any time: but the holy men of God spoke, inspired by the Holy Ghost (2 Pet. 1:19-21).

This passage is of capital importance for us, since it solemnly asserts that the Old Testament is inspired by the Holy Spirit.

In the Apocalypse, terms and images taken from the Old Testament, particularly from the Prophets, occur frequently, but the author does not quote texts referring to events that have taken place; this is understandable, since he himself was a prophet, whose mission it was to foretell the future.

SAINT PAUL

The writings of Saint Paul are of supreme importance for
our subject as their argument is continually based on the Old
Testament.

In addition to the advantage of a keen mind Saint Paul
brought to his task a remarkable preparation, as he had been
at the school for rabbis and had had for master one of the
most learned among them, the illustrious Gamaliel—"at the
feet of Gamaliel, taught according to the truth of the law of
the fathers" (Acts 22:3). Consequently he was equally at
home in simple exposition of doctrine or in conducting a discussion according to the rules of Rabbinic exegesis, which are
not always the same as ours.

In Acts 13 we find the substance of several of his sermons.
The method he used to convert his compatriots is related to
that found in the teaching of the other Apostles. The theme
of his sermon in the synagogue at Antioch in Pisidia is the
following:

In Jesus, the prophecies were fulfilled. The chiefs of the
Jewish people unknowingly contributed to their fulfillment
when they contrived the death of our Saviour through Pilate's
sentence. But God raised up Him who in the Psalms (2:7) He
already called His Son and who was not to suffer the corruption of the tomb (Ps. 15:10). It is through Jesus that, in
accordance with the prophecy of Isaias (55:3), God will bestow on His people the true and holy covenant that was
promised to David. If they refuse to accept the message, they
have only to "perish" as Habacuc (1:5) foretold, for God
will accomplish His admirable work nonetheless. As for Paul
himself, if the word of God, which he preaches, is rejected
by those who were first chosen and then made themselves
unworthy, he will turn to the Gentiles as Isaias foretold—
"Behold I have given thee to be the light of the Gentiles, that

thou mayest be my salvation even to the farthest part of the earth" (Isa. 49:6). This quotation from Isaias recalls the missionary program traced out by Jesus on the day of His Ascension (Acts 1:8).

In his sermon to the Jews in Rome, Saint Paul made use of another quotation from Isaias (6:9-10) in order to arrive at a similar conclusion:

> ... he [Paul] expounded, testifying the [doctrine of the] kingdom of God, and persuading them concerning Jesus, out of the law of Moses and the prophets, from morning until evening.
>
> And some believed the things that were said; but some believed not. And when they agreed not among themselves, they departed, Paul speaking this one word: Well did the Holy Ghost speak to our fathers by Isaias the prophet, Saying: Go to this people, and say to them: With the ear you shall hear, and shall not understand; and seeing you shall see, and shall not perceive. For the heart of this people is grown gross, and with their ears have they heard heavily, and their eyes they have shut; lest perhaps they should see with their eyes, and hear with their ears, and understand with their heart, and should be converted, and I should heal them (Acts 28:23-8).

In these terms is enunciated the principal theme of Pauline exegesis of the Bible. For Paul, a new Covenant had taken the place of the old, which had come to be beyond repair—not through God's fault, for He had kept His promises, but by reason of Israel's unbelief. In this new Covenant the partner without blame had changed his ally, taking in place of one who had disappointed him, one who would remain more faithful. It is in this sense that the New Testament fulfills the Old. This subject is given extensive treatment in Saint Paul's Epistles; we must now examine their principal lines of thought more closely, for they form the very heart and substance of the subject with which we are dealing.

In order to understand Saint Paul, it is important to bear in mind that he encountered opposition not only from the Jews who refused to recognize Jesus as the promised Messias but also from the Judaizers. These were the Jews who, though having become Christians and left the synagogue for the Church, brought with them all their old ties and remained so strongly attached to the practices of the Mosaic Law that they desired to impose them on all, even on converts from among the Gentiles.

With these partisans of obsolete practices, Saint Paul was obliged to engage in arduous controversy. Following his arguments in a superficial way, misunderstanding his statements in which the Law yields precedence to the Faith, might give the impression that he was an enemy of the Law. Such an impression would be quite wrong.

This champion of the new Law, this Apostle of the freedom of the children of God, still regarded the Old Testament as the word of God; he was even more closely attached to it than he had been when he sat at the feet of Gamaliel, as he now realized with far greater clarity the implications of God's promises to his people. Thus, when he was battling to deliver Christians from a burden that the fulfillment of the promises had rendered superfluous, he continued to rely on the Law and the Scriptures, on the miraculous history of that very Promise outlined in Israel's history and now perfected for the benefit of the "Israel of God," which is the people of Jesus Christ. Far from repudiating the Old Testament, Saint Paul glorified it in Him for whom the Holy Spirit destined this marvelous preparation.

Paul did not instruct Timothy, who had been schooled in the Scriptures by his Jewish mother and grandmother, to make no further use of the Old Testament; on the contrary, he

desired that his beloved disciple remain attached to these
books inspired by God which, properly interpreted, could
lead only to Christ. That is the full significance of the recom-
mendation contained in his last Epistle:

> But continue thou in those things which thou hast
> learned, and which have been committed to thee: knowing
> of whom thou hast learned them; And because from thy
> infancy thou hast known the holy scriptures, which can
> instruct thee to salvation, by the faith which is in Christ
> Jesus. All scripture, inspired of God, is profitable to teach,
> to reprove, to correct, to instruct in justice. That the man
> of God may be perfect, furnished to every good work
> (2 Tim. 3:14-17).

In mentioning the holy Scriptures in this passage, did Saint
Paul have in mind only the Gospels? He was careful, of
course, not to exclude them; indeed, in his former letter to
Timothy he quoted a saying of Jesus, reported by Saint Luke,
endowing it with equal authority with Deuteronomy (1 Tim.
5:18; Luke 10:7); but in requiring Timothy to train himself
in the school of the Scriptures, he was obviously thinking of
the Old Testament. This is quite clear if we compare the
passage quoted above with one he wrote not much earlier to
the Christians in Rome: "For what things soever were written,
were written for our learning: that through patience and the
comfort of the scriptures, we might have hope" (Rom. 15:4).

Among the hundreds of instances of Saint Paul's use of the
Old Testament, there are one hundred and twenty in
which he expressly quoted it. These quotations were not made
only for the Christians who had been converted from Judaism;
his arguments were addressed to all, Jews and Gentiles, and he
drew his proofs from the books of the Old Testament because
for all they are the word of God. Of course he did not fail to
quote Jesus' own words, but it is significant that he did not

assign to them, in relation to the other texts of Scripture, a
special value as proofs. It is understood that when Jesus is
speaking, this Truth is not shrouded in the same veils as was
the former revelation; but it is indeed the same God who is
speaking, and His word is sufficient for one capable of understanding it and who listens to it with submission.

Most frequently Saint Paul quoted the Prophets, and his
special fondness for Isaias is seen in the more numerous quotations from him; next come the Psalms in their twofold aspect
as prophecy, and religious and moral teaching; then the books
of the Pentateuch, both for the history they contain and the
laws they formulate; finally, the other historical books and
the sapiential books.

Although Saint Paul, like the rabbis, considered that every
text of Scripture possesses a value by what it asserts independ-
ently of its context, he did not disregard the course of Biblical
history. For him it moves toward Christ, so that Christ figures
in it throughout—sometimes directly prophesied, sometimes
prefigured by persons, actions, and things—with the result that
the Old Testament is given a weight undreamed of by the
synagogue. This can be seen, for example, in the lesson that
he drew from the episode recounted in chapter 34 of Exodus.
Here Moses is portrayed coming down from Mount Horeb
(or Sinai), where he had received the Lord's commands, with
his face veiled because it was shining so brightly that the
children of Israel would otherwise have been blinded by it.
Saint Paul wrote:

> And not as Moses put a veil upon his face, that the
> children of Israel might not steadfastly look on the face of
> that which is made void. But their senses were made dull.
> For, until this present day, the selfsame veil, in the reading
> of the old testament, remaineth not taken away (because
> in Christ it is made void). But even until this day, when

Moses is read, the veil is upon their heart. But when they shall be converted to the Lord, the veil shall be taken away. Now the Lord is a Spirit. And where the Spirit of the Lord is, there is liberty (2 Cor. 3:13-17).

Saint Paul did not deny that the Gospel too has its own veil, but it is only for those who refuse to believe, for those whose incredulity renders them in some sort blind like so many of his kinsmen.

When Saint Paul was concerned to confirm his teaching on morality and the ways of Providence with Biblical texts, he did not generally need to go much beyond the literal sense; but when it was a question of showing that the whole trend of the Scriptures is toward Christ, foretelling His coming as the shadow heralds the reality, he was obliged to go far beyond the literal sense because the Old Testament merely prefigures what the Revelation of the Gospel set forth in all clarity. Writing of certain practices of the Law, he said that they "are a shadow of things to come, but the body [reality] is of Christ" (Col. 2:17). By this he meant that men and things of the period of preparation correspond with those of the period of fulfillment, being so to say their pale and reduced projection, their prefiguration in the same way that a portent is related to its accomplishment. Thus, for those who possess this key, for those who have passed beyond the stage of the shadows and live in the period of fulfillment, it is possible to decipher the Biblical palimpsest, to discern in the sketches of the Old Testament the richest figures of the New and in this way to strengthen their Christian faith through the appeals of their Jewish hope.

In referring to these early images, these prophetic types which in the books of the old Covenant are promise of the new, Saint Paul frequently made use of the "spiritual sense"; and we have seen that the Gospels also have recourse to it.

As Pius XII wrote in his encyclical *Divino Afflante Spiritu:*

> All spiritual sense is not excluded from the Sacred Scripture. For what was said and done in the Old Testament was ordained and disposed by God with such consummate wisdom, that things past prefigured in a spiritual way those that were to come under the new dispensation of grace. Wherefore the exegete, just as he must search out and expound the literal meaning of the words, intended and expressed by the sacred writer, so also must he do likewise for the spiritual sense, provided it is clearly intended by God. For God alone could have known this spiritual meaning and have revealed it to us. Now Our Divine Saviour Himself points out to us and teaches us this same sense in the Holy Gospel; the Apostles also, following the example of the Master, profess it in their spoken and written words; the unchanging tradition of the Church approves it.

Moreover, the spiritual sense of Scripture occupies an essential place in the doctrinal construction of the New Testament; to remove from it the forms of reasoning where this sense is used would amount to a grave mutilation.

From the foregoing discussion it is possible to discern the main points of this doctrinal construction:

The history of God's relations with humanity do not begin with the Law, since long before it was revealed to Moses, Abraham, father of all believers, was justified by faith without the Law. The Law had its day and its role. The Lord assigned to it the function of "pedagogue" during the minority of Israel, His son, who owed obedience to the Law so long as he had not reached his majority. But the period under "tutors" is passed. The son who was a minor has come of age, and in emancipating him Christ bestowed on him the prerogatives of an heir. It is in Jesus that he becomes heir to the Promise that the chosen people was instructed to keep and pass on, and which is now fulfilled. (In passing, it is to be noted that Israel as a people is excluded from the new Covenant only to the extent that it persists in refusal to recognize Him who fulfilled the Promise.)

Though the Law, insofar as it imposed a burden of petty legal prescriptions, was abolished by the coming of Christ, as the shadow gives way to the coming of light, it does not follow that it was not fulfilled to the last jot or tittle, for the Law itself foretold its own abolition. As a consequence, Christ was, as Saint Paul says, "the end of the law . . . unto justice to every one that believeth" (Rom. 10:4) in the twofold sense of the word; he was the end because he both brought it to a close and was the objective at which it aimed.

This is the picture that the inspired authors of the New Testament give us of the Old. It is a complex one. On the one hand, they recognize that the Old Testament is abrogated in its letter but not in what it prefigures; on the other, they constantly appeal to it as the word of God, whose truth will never pass away. How are these two points of view to be reconciled? They are reconciled in Christ, who fulfills the ancient promise by giving grace to whoever believes in Him; in Christ who "fulfills" the Scripture by endowing with a full meaning what was hitherto fragmentary, and making real and efficacious what was only a figure.

Thus nothing is given up of what it has pleased God to reveal to men by the patriarchs and prophets, right down to the time when the hour came for Him to perfect this revelation by speaking "to us by his Son" (Heb. 1:2). Here, too, lies the explanation of the fact that the Church of Christ, which received the mission to "keep that which is committed to [her] trust" (1 Tim. 6:20), did not want to lose anything of the writings of the Old Testament and continues to assert them, in conjunction with those of the New, as the rule of her faith.

CHAPTER 2

The People of the Covenant: From Their Origins to Entry into the Promised Land

THE HISTORY of the Creator's dealings with man can be divided into four periods. In the first, God, who is love, creates man out of love in order that he shall be happy, but by reason of original sin, man eludes this happiness. The second period is that of the old Covenant, in which God, desiring to save man at all cost, chooses a people who would be entrusted with preserving His Revelation and giving a Saviour to the world. The third period is that of the new Covenant, in which God himself becomes man and by this means effects our redemption. The fourth period will be ushered in by Christ's return at the end of time, to realize the eternal happiness of the elect.

In the first five books of the Bible, the Pentateuch, God can be seen at work preparing and bringing the old Covenant into effect.

THE COVENANT WITH THE PATRIARCHS: GENESIS

Original sin did not result in the Creator's abandoning his creature. Not content with helping the first pair to adapt themselves to a new life, by making garments of skin for them, God deigned still to speak to them. He promised Adam a Redeemer; he accepted Abel's offerings and the prayers of

Enos. It was Enos, son of Seth, according to Genesis, who first bestowed on him the name of Yahweh,[1] which he was later to reveal to Moses. In this way relations were established between God and Seth's descendants, and it was through the latter that primitive tradition was handed down, but the word "Covenant" does not yet appear anywhere.

God uttered it for the first time after the Deluge, when Noe came out of the ark. He called on Noe to repopulate the earth and undertook, for his part, never again to lay it waste by flood. On this occasion the token that God gave of his promise was the rainbow, a natural phenomenon, to which he attached a peaceful significance. As described in Genesis, this "Covenant" embraced "all flesh," that is, every living creature that had survived the flood; even the animals received the assurance that they would not suffer destruction. Their inclusion shows clearly that there is no question here of a summons to any form of spiritual life, since animals are incapable of it. Although Noe was devout and showed Yahweh his gratitude by offering a holocaust, nothing seems to have been required of him in return for the divine generosity. It was entirely gratuitous, and the Covenant was unilateral. Noe and his family contracted only the obligation to increase and multiply, not to shed human blood, and to keep the natural law.

Sem, alone of the three sons of Noe, inherited God's special favor. It will be recalled that when Noe in his drunkenness threw off his coverings, Ham laughed at his father's nakedness, while Sem and Japheth respectfully covered him again. On awakening, Noe cursed Ham and blessed his other sons. To Sem he said, "Blessed be the Lord, the God of Sem," and turning to Japheth: "May God expand Japheth; let him dwell in the tents of Sem" (Gen. 9:26-7). The blessing bestowed

[1] See page 125.

on Sem designated him as the beneficiary of the divine Covenant. The blessing given to Japheth was to be carried into
effect, on the one hand, by the great civilized empires that
his descendants were to found among the Gentiles, and, on
the other, by the fact that it was from the descendants of Sem
that they were to receive the benefit of religious truth.

The Covenant entered into by Yahweh with Abram
(Abraham), Sem's descendant by Eber and Thare, was more
restricted than that with Noe, in the sense that it no longer
included living creatures without the power of reason and was
confined to the descendants of Abram.

One day when God brought this patriarch out of Ur of
the Chaldees, the land of his birth, he declared his intention
of being joined to him by a special bond. He promised even
greater things at Sichem when he showed Abram the land of
Chanaan, vowing to give it to him. The word "Covenant"
finally occurs in about the year 1850, it would seem, when
Abram encountered Melchisedec near Salem (or Jerusalem).
But this Covenant was only formally concluded when Abram,
already the father of Ismael (the son of Agar, the maid), received from Yahweh the promise of another posterity. This
was to issue from Isaac, whom Sara was to conceive in her old
age—Isaac, the first link in the chosen line. At this time God
changed the name of Abram to Abraham ("father of a multitude"). Abraham, on his side, as sign of the Covenant that
he had entered into, undertook to circumcise all the males of
his nation.

The sons of Ismael were also to be circumcised. They, too,
would be blessed, and God promised them that they would be
made fruitful. Nevertheless, it was to Isaac alone that the
Promise was made (Gen. 17:19-21).

God, like a friendly and trusting ally, kept Abraham informed of his purposes. Thus he revealed to him his intentions
regarding the city of Sodom, which was given over to un-

mentionable debauchery. For his part, Abraham evinced complete fidelity toward God. His complete trust and heroism carried him to the point of being willing to sacrifice the boy Isaac to God without concerning himself how the Promise could be fulfilled without this child. This faith was "accounted to him for righteousness." God rewarded him by heaping upon him fresh blessings and by declaring that in Isaac's posterity "all the nations of the earth shall be blessed" (Gen. 15:6; 22:18).

Subsequently, theophanies (or divine manifestations) renewed the Covenant in favor of Isaac and then of Jacob, his son; and it was under the name "God of Abraham, Isaac, and Jacob" that Yahweh in person was to reveal himself to Moses on Sinai.

Israel in Egypt

Three names are used to denote the heirs to the Promise: the Jewish people, the Hebrew people, the people of Israel.

The word "Jew" is derived from Juda, the son of Jacob, who gave his name to one of the twelve tribes. When the twelve tribes settled in Palestine, a southern province of this country was set apart for the tribes of Benjamin and Juda. After the death of Solomon, when schism divided the country in two, the part that was inhabited by the tribes of Benjamin and Juda came to be called by antinomy "the kingdom of Juda." Because of the increasing importance of Jerusalem, the capital of Juda, the name "Jews" was bestowed on all the inhabitants of Palestine and the name "Judea" was often given by the Romans to the whole of Palestine.

The origin of the word "Hebrew" is more uncertain. Some authorities believe it derives from Eber, a descendant of Sem and ancestor of Abraham. Indeed, Josephus calls Eber "the father of the Hebrews." Etymologically, Eber seems to mean the people coming "from beyond," a tribe of nomads which was possibly that of Abraham.

The word "Israelite" comes from the name given to Jacob on the occasion of his nocturnal struggle with the "angel." It was only at dawn that the latter overcame him. Jacob guessed that he had contended with God, and desired his blessing. God gave it to him, and before leaving, in remembrance of his courage, called him "Israel," that is, "strong against God," (Gen. 32: 24-9).

With the story of Joseph we come to the prelude to the conclusion of the Covenant in the proper sense of the term. Joseph, the son of Rachel (the second wife of Jacob-Israel) and the eleventh of the twelve sons of this patriarch, was his father's favorite. His brothers, in their hatred of him, sold him to Ismaelite traders, who took him to Egypt and resold him to Phutiphar, one of Pharao's officers. Joseph's brothers pretended to their father that there had been an accident. They dipped his tunic in goat's blood and sent it to Jacob, and it deceived him completely. "It is my son's tunic," he exclaimed. "A wild beast has devoured him!"

Joseph became Pharao's prime minister, and for seven years stored up corn in the royal granaries against a famine that was to last for the seven subsequent years. This famine affected the neighboring countries. Caravans from abroad flocked into Egypt where it was known that supplies were plentiful. Jacob sent his sons there, keeping at home only Benjamin his last-born. Joseph welcomed them without disclosing his identity. The passage of ten years had changed his features, and the Egyptian livery he wore made it even more difficult to recognize him. The sons of Jacob took away with them as much food as their camels could carry. Joseph merely required that the next time they come they bring with them Benjamin, who, like Joseph, was Rachel's son. On their second journey Benjamin accompanied them.

They presented [Joseph] with the gift they had with them in the house, and prostrated themselves before him. He inquired about their health, and said, "Is your father, the old man of whom you spoke, in good health? Is he still living?" "Your servant, our father, is well; he is still living," they said, bowing low to him. Then Joseph looked up and saw his brother Benjamin, the son of his own mother, and said, "So this is your youngest brother of whom you spoke to me? God be gracious to you, my son," he continued. Thereupon Joseph broke off and was on the verge of tears, for his heart yearned for his brother. He retired to his room and wept. . . .

Joseph could not control himself before all his attendants, so he exclaimed, "Let everyone withdraw from me." No one was with Joseph when he made himself known to his brothers. He wept aloud so that the Egyptians heard it, and the household of Pharao heard it.

Joseph said to his brothers, "I am Joseph. Is my father still alive?" But his brothers could not answer him because they were terrified in his presence. Then he said to them, "Come closer to me." When they drew near, he continued, "I am your brother Joseph, whom you sold into Egypt. Do not be distressed nor angry with yourselves that you sold me here; for God sent me before you to save life. For two years now the famine has been in the land, and for five more years there will be neither plowing nor reaping. God sent me before you to preserve a remnant for you in the land, and to deliver you in a striking way. Not you but God sent me here, and made me a father to Pharao, lord of all his house, and ruler over all the land of Egypt.

"Go quickly to my father and say to him, 'Your son Joseph sends you this message: God has made me master of all Egypt; come down to me, and do not delay. You shall live in the land of Gesen and be near to me, you, your sons, your grandsons, your flocks, your herds, and all that belongs to you. Five years of famine are still to come. I will provide for you there, that you, and your household, and all who belong to you may not be impoverished.' You yourselves see, and my brother Benjamin sees, that it is I who speak to you. Tell my father of my splendor in Egypt, and of all that you have seen. Hurry now and bring my father here." Then Joseph fell on the neck of his brother Benjamin and wept; and Benjamin wept on his neck. Joseph kissed all his brothers, weeping over each, and after that his brothers conversed with him. . . .

Then he sent his brothers on their way; and as they departed he said to them, "Do not quarrel on the way." So they went up from Egypt and came to their father Jacob in the land of Chanaan. They told him, "Joseph is still alive, and he is ruler over all the land of Egypt." But he was unmoved because he did not believe them. However, when they related to him all that Joseph had said to them, and when he saw the carts Joseph had sent to convey him, their father Jacob revived. "It is enough," said Israel. "My son Joseph is still alive; I will go and see him before I die" (Gen. 43:26-30; 45:1-8).

Jacob and his tribe left the land of Chanaan about the year 1700. On their arrival in Egypt they received from Pharao the land of Gesen, where they settled with their flocks. It was a frontier district, very fertile and situated, it appears, to the east of the Nile. Jacob lived another seventeen years. When he felt that death was upon him (Gen. 48:21-2; 49:1), he bestowed on each of his twelve sons a special blessing, but it was neither Ruben his first-born, nor Joseph his favorite, who received the promise of the Messias. The following words were addressed to Juda: "The sceptre shall not depart from Juda, nor the staff from between his feet, until he comes to whom it belongs. To him shall be the obedience of nations" (Gen. 49:10). In fact, Juda was the ancestor of David, who in turn was the ancestor of the Virgin Mary, the mother of the Messias.

The Departure from Egypt: Exodus

Four centuries went by. The Hebrews, who had increased greatly in numbers, retained their ethnic character without becoming merged with the Egyptians. The Pharaos saw in them a danger. Settled where they were, how would they behave in the case of invasion? If war broke out between the Chanaanites or the Syrians and the Egyptians, would they not make common cause with the invaders in order to recover their former privileges? The reigning Pharao, Ramses II (1301–1234), a great builder, decided to make use of the Hebrews in public works until such time as he had contrived to exterminate them.

> He said to his subjects, "Look how numerous and powerful the Israelite people are growing, more so than we ourselves!" . . .
>
> The Egyptians, then, dreaded the Israelites and reduced them to cruel slavery, making life bitter for them with hard work in mortar and brick and all kinds of field work—the whole cruel fate of slaves.
>
> The king of Egypt told the Hebrew midwives, one of whom was called Sephra and the other Phua, "When you act as midwives for the Hebrew women and see them giving birth, if it is a boy, kill him; but if it is a girl, she may live" (Exod. 1:9-16).

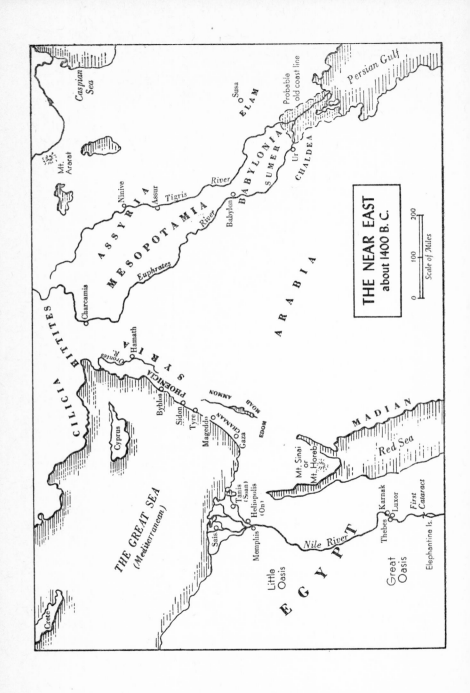

This decree, intended to destroy the chosen people, was used by God to save it. Moses, born in the tribe of Levi, was one of the children condemned to die.

[His mother] seeing that he was a goodly child, . . . hid him for three months. When she could hide him no longer, she took a papyrus basket, daubed it with bitumen and pitch, and putting the child in it, placed it among the reeds on the river bank. His sister stationed herself at a distance to find out what would happen to him.

Pharao's daughter came down to the river to bathe, while her maids walked along the river bank. Noticing the basket among the reeds, she sent her handmaid to fetch it. On opening it, she looked, and lo, there was a baby boy, crying! She was moved with pity for him and said, "It is one of the Hebrews' children." Then his sister asked Pharao's daughter, "Shall I go and call one of the Hebrew women to nurse the child for you?" "Yes, do so," she answered. So the maiden went and called the child's own mother. Pharao's daughter said to her, "Take this child and nurse it for me, and I will repay you." The woman therefore took the child and nursed it. When the child grew, she brought him to Pharao's daughter, who adopted him as her son and called him Moses; for she said, "I drew him out of the water" (Exod. 2:2-10).

At the royal palace Moses received the same education as the Egyptian princes, studying law, politics, diplomacy, and the military art, in short all that would serve to prepare him to become a leader of his people. In spite of all this, he had not ceased to consider himself a Hebrew.

After Moses had grown up, when he visited his kinsmen and witnessed their forced labor, he saw an Egyptian striking a Hebrew, one of his own kinsmen. Looking

about and seeing no one, he slew the Egyptian and hid him
in the sand. The next day he went out again, and now two
Hebrews were fighting! So he asked the culprit, "Why
are you striking your fellow Hebrew?" But he replied,
"Who has appointed you ruler and judge over us? Are
you thinking of killing me as you killed the Egyptian?"
Then Moses became afraid and thought, "The affair must
certainly be known." Pharao, too, heard of the affair and
sought to put him to death. But Moses fled from him and
stayed in the land of Madian (Exod. 2:11-15).

There Moses married the daughter of the priest Jethro. As
he was tending the flocks of his father-in-law, leading them
across the desert, he came to Horeb (or Sinai), the mountain
of God. The angel of Yahweh appeared to him as a flame of
fire coming out of a bush. Moses looked at it; the bush was on
fire but was not consumed. So he decided to go over and
look at this remarkable sight and see why the bush was not
burned. Yahweh saw him coming over and called out to
him from the bush: "Moses! Moses!" "Here I am," Moses
answered. Then Yahweh said, "Come no nearer! Remove the
sandals from your feet, for the place where you stand is holy
ground." He continued, "I am the God of your father, the
God of Abraham, the God of Isaac, the God of Jacob." Moses
thereupon hid his face for he was afraid to look at God.

But the Lord said, "I have witnessed the affliction of
my people in Egypt and have heard their cry of complaint
against their slave drivers. . . . So indeed the cry of the
Israelites has reached me, and I have truly noted that the
Egyptians are oppressing them. Come, now! I will send
you to Pharao to lead my people, the Israelites, out of
Egypt [into the land of the Chanaanites]."
But Moses said to God, "Who am I that I should go to
Pharao and lead the Israelites out of Egypt?" He answered,

"I will be with you. . . ." "But," said Moses to God, "when I go to the Israelites and say to them, 'The God of your fathers has sent me to you,' if they ask me, 'What is his name?' what am I to tell them?" God replied, "I am who am.". . .

Moses, however, said to the Lord, "If you please, Lord, I have never been eloquent. . . ." The Lord said to him, "Who gives one man speech and makes another deaf and dumb? . . .Go, then! It is I who will assist you in speaking and will teach you what you are to say" (Exod. 3:7-14; 4:10-11).

Together with Aaron his brother, who was more eloquent than he, Moses sought out Pharao (probably Merneptah, 1234–1225). The latter answered, "Who is the Lord that I should heed his plea to let Israel go? I do not know the Lord; even if I did, I would not let Israel go." But God obliged him to do so by inflicting on Egypt ten plagues, which succeeded one another in the following order: the water of the rivers and canals was turned into blood; frogs swarmed over the land; the dust of the earth was turned into gnats; Pharao's house and the whole land was infested with flies; pestilence ravaged the livestock of the Egyptians and it all died; festering boils broke out on man and beast; hail ruined the harvest; the east wind brought clouds of locusts which devoured what the hail had spared; then for three days the earth was covered with a darkness so thick that it could be felt, and the Egyptians were unable to see one another. In all these plagues, only the Egyptians were afflicted; the children of Israel were unharmed.

After the ninth plague Pharao sent for Moses and Aaron and said to them, "Go and worship the Lord. Your little ones, too, may go with you. But your flocks and herds must remain." Moses answered, "You must also grant us sacrifices

and holocausts to offer up to the Lord, our God. Hence, our
livestock also must go with us. Not an animal must be left
behind. Some of them we must sacrifice to the Lord, our God"
(Exod. 10:24-6).

Yahweh then said to Moses, "One more plague will I bring
upon Pharao and upon Egypt. After that he will let you
depart." Moses said, "Thus says the Lord: At midnight I will
go forth through Egypt; every first-born in this land shall die"
(Exod. 11:4-5).

The tenth plague is connected with the institution of the
Passover. God had said to Moses:

> "On the tenth of this month every one of your families
> must procure for itself a lamb, one apiece for each house-
> hold. If a family is too small for a whole lamb, it shall join
> the nearest household in procuring one. . . . The lamb must
> be a year-old male and without blemish. . . . They shall take
> some of its blood and apply it to the two doorposts and the
> lintel of every house in which they partake of the lamb.
> That same night they shall eat its roasted flesh with un-
> leavened bread and bitter herbs. . . . None of it must be
> kept beyond the next morning; whatever is left over in
> the morning shall be burned up. This is how you are to eat
> it: with your loins girt, sandals on your feet and your
> staff in your hand, you shall eat like those who are in flight.
> It is the Passover of the Lord" (Exod. 12:3-11).

When in the middle of the night Yahweh passed through
the land, he "slew every first-born in the land of Egypt, from
the first-born of Pharao on the throne to the first-born of the
prisoner in the dungeon, as well as all the first-born of the
animals" (Exod. 12:29). Only those houses were spared whose
doorposts and lintels were marked with the blood of the lamb.

During the night Pharao summoned Moses and Aaron
and said, "Leave my people at once, you and the Israelites

with you! Go and worship the Lord as you said. Take your flocks, too, and your herds, as you demanded, and begone; and you will be doing me a favor."

The Egyptians likewise urged the people on, to hasten their departure from the land; they thought that otherwise they would all die. The people, therefore, took their dough before it was leavened, in their kneading bowls wrapped in their cloaks on their shoulders. . . .

Now, when Pharao let the people go, God did not lead them by way of the Philistines' land, though this was the nearest; . . . Instead, he rerouted them toward the Red Sea by way of the desert road. In battle array the Israelites marched out of Egypt. Moses also took Joseph's bones along, for Joseph had made the Israelites swear solemnly that, when God should come to them, they would carry his bones away with them.

Setting out from Socchoth, they camped at Etham near the edge of the desert. The Lord preceded them, in the daytime by means of a column of cloud to show them the way, and at night by means of a column of fire to give them light. Thus they could travel both day and night (Exod. 12:31-4; 13:17-21).

The Hebrews had scarcely left before Pharao regretted having let them go. "What have we done!" he exclaimed, "Why, we have released Israel from our service!" So he set off in their pursuit with his chariots and soldiers, determined to make them turn back. The Hebrews espied the Egyptians when they themselves were at Phi-hahiroth, not far from the ford at Suez:

Then the Lord said to Moses, ". . . Lift up your staff and, with hand outstretched over the sea, split the sea in two, that the Israelites may pass through it on dry land. . . ."

Then Moses stretched out his hand over the sea, and the Lord swept the sea with a strong east wind throughout the night and so turned it into dry land. When the water was thus divided, the Israelites marched into the midst of the sea on dry land, with the water like a wall to their right and to their left. The Egyptians followed in pursuit; all Pharao's horses and chariots and charioteers went after them right into the midst of the sea. . . .

Then the Lord told Moses, "Stretch out your hand over the sea, that the water may flow back upon the Egyptians, upon their chariots and their charioteers." So Moses stretched out his hand over the sea, and at dawn the sea flowed back to its normal depth. The Egyptians were fleeing head on toward the sea, when the Lord hurled them into its midst. As the water flowed back, it covered the chariots and the charioteers of Pharao's whole army which had followed the Israelites into the sea. Not a single one of them escaped (Exod. 14:16-28).

As they made their way forward, the people of Israel encountered warlike tribes, particularly the Amalecites, who attacked them and suffered defeat.

Sinai, where the Israelites arrived about the year 1230, is a peninsula comprising in the north a desert tableland and in the south a mountainous district in which rises Gebel Musa, which appears to be Horeb, the mountain on which Moses spoke with God. We have come now to the very heart of the Old Testament.

In the third month after their departure from the land of Egypt, on its first day, the Israelites came to the desert of Sinai. . . .

Moses went up the mountain to God. Then the Lord called to him and said, "Thus shall you say to the house of Jacob; tell the Israelites: You have seen for yourselves

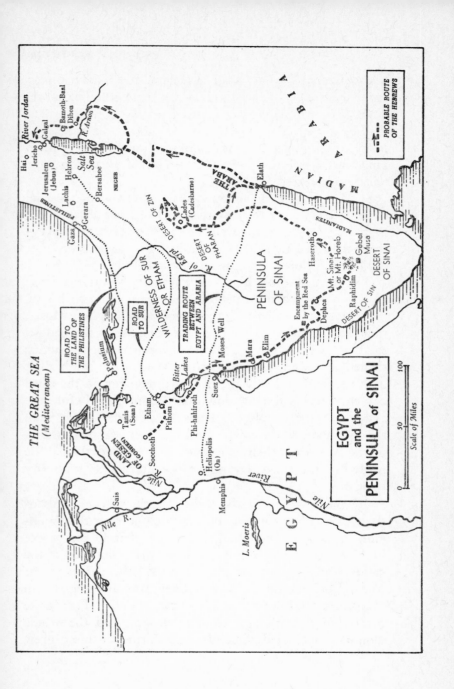

EGYPT
and the
PENINSULA of SINAI

THE GREAT SEA
(Mediterranean)

ARABIA

MADIAN

River Jordan

Hai
Jericho
Galgal
Bamoth-Baal
Dibon
R. Arnon

Jerusalem
(Jebus)
Hebron
Salt
Sea

Lachis
Bersabee
NECEB

Gaza
Gerara

Pelusium

Elath

THE ARABA

MADIANITES

Kades
(Cadesbarne)

DESERT OF ZIN

DESERT OF PHARAN

R. of Egypt

PENINSULA
OF SINAI

Haseroth
Mt. Sinai
or Mt. Horeb
Gebel
Musa

DESERT
OF SINAI

ROAD TO
THE LAND OF
THE PHILISTINES

WILDERNESS OF SUR
OR ETHAM

ROAD
TO SUR

TRADING ROUTE
BETWEEN
EGYPT AND ARABIA

Moses Well

Encampment
by the Red Sea

Dephca
Raphidim
DESERT OF SIN

Mara
Elim

Bitter
Lakes

Suez

Pithom
Phi-hahiroth

Etham

Tanis
(Soan)

Socchoth

LAND
OF
GESEN
(GOSHEN)

Heliopolis
(On)

EGYPT

Sais

Nile R.

Memphis

L. Moeris

Nile River

Nile R.

PROBABLE ROUTE
OF THE HEBREWS

0   50   100
Scale of Miles

how I treated the Egyptians and how I bore you up on eagle wings and brought you here to myself. Therefore, if you hearken to my voice and keep my covenant, you shall be my special possession, dearer to me than all other people, though all the earth is mine. You shall be to me a kingdom of priests, a holy nation. That is what you must tell the Israelites."

So Moses went and summoned the elders of the people. When he set before them all that the Lord had ordered him to tell them, the people all answered together, "Everything the Lord has said, we will do." Then Moses brought back to the Lord the response of the people.

The Lord also told him, "I am coming to you in a dense cloud, so that when the people hear me speaking with you, they may always have faith in you also." When Moses, then, had reported to the Lord the response of the people, the Lord added, "Go to the people and have them sanctify themselves today and tomorrow. Make them wash their garments and be ready for the third day; for on the third day the Lord will come down on Mount Sinai before the eyes of all the people. . . . Then Moses came down from the mountain to the people and had them sanctify themselves and wash their garments. He warned them, "Be ready for the third day. Have no intercourse with any woman."

On the morning of the third day there were peals of thunder and lightning, and a heavy cloud over the mountain, and a very loud trumpet blast, so that all the people in the camp trembled. But Moses led the people out of the camp to meet God, and they stationed themselves at the foot of the mountain. Mount Sinai was all wrapped in smoke, for the Lord came down upon it in fire. The smoke rose from it as though from a furnace, and the whole mountain trembled violently. The trumpet blast grew louder, while Moses was speaking and God answering him with thunder. When the Lord came down to the top of Mount Sinai, he summoned Moses to the top of the mountain, and Moses went up to him. . . .

Then God delivered all these commandments:

"I, the Lord, am your God, who brought you out of the land of Egypt, that place of slavery. You shall not have other gods besides me. You shall not carve idols for yourselves in the shape of anything in the sky above or on the earth below or in the waters beneath the earth; you shall not bow down before them or worship them. For I, the Lord, your God, am a jealous God, inflicting punishment for their fathers' wickedness on the children of those who hate me, down to the third and fourth generation; but bestowing mercy down to the thousandth generation, on the children of those who love me and keep my commandments.

"You shall not take the name of the Lord, your God, in vain. For the Lord will not leave unpunished him who takes his name in vain.

"Remember to keep holy the Sabbath day. Six days you may labor and do all your work, but the seventh day is the Sabbath of the Lord, your God. No work may be done then either by you, or your son or daughter, or your male or female slave, or your beast, or by the alien who lives with you. In six days the Lord made the heavens and the earth, the sea and all that is in them; but on the seventh day he rested. That is why the Lord has blessed the Sabbath day and made it holy.

"Honor your father and your mother, that you may have a long life in the land which the Lord, your God, is giving you.

"You shall not kill.

"You shall not commit adultery.

"You shall not steal.

"You shall not bear false witness against your neighbor.

"You shall not covet your neighbor's house. You shall not covet your neighbor's wife, nor his male or female slave, nor his ox or ass, nor anything that belongs to him."

When the people witnessed the thunder and lightning, the trumpet blast and the mountain smoking, they all feared and trembled. So they took up a position much farther away and said to Moses, "You speak to us, and we will listen; but let not God speak to us, or we shall die." Moses answered the people, "Do not be afraid, for God has come to you only to test you and put his fear upon you, lest you should sin." Still the people remained at a distance, while Moses approached the cloud where God was (Exod. 19:1-20; 20:1-21).

It was on the occasion of this first absence of Moses that the people for the first time broke the Covenant; but at the prayer of the mediator the Lord restored it.

When the people became aware of Moses' delay in coming down from the mountain, they gathered around Aaron and said to him, "Come, make us a god who will be our leader; as for the man Moses who brought us out of the land of Egypt, we do not know what has happened to him." Aaron replied, "Have your wives and sons and daughters take off the golden earrings they are wearing, and bring them to me." So all the people took off their earrings and brought them to Aaron, who accepted their offering, and fashioning this gold with a graving tool, made a molten calf. Then they cried out, "This is your God, O Israel, who brought you out of the land of Egypt." On seeing this, Aaron built an altar before the calf and proclaimed, "Tomorrow is a feast of the Lord.". . .

With that, the Lord said to Moses, "Go down at once to your people, whom you brought out of the land of Egypt, for they have become depraved. They have soon turned aside from the way I pointed out to them. . . . I see how stiff-necked this people is. . . . Let me alone, then, that my wrath may blaze up against them to consume them. . . ."

But Moses implored the Lord, his God, saying, "Why, O Lord, should your wrath blaze up against your own people, whom you brought out of the land of Egypt with such great power and with so strong a hand? Why should the Egyptians say, 'With evil intent he brought them out, that he might kill them in the mountains and exterminate them from the face of the earth'? Let your blazing wrath die down; relent in punishing your people. Remember your servants Abraham, Isaac and Israel, and how you swore to them by your own self, saying, 'I will make your descendants as numerous as the stars in the sky; and all this land that I promised, I will give your descendants as their perpetual heritage.' " So the Lord relented in the punishment he had threatened to inflict on his people (Exod. 32:1-14).

Moses ordered expiation to be made for the apostasy of the people and some three thousand were put to death. The tribe of Levi, which had remained faithful, was entrusted with execution of the order; from this time dates the special consecration of this tribe to the Lord. Next the "Tabernacle" was constructed. The tablets of the Law were enclosed by Moses in a rectangular casket, which was called the Ark of the Covenant because it contained the testimony of the covenant of Yahweh with his people. The Ark of the Covenant was first placed in a tent or tabernacle (from the Latin *tabernaculum*, meaning tent). It was around this tent (the Meeting Tent) that the Jews reunited as long as they were in the desert. Later the Temple in Jerusalem was built to contain the Ark of the Covenant, replacing the primitive tent.

Henceforward the essential features of the Covenant were settled, and Moses began to play the part that was to be his for nearly half a century.

Israel, which was founded to preserve monotheism, was not called by God to exert a material or political influence. Its mission was purely religious: "You shall be my special possession, dearer to me than all other people. . . . You shall be to me a kingdom of priests, a holy nation" (Exod. 19:6).

Moses was not only the mediator of the Covenant, he was also its legislator and organizer.

It should not be thought that all the legislation contained in the Book of Exodus dates from the same period as the promulgation of the Decalogue. Between this promulgation by the voice of God (chapter 20) and the ceremony of the Covenant (chapter 24) there has been inserted a first series of laws, known as the "Code of the Covenant." But it seems probable that these chapters are out of order, as the laws they contain were almost certainly promulgated at the end of Moses' life when, on the plains of Moab, before crossing the Jordan, the tribes of Ruben and Gad received their share of the territory (Transjordan). This circumstance explains the character of the Code. Several of its features imply the settled mode of life of farmers rather than that of a wandering pastoral people; for example, there are prescriptions concerning fields to be left fallow every seven years and those in connection with the harvest festival. Moses would seem to have set down in writing rules that he had given the people in the course of his long career. Some of them reflect what he learned at Pharao's court, which was in close touch with the great eastern empires. Thus, in the Code of the Covenant there are traces of the influence of the Hittite code.

THE OTHER BOOKS OF THE LAW: LEVITICUS, NUMBERS, DEUTERONOMY

Leviticus interrupts the account of the events that happened in the desert in order to insert the ritual to be followed by the priests of the tribe of Levi. It describes in great detail the holocaust or sacrifice of animals burned in their entirety in honor of Yahweh and the oblation of fine flour without leaven. These are very ancient forms of offering to the divinity; the first is connected with pastoral, the second with agricultural life. Very ancient, too, is the original idea of the sacrifice of communion or the peace offering, in which one part of the victim is reserved for the offerer and the other for Yahweh. A newer idea is that of the sacrifice for sin ("sin offering"), the sacrifice of reparation. It was concerned with a sin "against the Law," against, that is, rights of a higher order, or against the rights of a neighbor. All guilty of such offense—not excluding the "prince" or head of the tribe—were obliged to make this sacrifice of reparation. The offense might even involve the responsibility of the whole "community," that is, of the whole company of Israel. The moral and religious nature of these acts appears to be of a very high order in comparison with the sacrifices of neighboring peoples.

The same character is found in the law of holiness, whose prescriptions, coupled with severe sanctions, safeguard the dignity of the conjugal union, and in the regulations concerning the priesthood and acts of worship. In Leviticus there are detailed rules regarding the festivals, most of which are intended to commemorate the events of the Covenant and the goodness of Yahweh with respect to Israel. The blessings and curses that conclude the book also refer to the Covenant; God promises that his way with the Hebrew people will depend upon their ways, that he will show himself generous if they keep their promises but severe if they break them.

The Book of Numbers takes its name from the two enu-
merations or censuses that it contains. It includes also chapters giving the regulations for the Levites. The Levites formed
a considerable body and were recruited from the tribe of Levi;
they were entrusted with the service of the Tabernacle under
the direction of the priests, who were chosen from among the
descendants of Aaron. In addition to this legislative section
there are accounts relating how the Hebrews disobeyed and
rebelled, and how God punished them. Because they mur-
mured and blasphemed, he decided to prolong their sojourn
in the desert to forty years. As punishment for a certain lack
of faith Moses and Aaron were not to enjoy the happiness of
entering the Promised Land. One of the most fearful acts of
divine vengeance occurred when the Hebrews, triumphant
over their enemies and occupying the plains of Moab, attempted a form of religious syncretism[2] which constituted a
betrayal of monotheism.

> While Israel was living at Sattim, the people degraded
> themselves by having illicit relations with the Moabite
> women. These then invited the people to the sacrifices of
> their god, and the people ate of the sacrifices and wor-
> shiped their god. When Israel thus submitted to the rites
> of Baal-Phogor, the Lord's anger flared up against Israel,
> and he said to Moses, "Gather all the leaders of the people,
> and hold a public execution of the guilty ones before the
> Lord, that his blazing wrath may be turned from Israel."
> So Moses told the Israelite judges, "Each of you shall kill
> those of his men who have submitted to the rites of Baal-
> Phogor."
> Yet a certain Israelite came and brought in a Madianite
> woman to his family in the view of Moses and of the

[2] Syncretism is a system of philosophy or religion which fuses together
conflicting beliefs.

whole Israelite community, while they were weeping at the entrance of the Meeting Tent. When Phinees, son of Eleazar, son of Aaron the priest, saw this, he left the assembly, and taking a lance in hand, followed the Israelite into his retreat where he pierced the pair of them, the Israelite and the woman. Thus the slaughter of Israelites was checked; but only after twenty-four thousand had died.

Then the Lord said to Moses, "Phinees, son of Eleazar, son of Aaron the priest, has turned my anger from the Israelites by his zeal for my honor among them; that is why I did not put an end to the Israelites for the offense to my honor. Announce, therefore, that I hereby give him my pledge of friendship, which shall be for him and for his descendants after him the pledge of an everlasting priesthood, because he was zealous on behalf of his God and thus made amends for the Israelites" (Num. 25:1-13).

The second census, at the end of the Book of Numbers, shows the variations in population among the Hebrews during their long sojourn in the Desert of Sin.

In the course of time additional laws, both religious and civil, were made. One law settled the question of the successor to Moses as head of the community: Moses' powers passed to Josue, while Aaron's priestly powers were given to Eleazar and his descendants. By another law the tribes of Ruben, Gad, and Manasse were given possession of their share of territory in the already conquered region of Transjordan. A further law regulated division of the land on the other side of the Jordan when it should be occupied. The establishment of Israel in the land of Chanaan was only completed under Josue, but the methods by which it was carried out were settled in the time of Moses, so it can be said that the Books of the Law settled all fundamental matters, although new laws would still be needed to deal with new situations.

Deuteronomy (the name means "second Law") is a partial repetition or recapitulation of the three preceding books of the Pentateuch, given in the form of three important speeches by Moses. In the second the promulgation of the Ten Commandments is renewed, introduced by the phrase, "Hear, O Israel," which was to become the Jews' habitual introduction to prayer. These speeches, wholly imbued with the idea of the Covenant, are a confirmation of the Law as promulgated. They emphasize God's love for man and the love that man owes to God.

The proximity of the Chanaanites, with their idols, superstitions, and sacrifices of children, offered Israel frequent occasions for infidelity. To preserve the Covenant from these dangers, several passages of Deuteronomy strongly prohibit the use of high places (the cult of false gods was ordinarily celebrated on high places), sacred pillars and sacred poles, graven images; the adoration of the "heavenly host" (worship of the stars); and all the practices of idolatry. Worship, according to Deuteronomy, does not consist solely in ritual prescriptions; the circumcision on which Yahweh insists is a circumcision of the heart, combined with an effective love of the weak.

A single place of worship is authorized by Deuteronomy; there alone are sacrifices to be offered, and the Levites, who in all the cities, living on the offerings of the faithful, maintain the worship of Yahweh, can officiate only in the place chosen by him.

In addition to the Levitical priesthood, there is mention of the activity of the prophets. But a distinction is made between the good prophets and the bad, or "dreamers." The latter, who would lead the people to gods other than Yahweh, are to be put to death, just as every other tempter, even a near relation, who desires to seduce Israel into idolatry is to be stoned. The true prophet, raised up by Yahweh, is to be recognized by the agreement between his utterances and the Law and by the fulfillment of the things that he foretells. Such a one is to be heard, especially the greatest Prophet of all, the one whom Moses spoke of as "a prophet like me," in a passage that can be applied to any authentically inspired prophet, but of which Jesus claimed to be the perfect realization.

Certain prescriptions are given to the "kings": they are warned against excessive luxury and directed to teach fidelity to the Law through their example. Those who neglect their duty will be punished. But all who return to their God with sincere heart will be forgiven. Yahweh, for his part, will never forget the Covenant, and will remember the Jews till "the end of time."

The scroll of the Law, laid beside the Ark of the Covenant in the Tabernacle, bore witness to these promises, threats, and exhortations, as did the magnificent Song of Moses with which Deuteronomy concludes. It is one of the finest examples of Jewish poetry:

> Give ear, O heavens, while I speak;
> > let the earth hearken to the words of my mouth!
> May my instruction soak in like the rain,
> > and my discourse permeate like the dew,
> Like a downpour upon the grass,
> > like a shower upon the crops:
>
> For I will sing the Lord's renown.
> > Oh, proclaim the greatness of our God!
> The Rock—how faultless are his deeds,
> > how right all his ways!
> A faithful God, without deceit,
> > how just and upright he is! ...

Think back on the days of old,
    reflect on the years of age upon age.
Ask your father and he will inform you,
    ask your elders and they will tell you. . . .
[For] the Lord's own portion was Jacob,
    His hereditary share was Israel.

He found them in a wilderness,
    a wasteland of howling desert.
He shielded them and cared for them,
    guarding them as the apple of his eye.

As the eagle incites its nestlings forth
    by hovering over its brood,
So he spread his wings to receive them
    and bore them up on his pinions.

The Lord alone was their leader,
    no strange god was with him.
                        (Deut. 32:1-12)

Having reminded the Israelites of the goodness of God toward them, Moses proceeded to threaten them. He placed the
following words in the mouth of Yahweh:

He will say, "Where are their gods
    whom they relied on as their 'rock'?
Let those who ate the fat of your sacrifices
    and drank the wine of your libations
Rise up now and help you!
    Let them be your protection!

"Learn then that I, I alone, am God,
    and there is no god besides me.
It is I who bring both death and life,
    I who inflict wounds and heal them,
    and from my hand there is no rescue.

"To the heavens I raise my hand and swear:
 As surely as I live forever,
I will sharpen my flashing sword,
 and my hand shall lay hold of my quiver.

"With vengeance I will repay my foes
 and requite those who hate me.
I will make my arrows drunk with blood,
 and my sword shall gorge itself with flesh—
With the blood of the slain and the captured,
 Flesh from the heads of the enemy leaders."

Exult with him, you heavens,
 glorify him, all you angels of God;
For he avenges the blood of his servants
 and purges his people's land.

(Deut. 32:37-43)

JOSUE AND ENTRY INTO THE PROMISED LAND

The spirit of the Book of Josue is identical with that of Deuteronomy, and the role of Josue himself is in some sort a repetition of that of Moses.

When in full view of the Promised Land the Hebrews encountered the obstacle formed by the river Jordan, Josue called on them to purify themselves, as Moses had done on approaching Sinai.

As had happened at the Red Sea, the waters of the Jordan ceased to flow and the people crossed dry-shod. Finally, the Ark of the Covenant led the Hebrews, as earlier the cloud had led them in the desert. It is true that manna had ceased to fall, but the crops of the earth took its place; this was also a proof that Yahweh keeps his promises.

Josue began his mission by preaching fidelity to the Mosaic Law. It was on condition of such fidelity alone, he told the

people, that God would help them to conquer the Promised
Land. None showed himself more obedient than he to the
commands of God.

As soon as they had crossed the Jordan, the Hebrews
settled at Galgal. With twelve stones taken from the bed of
the river, they raised a monument intended to commemorate
the miracle worked for their benefit. All those who had not
yet been circumcised now underwent this ceremony. The
Passover was celebrated in accordance with the rites of the
first Passover in Egypt, since wheat with which to make unleavened bread was now at hand. Later on, when the land of
Chanaan had been conquered and shared out among the
twelve tribes, and Josue was coming to the end of his days
and the conclusion of his mission, he called all the people
together at Sichem and renewed the Covenant with the greatest solemnity. The choice of site is significant. The ceremony
took place under the terebinth of More, on the very spot
where Yahweh had promised Abraham that he would give this
country to his posterity and where the patriarch had raised
an altar to his divine benefactor (Gen. 12:7). Again in this
instance, Josue was obeying Moses who, in the second speech
ascribed to him in Deuteronomy (11:29-30), had asked that
a "blessing" come down on and remain in this place.

It should be noted that the law of a single sanctuary, regarded by the authors of Josue and Deuteronomy as the
safeguard of monotheistic religion, remained in full force. This
one sanctuary was the Tabernacle containing the Ark of the
Covenant. It was transferred from Galgal to Silo and then
to Sichem. The day came when the Transjordan tribes (those
of Ruben and Gad) returned to their own territory after
helping their brethren with the conquest of the land over the
Jordan. They then wished to raise an altar to Yahweh on
their side of the Jordan. At once the "community" of Israel
asserted its readiness to make war on them as rebels against

the Law. The Rubenites and the Gadites were obliged to declare that they would not set up altar against altar. Nothing else would satisfy the Hebrews of the other ten tribes for they were resolute that they would obey Josue, as he had obeyed Moses.

CHAPTER 3

The People of the Covenant:
From the Judges to the Exile

THE PERIOD OF JUDGES AND SAUL

IN THE Biblical sense of the term, the "judge" is not only one who dispenses justice. He is also a noted man who emerges from among his fellows to inspire them with hope and remind them of their duty; the liberator, on occasion; the leader who arises here and there and succeeds in exercising authority over one or several tribes.

The period known as that of the Judges extends from the entry of the Israelites into the Promised Land until the advent of royalty, that is, from Josue to Saul, 1200 to 1025.

It was a difficult period for the Hebrews. They were scattered over a territory that only partially belonged to them, and beset by a host of enemies who, materially and militarily, were in a more advanced state than they. These enemies were the Chanaanites, who still retained a large part of the country; the Philistines, who had come from Crete and settled on the Mediterranean coast; and the Amorrites, Ammonites, Moabites, Edomites, and Madianites, etc., who continually exerted pressure on the frontiers. The position of the Hebrews was especially weak and vulnerable because politically they were ruled by no central government; and religiously no visible authority compelled the recognition of all in order to keep them faithful to the laws of Yahweh.

During this period the greater number of them practically

PALESTINE
Divided Among the
TWELVE TRIBES

0   10   20
Scale of Miles

Sidon
Mt. Lebanon
Anti-Lebanon
Damascus

Sarephta

Cana
Lesem (Dan)

Cedes

BASAN

Achzib
ASER
Jeron
NEPHTHALI

Rohob
Golan

Achsaph
Remmon
Astharoth

Halcath
ZABULON
Edrai

Dor
Carmel
Sarid
Mt. Tabor
Endor
Villages of Jair

THE GREAT SEA
(Mediterranean)
Sunam
Mt. Gelboe
MANASSE

Mageddo
Cison R.
ISSACHAR
Ramoth-Galaad

Thaanach
Jesrael
Beth-San

Plain of Sharon
MANASSE
Thersa

Mt. Ebal
Sichem
Janoe

Mt. Garizim
Silo

Joppe
EPHRAIM
GAD

Mt. Ephraim
Phanuel

Bethel

Beth-Horon
Gabaon
Sattim

DAN
Ramatha
Jericho
Mephaath

Saraa
BENJAMIN
Galgal

Beth-Sames
Cariath-jarim
Jerusalem (Jebus)
Hesebon

Azotus
Bamoth-baal
Beth-baal-maon

Ascalon
Bethlehem
Mt. Nebo
Medaba

Eglon
JUDA
RUBEN

Lachis
Hebron
Dibon

Gaza
Ziph
R. Arnon
Aroer

Carmel

PHILISTINES
Salt Sea

SIMEON

MOAB

R. of Egypt

EDOM

AMMON

Jordan River

gave up the religion of Sinai. Sacrifices were offered on the
high places of Chanaan; images of Yahweh were made, and
he was brought to the level of the local gods (Baals); human
sacrifices were offered; witchcraft and necromancy were
practiced. All this the Book of Judges sums up in the phrase,
inspired by Deuteronomy: "The Israelites offended the Lord."
These words are applied sometimes to one tribe, sometimes
to another. In like manner, liberation from the yoke of a
hostile nation was effected sometimes in favor of one tribe,
sometimes in favor of another, according to whether this
judge or that had been raised up by Yahweh and endowed
with his "spirit." In all this diversity there was uniformity
in one particular: God's attitude is unchanging; faithful to
the Covenant, he abandons the people to the consequences of
their sins when they "fornicate" with strange gods, and he
stretches forth his arm to save them when they show repentance.

Amidst all this apostasy and culpable syncretism there
emerged some striking figures who remained faithful to
Yahweh. Such a one was the prophetess Debora. In the
canticle in which, while blaming the lack of unity among
the tribes, she celebrates her victory over the Chanaanites
(Judg. 5), not only does she praise Yahweh with fitting
gratitude but she mentions "those who love [him]" in the same
terms as the first article of the Law. A further example of
fidelity is given by Samson's parents, who consecrated their
son to the Lord and evinced a truly religious sense in keeping
their promise.

Among the Judges, let us recall particularly Gedeon,
Samson, and Samuel.

Gedeon received from Yahweh's angel this order: "Go
with the strength you have and save Israel from the power of
Madian" (Judg. 6:14). Accompanied by ten of his servants,
he set out to destroy the altar of Baal put up by his father and

the sacred pole in honor of the goddess Astarte; then he offered a holocaust to Yahweh on the remains of this pagan altar, sacrificing a bullock. This action did not infringe the rule of a single altar since on this occasion it was commanded by Yahweh himself. But after Gedeon's death, attempts were made to set up centers for the worship of Yahweh in places other than where the Ark of the Covenant rested. This constituted, in the words of the Bible, a "prostitution," that is, idolatrous syncretism.

Samson's birth was accompanied by certain supernatural manifestations:

> There was a certain man from Saraa, of the clan of the Danites, whose name was Manoe. His wife was barren and had borne no children. The Angel of the Lord appeared to the woman and said to her, "Though you are barren and have had no children, yet you will conceive and bear a son. Now, then, be careful to take no wine or strong drink and to eat nothing unclean. As for the son you will conceive and bear, no razor shall touch his head, for this boy is to be consecrated to God from the womb. It is he who will begin the deliverance of Israel from the power of the Philistines (Judg. 13:2-5).

In Samson's time the Philistines were masters of the plains and had dominion over Israel. Although Samson, through the exploits he accomplished by reason of his great strength, was unable to change this state of affairs, he at least personified the resistance of the chosen people to pagan domination and in this way fostered their hope. Unfortunately, he revealed his vow as a Nazirite. A woman was his downfall. As a Nazirite he had undertaken not to have his hair cut—and not to drink alcohol. When Dalila, the Philistine whom her compatriots had bribed to beguile him, learned of his vow, she cut his hair, and God took away from him the strength that he attached to observance of the Nazirite vow. The Philistines gouged out his eyes and put him to grinding corn in his prison.

The lords of the Philistines assembled to offer a great sacrifice to their god Dagon and to make merry. They said, "Our god has delivered into our power Samson our enemy." When their spirits were high, they said, "Call Samson that he may amuse us." So they called Samson from the prison, and he played the buffoon before them. When the people saw him, they praised their god. For they said, "Our god has delivered into our power our enemy, the ravager of our land, the one who has multiplied our slain."

Then they stationed him between the columns. Samson said to the attendant who was holding his hand, "Put me where I may touch the columns that support the temple and may rest against them." The temple was full of men and women: all the lords of the Philistines were there, and from the roof about three thousand men and women looked on as Samson provided amusement. Samson cried out to the Lord and said, "O Lord God, remember me! Strengthen me, O God, this last time that for my two eyes I may avenge myself once for all on the Philistines."

Samson grasped the two middle columns on which the temple rested and braced himself against them, one at his right hand, the other at his left. And Samson said, "Let me die with the Philistines!" He pushed hard, and the temple fell upon the lords and all the people who were in it. Those he killed at his death were more than those he had killed during his lifetime.

All his family and kinsmen went down and bore him up for burial in the grave of his father Manoe between Saraa and Esthaol. He had judged Israel for twenty years (Judg. 16:23-31).

Samuel, the Judge, of the tribe of Ephraim, whom before his birth his mother Anna had consecrated to Yahweh as some kind of Nazirite, was also a "prophet of God."

Prophecy was to be found in Israel at this time, in contrast with the period immediately preceding when the "word of the Lord" was rarely heard (1 Sam. 3:1). There were in existence in this period companies of prophets, and Samuel on occasion presided over them (19:20); but it is not through them that he acquired the gift, nor did he make use of musical instruments, as they did, in order to provoke ecstasy. His prophetic charism was in evidence from childhood. He differed from his predecessors in that he exercised authority as "judge" over the whole of Israel, prefiguring the state of a unified community, which was achieved only under David and, particularly, Solomon.

The Tabernacle, at the time of Samuel's vocation as a prophet, was at Silo, and the priesthood was exercised by Heli, who was feeble and old. Heli's extreme indulgence for his sons, whom he allowed to take from Yahweh the fat of the sacrificial victims, was punished by a victory of the Philistines, who seized the Ark of the Covenant and destroyed the Tabernacle of Silo. After the Philistines sent the Ark back, it was temporarily set down at Cariath-jarim. From this time the people did not assemble before the Ark, but elsewhere, generally at Maspha, sometimes at Bethel or at Galgal. Samuel himself resided at Ramatha, where he set up an altar. Circumstances were scarcely favorable to unity of sanctuary, and the author of the Book of Samuel makes no attempt to disguise this multiplication of altars. It is evident that sacrifices were offered in different families and tribes, for example, in the house of Isai, David's father, and the sacred writer does not censure it. The practice of consulting Yahweh by a species of divination (or sortilege), according to a method that has remained a mystery, was much in use. Vestiges of idolatry were difficult to eradicate. Samuel was instrumental in abolishing the images of "strange gods," the idols of Baal and Astarte, so that adoration should be given to Yahweh alone (1 Sam. 7:3-4); but we find Michol, Saul's daughter and David's wife, keeping one of these idols, called "teraphim" (19:13), which Samuel had denounced as criminal (15:23).

Although Samuel's authority settled the religious problem, the lack of cohesion among the tribes made political unification desirable. With a view to achieving this, there had been some thought of giving Gedeon, during his period of office, the title of king, even though certain elements of the community of Israel were reluctant to adopt this somewhat novel solution. Samuel had at first been opposed to it, and he acceded to the requests of those in favor of a king only when Yahweh himself consented.

The king chosen by Yahweh and designated by the drawing of lots was Saul of the tribe of Benjamin. Saul, who possessed great physical strength and valor, succeeded in bestowing on the nation a certain military and political cohesion, and he won outstanding victories. But he did not conform with sufficient docility to all the requirements of the concept of theocratic kingship and was cast off by Yahweh for his misconduct in the strictly religious sphere. For example, at Galgal he himself had offered the holocausts, without awaiting Samuel's coming, although the latter had arranged to meet him there. Later, he asked the witch of Endor to conjure up the shade of Samuel. All this reveals with what difficulties spiritual progress is achieved even among those who are reputed the best. Yet since Saul was Yahweh's anointed, he was on this account held in respect until the end, in spite of his mental derangement and his sins. Even at Gelboe, where the king was defeated by the Philistines, his armorbearer refused to raise his hand against the Lord's anointed and help him to commit suicide.

DAVID AND SOLOMON

The dynasty of Saul was short-lived. The future belonged to David (1010-970), the descendant of Juda, that son of Jacob to whom his father's blessing had passed on the promise of the Messias.

David, Saul's son-in-law, while still young had achieved glory through his victory over Goliath, the Philistine giant. David was a valiant soldier and an astute diplomat as well as a talented musician and a great poet. Owing to the jealousy of Saul, his father-in-law, he had been obliged to flee and take refuge among the Philistines in order to save his life. By divine protection he was preserved from all dangers, won many victories, and achieved recognition as king by the tribe of Juda and then by the tribes in the north.

The capture of Jerusalem, from which he drove out the Jebusites, had important results. David transformed this stronghold into the capital of his unified kingdom; he also desired that it become the center of religious unity. He brought the Ark of the Covenant there and planned to build a fine temple to Yahweh. He even bought the site on which the Temple was to be built, but it was Solomon, his son, who was to bring this plan to a successful conclusion.

By taking the Ark to Jerusalem, David fulfilled a vow that he had made:

I will not enter the house I live in,
    nor lie on the couch where I sleep:
I will give my eyes no sleep
    my eyelids no rest,
Till I find a place for the Lord,
    a dwelling for the Mighty One of Jacob.

(Ps. 131:3-5)

From Psalms 67 and 23 we can form an idea of the scene on the arrival of the Ark at Sion-Jerusalem:

> The singers lead, the minstrels follow,
>> in their midst the maidens play on timbrels.
> In your choirs bless God;
>> bless the Lord, you of Israel's wellspring!
> There is Benjamin, the youngest, leading them;
>> the princes of Juda in a body,
>> the princes of Zabulon, the princes of Nephthali.
>>> (Ps. 67:26-8)
> Lift up, O gates, your lintels;
>> reach up, you ancient portals,
>> that the king of glory may come in!
> Who is this king of glory?
>> The Lord of hosts; he is the king of glory.
>>> (Ps. 23:7-10)

As a reward to David for his good intentions, Yahweh, by the mouth of the prophet Nathan, promised him that he would be the founder of a dynasty:

> And when thy days shall be fulfilled, and thou shalt sleep with thy fathers, I will raise up thy seed after thee, which shall proceed out of thy bowels, and I will establish his kingdom. He shall build a house to my name, and I will establish the throne of his kingdom for ever. I will be to him a father, and he shall be to me a son: and if he commit any iniquity, I will correct him with the rod of men, and with the stripes of the children of men. But my mercy I will not take away from him, as I took it from Saul, whom I removed from before my face. And thy house shall be faithful, and thy kingdom for ever before thy face, and thy throne shall be firm for ever (2 Sam. 7:12-16).

This prophecy goes beyond the person of Solomon and foretells the Messias. Consequently, the author of Paralipomenon in mentioning it employs the word "covenant," which since the days of Moses was used in a very special sense (2 Par. 13:5).

As his power increased, David added to the number of his wives, after the manner of eastern potentates. His lust caused him to commit a serious crime. He took Bethsabee from her husband Urias, and then had him killed in order to hush up the scandal. But he repented of this grave sin and of many other serious faults, and the beautiful prayers that he composed to express his repentance are still those we use to express our own.

David was succeeded by Solomon (970-931), the adulterine son of Bethsabee. No reign in all the history of Israel, externally at least, was so glorious. This king, who governed an apparently united nation, was a great builder. He was admired on all sides for his wisdom and the ostentatious wealth of his court. An astute policy of alliances enabled him to enjoy friendly and useful relations with neighboring kingdoms. Yet Solomon, unrestrained man that he was, filled his harem with foreign women and built for them idolatrous sanctuaries in which they could worship their own gods. These "abominations" were highly objectionable to the better of his subjects; many were outraged at being obliged to pay the expenses of all his luxury and magnificence; disaffection spread; disagreement increased between the tribes of the north and those of the south; and schism, which had been brewing for some time, openly occurred in 931, on the accession of Roboam, Solomon's successor.

The Kingdoms of Israel and Juda

Thus, Palestine was divided into two kingdoms: the kingdom of Israel, made up of the tribes in the north, with Samaria as its capital; the kingdom of Juda, in the south, made up of the tribes of Juda and Benjamin, with Jerusalem as its capital. The former lasted for two centuries, until its destruction by the Assyrians; the latter, three and a half centuries, until its destruction by the Babylonians.

The Kingdom of Israel (931-721).

The religious consequences of the schism were disastrous, more so in the north than in the south, which remained in possession of the Ark of the Covenant and the Temple in Jerusalem, the only place in which Yahweh desired to receive the worship of his adorers.

For political reasons, the kings of Israel sought to prevent their subjects from going to Jerusalem to worship. The Levites, however, went into exile in order to follow the Ark of the Covenant, and many other fervent Hebrews imitated them so as to be able to continue going up to the Temple. The situation in Israel became such that those who believed in the pure worship of Yahweh had to go into hiding to practice monotheism.

Nine dynasties, one after another, headed the kingdom of Israel. All of them were condemned by the authors of the relevant books of the Bible.

Jeroboam I (931-910), the author of the schism, dedicated two sanctuaries to Yahweh, one in the south at Bethel, the other in the north at Dan. He himself officiated in them before a golden calf, which, like the ox Apis in Egypt and the bullock Hadad in Syria, was supposed to represent the deity.

Of Nadab, son of Jeroboam I, Scripture says "He did evil in the sight of the Lord, and walked in the ways of his father,

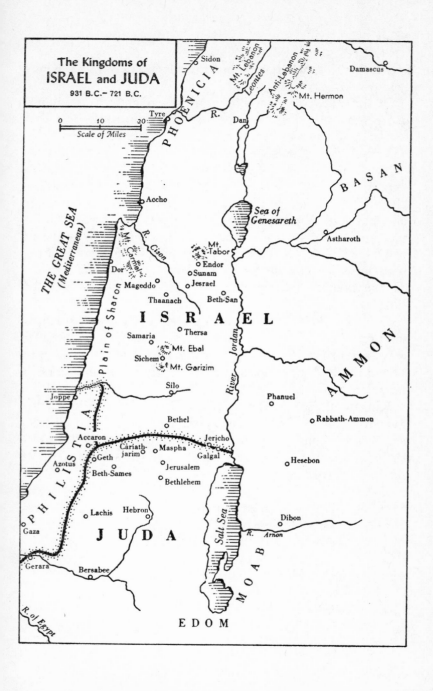

The Kingdoms of
ISRAEL and JUDA
931 B.C.– 721 B.C.

0   10   20
Scale of Miles

Sidon

Mt. Lebanon

Leontes R.

Anti-Lebanon

Damascus

Mt. Hermon

Tyre

Dan

R.

PHOENICIA

BASAN

Accho

Sea of
Genesareth

THE GREAT SEA
(Mediterranean)

R. Cison

Mt. Carmel

Mt. Tabor

Endor

Sunam

Jesrael

Astharoth

Dor

Mageddo

Thaanach

Beth-San

I S R A E L

Samaria

Thersa

Mt. Ebal

Sichem

Mt. Garizim

Silo

Plain of Sharon

River Jordan

AMMON

Joppe

Bethel

Phanuel

Accaron

Cariath-
jarim

Maspha

Jericho

Galgal

Rabbath-Ammon

PHILISTIA

Azotus

Geth

Beth-Sames

Jerusalem

Bethlehem

Hesebon

Gaza

Lachis

Hebron

Dibon

J U D A

Salt Sea

R. Arnon

Gerara

Bersabee

M O A B

R. of Egypt

E D O M

and in his sins, wherewith he made Israel to sin" (3 Kings 15:26).

Of Amri (885-874), an important sovereign in the temporal order, the Book of Kings confines its account to the fact that he founded Samaria, and "acted wickedly above all that were before him" (3 Kings 16:25).

Nevertheless, he was surpassed in wickedness by Achab (874-853), a man of some political and military standing. Under the influence of his wife, the dreadful Jezabel, daughter of a priest of Astarte, he set up in Samaria a sacred pole to this goddess. In the same city he built a temple to Baal and worshiped him. He continued the policy of reconciliation with Jerusalem, begun by his predecessor, and gave Athalia, his daughter, in marriage to Joram, son of Josaphat, king of Juda.

Ochozias, Achab's son, was reproved by Yahweh for having prayed for his cure to the Baal of Accaron in Philistia. It may be remarked in passing that this Baal is the Beelzebub to whom the Philistines were one day to attribute our Saviour's miracles.

King Jehu (841-814) carried out the divine threat that lay over the family of Ochozias by slaying Jezabel and all who survived of Achab's descendants. He put down the Baals and their priests, but he was also wicked and earned the reproofs of the Scriptures.

Yahweh punished Israel's unfaithfulness by laying waste Samaria, which fell into the power of the Assyrians. It was first besieged by Shalmaneser V, king of Ninive, who compelled Osee (732-724), Israel's last sovereign, to pay him tribute. In 721, under Sargon II, the conquest was completed, and the Jews of the northern kingdom were deported.

Colonists from Babylon and Syria were sent to north Palestine to occupy the land vacated by the Jews. These misinstructed immigrants, taught by the syncretist Israelites who had remained in Samaria to obey the demands of the "local god," could not do otherwise than practice syncretism in their turn. This led to the schismatic worship which from that time was adopted by the Samaritans.

The Kingdom of Juda (931-587).

The religious history of the kingdom of Juda is less uniformly gloomy than that of Israel, and it contains some fine chapters, which do credit to the people of God.

Roboam (931-913) and his son Abiam practiced a syncretist form of worship to which Roboam, like his father Solomon, had been seduced by his foreign concubines. The invasion carried out by Sesac, pharao of Egypt, who sacked the Temple and the palace at Jerusalem, as the prophet Semeias had foretold, was the punishment for this infidelity.

Asa, son of Abiam, and Josaphat, son of Asa, proved to be true worshipers of Yahweh, hostile to any compromise with idolatry, but neither of them was successful in abolishing worship in those "high places" where altars had been set up. Asa, who at the outset of his reign was praised by the author of Paralipomenon for restoring the pure worship of Yahweh, was later reproved by him, as he was by the prophet Hanani. Asa had sought an alliance with the king of Syria instead of relying on the Covenant, which he had renewed with Yahweh, and in his last illness he had recourse to medicine, which at that time was held to be magic.

Josaphat (870-848), in order to make knowledge of the Law more general, sent priests and Levites traveling through the country, taking with them the Torah of Yahweh, "the book of the law of the Lord" (2 Par. 17:9), and he set up in Jerusalem a court of judges to interpret it in disputed cases. By means of fasting, prayer, and the singing of psalms he won a bloodless victory over a coalition of Moabites and Edomites; but he was unsuccessful in a project for maritime trade be-

cause he had undertaken it in partnership with Ochozias of
Israel. The prophet Eliezer had foretold this failure, which was
no doubt due to natural causes, perhaps a storm or lack of
seamanship; but it is not on this "realistic" plane that the
prophets and chronicler see events. Josaphat entered into a
political and military alliance with Achab, king of Israel, and
married his son Joram to Athalia, Achab's daughter by Jezabel.
This mistake was to have consequences that the devout king
had not foreseen. Athalia exerted a baleful influence over her
husband, persuading him to kill all his brothers and re-establish
idolatrous worship. Joram's reign ended with a military disaster, and he was struck with an incurable disease; these were
in fact divine punishments.

After the short reign of Ochozias, the son of Joram, Athalia
(841-835) seized power, and to ensure that she would enjoy
it alone for some time, she put to death all the members of
the royal family. She also built in Jerusalem a temple to Baal
of the Phoenicians. But the boy Joas, son of Ochozias, had
escaped the massacre of his relations. Hidden in Yahweh's
Temple, he was brought up by the high priest Joiada who,
when the boy was seven years old, showed him to the people.
They acclaimed him king, and "Athalia was slain with the
sword in the king's house."

Having been brought up under such excellent conditions,
Joas showed his love for Yahweh by restoring the Temple,
which had fallen into disrepair during Athalia's reign, but he
was unsuccessful in suppressing all the private sanctuaries.
After the death of Joiada he fell into syncretist worship, and
when the high priest Zacharias, Joiada's son, reproached him
for it, he showed no hesitation in putting him to death in the
courtyard of the Temple. Joas was punished for this by an
invasion of the Assyrians and by a plot against him on the part
of his discontented subjects, who put him to death in his turn.
In his successors, Amasias, Ozias, and Joatham, with their suc-

cessive phases of true worship of Yahweh, unfaithfulness, and punishment, the story of Joas was repeated.

Achaz (736-716) left the reputation of a wicked king, "grievous to men, . . . to my God also," as Isaias said (7:13). To defend himself against the alliance of Syria and Israel, from which Isaias had assured him he had nothing to fear, he turned to the Assyrians. From this time Juda became the vassal of Assyria—at the very time when Israel disappeared from the political scene. Achaz, not content with worshiping "strange gods," shut the Temple and even practiced human sacrifice, offering his own son to Moloch of the Chanaanites.

The reign of Ezechias (716-687) was one of the most religious in the history of the kingdom of Juda. On the advice of Isaias, Ezechias undertook the difficult task of restoring the Temple and of banishing from the country the "abominations" that his predecessor had introduced. He renewed the Covenant (2 Par. 29:10), re-established the celebration of the festivals, and had the Scriptures that were in circulation carefully committed to writing (Prov. 25:1). He was anxious to be free of the vassalage of the Assyrians and sought to discontinue paying them tribute. Sennacherib, their king, reacted vigorously, and a triumphant campaign brought him, in 700, to the very gates of Jerusalem. He was unable, however, to effect an entry because the hand of Yahweh, against whom he had blasphemed, was upon him; a sudden outbreak of the plague forced him to raise the siege. Although the religious policy of Ezechias was successful insofar as rites and external practices were concerned, it does not appear to have greatly affected the interior disposition of his subjects. Micheas, who deplored this, as did Isaias, went so far as to foretell that as a punishment for their impiety the Jews would one day witness the destruction of the Temple and of Jerusalem (Mic. 3:9-12).

It was probably because of the superficial nature of Ezechias' restoration of the true worship of Yahweh that it did not survive its author, and that the reign of his son Manasse shows a reaction that the Scriptures clearly brand as wicked. Increasingly under the domination of Assyria, Manasse copied from that country the worship of the heavenly bodies, setting up in the courtyard of the Temple altars to "all the host of heaven" (4 Kings 21:3-5). To their worship he joined that of the Chanaanite idols, sacrificed his son to Moloch, and shed the blood of several of his subjects who had remained faithful to Yahweh. A Jewish tradition has it that it was on his order that the great prophet Isaias was sawn in two.

Josias (640-609), the grandson of Manasse, returned to the principles of Yahwism. He cleansed the country of all traces of idolatry and undertook the restoration of the Temple. In the course of this restoration the book of the Law, that is, Deuteronomy, was unearthed. It was probably a copy written at the time when Ezechias' agents were taking down in books the traditions and Mosaic narratives, which until that time the Jews had transmitted orally. The rediscovered "Book of the Covenant" was solemnly read in the presence of the people, and the Covenant was renewed. At the same time a religious reformation was systematically carried out: idolatrous altars, the crematorium set up for the sacrificing of children, and all other traces of syncretism were destroyed. The reform extended not only to Jerusalem and Judea but as far as Bethel and the region bordering on Samaria which Josias had added to his kingdom. Nechao II of Egypt, desiring to bring help to Ninive, the capital of Assyria, which in 612 had fallen to the onslaught of the Chaldeans and the Medes, demanded of Josias passage through the country. Josias offered armed resistance; he was defeated and killed at the battle of Mageddo.

Joakim (609-598) was a tool of Egypt, and he permitted the very worst syncretism to gain the upper hand. The prophet Jeremias, who was active at this time, had to denounce not only idolatrous practices but also a formalist and magical view of the worship of Yahweh which was bound up with them, a view which regarded the Temple as a kind of fetish under whose protection all kinds of wickedness were allowed. The same prophet was no less severe against the supporters of Egypt, whose imprudent activities were to draw down on Palestine the scourge of Nabuchodonosor (Nebuchadnezzar), the new king of Babylon and victor over the Egyptian ruler at Charcamis (605). The pro-Egyptian group, more firmly attached to its all too human viewpoint than to the will of Yahweh, would listen only to the time-serving prophets, whom Micheas said "divined for money" (Mic. 3:11). It instigated the bitter persecution of Jeremias though it did not succeed in harming his prestige. In 598 Joakim endeavored to throw off the yoke of Babylon. He was dead by the time Nabuchodonosor, to punish him, came to lay siege to Jerusalem.

Joakin, son of Joakim, was in the first group of Jews Nabuchodonosor carried off to Babylon. With him were all the leading men of the nation and all its metal workers. The victor also took with him the valuable ornaments and treasures belonging to the Temple.

Sedecias (598-587), the last king of Juda, was a puppet placed on the throne by Nabuchodonosor. A weakling, he consulted Jeremias in secret while leaving him to the mercies of his persecutors. Unable to withstand the intrigues of the Egyptians against the powerful sovereign to whom he owed the throne, he revolted against him. In 589 Nabuchodonosor appeared once more before the holy city, and, despite the heroism of its defenders, he took it in 587. In the Lamentations and the narrative portions of Jeremias we have moving accounts of the suffering endured by the people of Jerusalem during the siege. Great numbers were taken to Nabuchodonosor at Reblatha and massacred. Here Sedecias' eyes were put

out, and then he was carried off to Babylon with a great
number of the inhabitants of Juda. The city and Temple were
sacked and then burned. A governor, Godolias, was placed at
the head of the poor and the peasants, who alone remained in
the country. He was obliged to take up his residence in
Maspha, where he endeavored with the help of Jeremias,
now out of prison, to give fresh heart to the people by restoring the true worship of Yahweh, but he was soon assas-
sinated by pro-Egyptian fanatics. The latter, to elude reprisal
on the part of Nabuchodonosor, carried off to Egypt as many
as they could of those who remained of the nation—this in
spite of Jeremias, whom they obliged to accompany them and
who, even in Egypt, never ceased to reprove them for com-
promising with idolatry (Jer. 44). According to an unreliable
tradition, they finally stoned him to death. A third band of
exiles was taken to Babylon in 582/581. As Jeremias had foretold (25:11; 29:10), the exile in Babylon was to last about
seventy years.

THE PROPHETS

In the Bible we find mentioned "sons of the prophets,"
"false prophets," and "prophets of Yahweh."

The "sons of the prophets" were devout men living in community; some of their religious exercises, like music and
dancing, provoked a kind of ecstasy. No "prophet of Yahweh"
arose from among their ranks, but certain leaders, for example,
Elias and Eliseus, made use of their services on occasion.

The "false prophets" made of prophecy a lucrative busi-
ness to which they clung at all cost. Some of them claimed
to be inspired by Yahweh, while suiting their words to the
desires of the kings and people. Others devoted all their
ministry to the service of the Baals.

The "prophet of Yahweh," on the other hand, did not

choose his state; often he would embrace it with extreme
reluctance, as Amos did. He alone could call himself the
mouthpiece of Yahweh, because Yahweh had charged him
with a mission and spoke through his mouth. For all the
prophets of Yahweh this mission was to maintain and renew
the spirit of the Covenant; for some, it included also preaching the Messianic hope. Here we shall mention only a few of
the prophets of the Covenant.

The first great prophet is Elias, one of the most important
figures in Biblical history. He was sent to the kingdom of
Israel at the time of Achab and Jezabel. An uncouth ascetic,
clothed in coarse garments and enduring all sorts of priva-
tions, he preferred to live far from men in the solitude of
Mount Carmel. He became the uncompromising champion of
the one God against the Baals and other false gods. One of the
most celebrated episodes of his career took place on Carmel.

Elias had predicted to Achab that there would be a great
drought as a punishment to him and his kingdom for their
apostasy. "There shall not be dew nor rain these years, but
according to the words of my mouth." The king sent to seek
him out in order to put him to death.

After many days the word of the Lord came to Elias,
in the third year, saying: Go and shew thyself to Achab,
that I may give rain upon the face of the earth. And Elias
went to shew himself to Achab....

And when he had seen him, he said: Art thou he that
troublest Israel? And he said: I have not troubled Israel,
but thou and thy father's house, who have forsaken the
commandments of the Lord, and have followed Baalim.
Nevertheless send now, and gather unto me all Israel, unto
mount Carmel, and the prophets of Baal four hundred and
fifty, and the prophets of the groves four hundred, who
eat at Jezabel's table. Achab sent to all the children of

Israel, and gathered together the prophets unto mount Carmel.

And Elias coming to all the people, said: How long do you halt between two sides? if the Lord be God, follow him; but if Baal, then follow him. And the people did not answer him a word. And Elias said again to the people: I only remain a prophet of the Lord: but the prophets of Baal are four hundred and fifty men. Let two bullocks be given us, and let them choose one bullock for themselves, and cut it in pieces and lay it upon wood, but put no fire under: and I will dress the other bullock, and lay it on wood, and put no fire under it. Call ye on the names of your gods, and I will call on the name of my Lord: and the God that shall answer by fire, let him be God. And all the people answering said: A very good proposal.

Then Elias said to the prophets of Baal: Choose you one bullock and dress it first, because you are many: and call on the names of your gods, but put no fire under. And they took the bullock which he gave them, and dressed it: and they called on the name of Baal from morning even till noon, saying: O Baal, hear us. But there was no voice, nor any that answered: and they leaped over the altar that they had made. And when it was now noon, Elias jested at them, saying: Cry with a louder voice: for he is a god, and perhaps he is talking, or is in an inn, or on a journey, or perhaps he is asleep, and must be awaked. So they cried with a loud voice, and cut themselves after their manner with knives and lancets, till they were all covered with blood. And after midday was past, and while they were prophesying, the time was come of offering sacrifice, and there was no voice heard, nor did any one answer, nor regard them as they prayed.

Elias said to all the people: Come ye unto me. And the people coming near unto him, he repaired the altar of the

Lord, that was broken down. And he took twelve stones according to the number of the tribes of the sons of Jacob, to whom the word of the Lord came, saying: Israel shall be thy name. And he built with the stones an altar to the name of the Lord: and he made a trench for water, of the breadth of two furrows round about the altar. And he laid the wood in order, and cut the bullock in pieces, and laid it upon the wood. And he said: Fill four buckets with water, and pour it upon the burnt offering, and upon the wood. And again he said: Do the same the second time. And when they had done it the second time, he said: Do the same also the third time. And they did so the third time. And the water ran round about the altar, and the trench was filled with water.

And when it was now time to offer the holocaust, Elias the prophet came near and said: O Lord God of Abraham, and Isaac, and Israel, show this day that thou art the God of Israel and I thy servant, and that according to thy commandment I have done all these things. Hear me, O Lord, hear me: that this people may learn, that thou art the Lord God, and that thou hast turned their heart again.

Then the fire of the Lord fell, and consumed the holocaust, and the wood, and the stones, and the dust, and licked up the water that was in the trench. And when all the people saw this, they fell on their faces, and they said: The Lord he is God, the Lord he is God. And Elias said to them: Take the prophets of Baal, and let not one of them escape. And when they had taken them, Elias brought them down to the torrent Cison, and killed them there (3 Kings 18: 1-2, 18-40).

Elias was carried up to heaven on a fiery chariot:

When the Lord would take up Elias into heaven by a whirlwind, . . . Elias and Eliseus were going from Galgal.

And Elias said to Eliseus: Stay thou here, because the
Lord hath sent me as far as Bethel. And Eliseus said to him:
As the Lord liveth, and as thy soul liveth, I will not
leave thee. And when they were come down to Bethel, the
sons of the prophets, that were at Bethel, came forth to
Eliseus, and said to him: Dost thou know that this day
the Lord will take away thy master from thee? And he
answered: I also know it: hold your peace.

And Elias said to Eliseus: Stay here, because the Lord
hath sent me to Jericho. And he said: As the Lord liveth,
and as thy soul liveth, I will not leave thee. And when they
were come to Jericho, the sons of the prophets, that were
at Jericho, came to Eliseus, and said to him: Dost thou
know that this day the Lord will take away thy master
from thee? And he said: I also know it: hold your peace.

And Elias said to him: Stay here, because the Lord hath
sent me as far as the Jordan. And he said: As the Lord
liveth, and as thy soul liveth, I will not leave thee: and
they two went on together. And fifty men of the sons of
the prophets followed them, and stood in sight at a distance: but they two stood by the Jordan. And Elias took
his mantle and folded it together, and struck the waters,
and they were divided hither and thither, and they both
passed over on dry ground.

And when they had gone over, Elias said to Eliseus:
Ask what thou wilt have me to do for thee, before I be
taken away from thee. And Eliseus said: I beseech thee
that in me may be thy double spirit. And he answered:
Thou hast asked a hard thing: nevertheless, if thou see me
when I am taken from thee, thou shalt have what thou
hast asked; but if thou see me not, thou shalt not have it.

And as they went on, walking and talking together, behold a fiery chariot, and fiery horses, parted them both
asunder: and Elias went up by a whirlwind into heaven.

And Eliseus saw him, and cried: My father, my father, the
chariot of Israel, and the driver thereof. And he saw him
no more: and he took hold of his own garments, and rent
them in two pieces. And he took up the mantle of Elias,
that fell from him . . . (4 Kings 2:1-13).

The return of Elias was to form one of the constant themes
of Jewish apocalyptic literature; one hears its echoes in the
Gospels. Elias appears in them as the typical prophet; the
archangel Gabriel and Jesus himself refer to his mission to
show the importance of that of John the Baptist. At our
Saviour's transfiguration Peter, James, and John saw Moses
and Elias on either side of him, one the personification of the
Law, the other of the Prophets.

Eliseus, disciple of Elias, resembled him in many ways, although he led a less solitary life and on occasion made use
of music to induce ecstasy and prophecy (4 Kings 3:15). He
too performed many miracles in order to bear witness to
Yahweh's infinite power; he too was held responsible for the
disasters that he had foretold; he too answered by predict-
ing the arrival of help, in which no one believed and which
nevertheless came just as he had said. On occasion he could
relax his severity, as he did, for example, when he spared the
Syrians, showing such mercy as was unknown among victors
in ancient times; or when he restored her child alive to the
Sunamite woman:

Eliseus therefore went into the house, and behold the
child lay dead on his bed. And going in he shut the door
upon him, and upon the child, and prayed to the Lord.
And he went up, and lay upon the child: and he put his
mouth upon his mouth, and his eyes upon his eyes, and
his hands upon his hands: and he bowed himself upon
him, and the child's flesh grew warm. Then he returned
and walked in the house, once to and fro: and he went up,

and lay upon him: and the child gaped seven times, and opened his eyes. And he called Giezi, and said to him: Call this Sunamitess. And she being called, went in to him: and he said: Take up thy son. She came and fell at his feet, and worshipped upon the ground: and took up her son, and went out (4 Kings 4:32-7).

There were other prophets in the same period. One was the first Micheas, the son of Jemla, who alone, in opposition to the time-serving prophets, foretold the defeat of Achab at Ramoth-Galaad. Like Elias and Eliseus, these prophets are known to us only by what we are told of them, for they left no writings.

The first of the writer prophets is Amos, who exercised his ministry in the kingdom of Israel under Jeroboam II in about the year 750. He was unable to resist the call of God for, as he says, "The lion shall roar, who will not fear? The Lord God hath spoken, who shall not prophesy?" (Amos 3:8).

I am not a prophet, nor am I the son of a prophet; but I am a herdsman plucking wild figs. And the Lord took me when I followed the flock, and the Lord said to me: Go, prophesy to my people Israel. And now hear thou the word of the Lord (Amos 7:14-16).

The kingdom of Israel was enjoying a period of prosperity. The nobles feasted in their palaces in Samaria and the poor starved. In the sanctuaries Yahweh was represented in the form of a golden calf. The merchants made use of false measures; the rich brought the poor to slavery (8:5-6).

Since the idolatrous nations had been punished for their sins, Amos declared, the Jews should learn from this that a similar fate awaited them. In any case they were not to flatter themselves that their legal observances would suffice to save them. Yahweh instructed them by the mouth of Amos:

I hate, and have rejected your festivities:
> and I will not receive the odor of your assemblies.
And if you offer me holocausts, and your gifts,
> I will not receive them:
> neither will I regard the vows [sacrifices] of your
> > fat beasts.
Take away from me the tumult of thy songs:
> and I will not hear the canticles of thy harp.
But judgment shall be revealed as water,
> and justice as a mighty torrent.
> > (Amos 5:21-4)

This is, he says, because they have "cast away the law of the Lord, and have not kept his commandments; for their idols have caused them to err ..."; it is because they have "sold the just man for silver, and the poor man for a pair of shoes ..." (2:4-6). For this reason Israel will be punished and will "go into captivity beyond Damascus" (5:27) into Assyria, despite the fact of God's choosing this people for his own. For this choice is not a privilege needing no return on their part, and they delude themselves who await the "day of the Lord" saying, "The evils shall not approach, and shall not come upon us" (9:10). On the other hand, those who do good can still hope and await the Lord's intervention in favor of "the tabernacle of David that is fallen" (9:11):

Hate evil, and love good,
> and establish judgment in the gate:
> it may be the Lord the God of hosts
> may have mercy on the remnant of Joseph.
> > (Amos 5:15)

The "remnant" of Israel, the "day of the Lord" (5:18) are used here for the first time. We shall find that they recur frequently in prophetical literature.

Such views imply that the idea of the Covenant was alive.
Osee, who prophesied a few years later, spoke in much the
same way. He too repeats that Yahweh cares little for a
worship that is merely external and a formality:

> For I desire mercy [love], and not sacrifice:
>   and the knowledge of God more than holocausts.
>   (Osee 6:6)

That sentence was to be repeated by Jesus and adopted as
his own. But what stamps Osee's prophecy with an accent all
its own is his insistent portrayal of the Covenant of Yahweh
with his people as a love match, and of the faithlessness of
Israel, running after false gods and foreign help, as adultery—
like a lost woman seeking her lovers. The prophet's marriage
with Gomer, a prostitute, whom he was unable to prevent
himself loving, and whom he took back after proving her, is
a symbol of Yahweh's passion for a faithless people whom
punishment alone will bring back to their divine bridegroom:

> I will allure her, and will lead her into the wilderness:
> And I will speak to her heart. . . .

> And I will espouse thee to me in justice, and judgment,
>   and in mercy, and in commiserations [in tenderness
>   and in love],
> And I will espouse thee to me in faith:
>   and thou shalt know that I am the Lord.
>   (Osee 2:14-20)

With Osee, this image entered into the treasure house of the
Bible; there it was to remain. It is to be found in all the great
prophets and in the Canticle of Canticles; and it appears in full
beauty in the New Testament, where Jesus and his Church
appear as Bridegroom and Bride, as were Yahweh and his
people.

The work of Isaias, who was a prophet in the kingdom of Juda, is too important to be dealt with solely in this chapter, and we shall return to it again.[1] Here we will confine our discussion to the place he occupied among the prophets of the Covenant. His vocation came to him during a vision in the Temple in 740:

> In the year that king Ozias died, I saw the Lord sitting upon a throne high and elevated: and his train filled the temple. Upon it stood the seraphims: the one had six wings, and the other had six wings: with two they covered his face, and with two they covered his feet, and with two they flew. And they cried one to another, and said:

> Holy, holy, holy, the Lord God of hosts,
>   all the earth is full of his glory.

> And the lintels of the doors were moved at the voice of him that cried, and the house was filled with smoke. And I said:

> Woe is me [I am lost],
>   because I have held my peace;
>   because I am a man of unclean lips,
>   and I dwell in the midst of a people that have
>   unclean lips,
>   and I have seen with my eyes the King the
>   Lord of hosts.

> And one of the seraphims flew to me, and in his hand was a live coal, which he had taken with the tongs off the altar. And he touched my mouth, and said:

> Behold this has touched thy lips,
>   and thy iniquities shall be taken away,
>   and thy sin shall be cleansed.

[1] See pages 164-70.

And I heard the voice of the Lord, saying:

Whom shall I send?
  and who shall go for us?

    And I said:

Lo, here am I, send me.

(Isa. 6: 1-8)

Although Isaias does not explicitly mention the Covenant, it is obvious that he is referring to it. From the first words of his book, the children of Israel are vehemently reproved as unfaithful: "I have brought up children, and exalted them: but they have despised me. . . . a wicked seed, ungracious children: they have forsaken the Lord" (1:2-4). This unfaithfulness on the part of Jerusalem is "prostitution": "How is the faithful city . . . become a harlot?" (1:21). The sacrifices offered to the Lord do not please him; they are only an empty ritualism if there is not joined with them an active concern for justice and charity:

To what purpose do you offer me the multitude of your
                              victims?
      saith the Lord.
I am full, I desire not holocausts of rams,
      and fat of fatlings . . .
      for your hands are full of blood.

Wash yourselves, be clean,
      take away the evil of your devices from my eyes:
      cease to do perversely,
      learn to do well:
      seek judgment, relieve the oppressed,
      judge for the fatherless, defend the widow.

(Isa. 1: 11-17)

We can discern here the principal themes of Osee. An instance of another is the comparison of Israel with an "empty vine" that will one day become the "choicest vine," for even the sternest prophecy hints at forgiveness for a repentant Israel.

Isaias, one of the great lyric poets of the world, gives striking proof of a religious spirituality worthy of the highest of the mystics. He evolved definitive statements some of which were repeated by our Lord himself: "This people draw near me with their mouth, and with their lips glorify me, but their heart is far from me, and they have feared me with the commandment and doctrines of men..." (29:13).

Those whom Yahweh uses to punish his people—the Assyrian to whom he "whistles" from the ends of the earth (5:26), as he "hissed" for the flies in Egypt (7:18), "the razor" that he hired beyond the Euphrates (7:20), and the "rod and staff" of his anger (10:5)—are only instruments. They are not to grow proud. Once their mission is completed, they will be broken: Assur will be smitten by the sword; those whose purpose it was to lay waste the fortified towns, when it was Yahweh's will that they should do so, will find that he will put a ring in their nose and a bit between their lips because, in their pride, they thought that they could prevail against him and his people; by the way that he came, Sennacherib would return (37:26-9).

Jeremias, the other great prophet, the "man of sorrows" who witnessed the disappearance of the kingdom of Juda, was also a prophet of the Covenant. He was profoundly influenced by Deuteronomy, which was rediscovered at the time of his youth; the phrase: "Hearken to my voice: and I will be your God and you shall be my people," which is the affirmation of the Covenant, is constantly on his lips. For Jeremias, fidelity to the Covenant meant a return to the spirit of Mosaic times: "Thus saith the Lord: I have remembered thee, pitying thy youth, and the love of thy espousals, when thou fol-

lowedst me in the desert . . ." (2:2). He sees the nations who
wish to attract the people of Israel with the promise of their
support as "lovers" who run after the guilty "bride" to dis-
honor her and wish even to do her to death. But let the wife
embrace her husband, and the divine Bridegroom will show
her nothing but mercy (3:12-13).

Moreover, neither the Temple, nor burnt offerings, nor the
Law, nor circumcision of the flesh, will avail to save a people
whose will is rooted in sin (4:4; 7:4; 8:8; 9:24). Israel will
be treated like the two baskets offered as first fruits in the
Temple:

> The Lord showed me: and behold two baskets full of
> figs, set before the temple of the Lord. . . . One basket had
> very good figs, like figs of the first season: and the other
> basket had very bad figs, which could not be eaten, be-
> cause they were bad. . . .
>
> And the word of the Lord came to me, saying: Thus
> saith the Lord the God of Israel: Like these good figs, so
> will I regard the captives of Juda, whom I have sent forth
> out of this place into the land of the Chaldeans, for their
> good. And I will set my eyes upon them to be pacified,
> and I will bring them again into this land: And I will
> build them up, and not pull them down: and I will plant
> them, and not pluck them up. And I will give them a heart
> to know me, that I am the Lord: and they shall be my
> people, and I will be their God: because they shall return
> to me with their whole heart.
>
> And as the very bad figs, that cannot be eaten, because
> they are bad: thus saith the Lord: So will I give Sedecias
> the king of Juda, and his princes, and the residue of
> Jerusalem, that have remained in this city, and that dwell
> in the land of Egypt. And I will deliver them up to vexa-
> tion, and affliction, to all the kingdoms of the earth: to be

a reproach, and a byword, and a proverb, and to be a
curse in all places to which I have cast them out. And I
will send among them the sword, and the famine, and the
pestilence: till they be consumed out of the land which I
gave to them and to their fathers (Jer. 24: 1-2; 4-10).

Thus, after the seventy years' exile, God will lead his people
back to Palestine; Jerusalem will be rebuilt; and, in the north
and in the south, sacrifices of thanksgiving will once more be
offered. There will be no Ark of the Covenant, but a new day
will dawn in which external actions will be of less importance
than sincerity of heart, and in which God will deal far more
with individuals, without lessening the role of the community
as such.

Behold the days shall come, saith the Lord, and I will
make a new covenant with the house of Israel, and with
the house of Juda. . . . I will give my law in their bowels,
and I will write it in their heart: and I will be their God,
and they shall be my people. And they shall teach no more
every man his neighbour, and every man his brother, saying: Know the Lord: for all shall know me from the least
of them even to the greatest, saith the Lord: for I will
forgive their iniquity, and I will remember their sin no
more (Jer. 31:31-4).

Here is foretold the coming of that personal, spiritual religion, the religion of the new Covenant, of which Jesus was
to speak at the Last Supper.

CHAPTER 4

The People of the Covenant:
From the Exile to the Coming of Christ

THE ISRAELITES AND THE PROPHETS
DURING THE EXILE

W E KNOW hardly anything of the Jews of the kingdom of Israel who were carried off to Ninive. Ill-equipped
for such a trial because of the inferior level of religion that had
existed in Samaria, they probably lost, among the Assyrians,
what little remained of Yahwism and national conscience.

We are better informed concerning the Jews of Juda who
were deported to Babylon. Not all learned from their mis-
fortune the lessons that it had to teach. Some adapted themselves to the Chaldean country, in which trade and husbandry
flourished. The relative freedom left to them enabled them to
engage in commerce. They were extremely successful, forgot
their former homeland, and became completely pagan.

Others, on the contrary, remained faithful to Yahweh.
Their love for their lost homeland was but increased, and
they looked back with longing to Sion (Jerusalem) and the
Temple ceremonies, refusing any religious contact with their
oppressors:

By the streams of Babylon
    we sat and wept
    when we remembered Sion.
On the aspens of that land
    we hung up our harps,

Though there our captors asked of us
    the lyrics of our songs,
And our despoilers urged us to be joyous:
    "Sing for us the songs of Sion!"

How could we sing a song of the Lord
    in a foreign land?
If I forget you, Jerusalem,
    may my right hand be forgotten!
May my tongue cleave to my palate
    if I remember you not,
If I place not Jerusalem
    ahead of my joy. . . .

O daughter of Babylon, you destroyer,
    happy the man who shall repay you
    the evil you have done us!
Happy the man who shall seize and smash
    your little ones against the rock!
                (Ps. 136:1-9)

There was no longer any question of the exiles' performing the ritual acts that could take place only in the Temple, but those of their priests who had survived the massacre of Reblatha (Jer. 52:24-7) had by no means lost their prestige. Frequently they became the spiritual leaders of the exiles. In addition, the scribes and doctors of the Law, from both within and without the ranks of the priesthood, came to assume a role of increasing importance.

Up to this time the Scriptures were transmitted principally by being memorized and passed on by word of mouth, not by writing. Copies of the Law had always been scarce and many perished in the disaster. To preserve the decrees of the Mosaic Law and all that was remembered of national history from further disasters, writers or "scribes" copied onto scrolls

the different versions in circulation. Although these agreed
fundamentally, there were variations in detail: in one tribe
God was called *Yahweh* and in another *'Elohim;* again,
some aspect of the history of Israel may have been accorded
greater importance in one tribe than in another. The scribes,
guided by their scrupulous reverence for the sacred "word,"
put down, like mere collectors of texts, exactly what they
were told, without eliminating divergencies or reducing variations in the versions to uniformity.

Since many passages of the Law needed interpretation
when they were applied to concrete situations of the time,
groups of jurists and casuists were established on whom devout
Jews relied for the direction of their consciences. These authorized interpreters were called "doctors of the Law." One
of these was the priest Ezechiel, who among the Babylonian
exiles was outstanding as a legal authority. He was also endowed with the charism of prophecy.

God continued to send prophets to Israel. In this way was
ensured the continuity in the designs of Providence for this
people which one might have thought no longer existed as a
nation, but which, on the contrary, was increasingly finding
its feet.

The great prophets of the Exile are Jeremias, Ezechiel, and
the "second Isaias."

Jeremias, who was not included among the Babylonian
exiles, sent messages to them. Unlike the complaisant prophets
who foretold that the captivity would be short, he asserted
that it would last for decades and he advised his fellow
countrymen to settle on the banks of the Euphrates, to plant
trees, build houses, and found families in order to safeguard the
future. Increasingly, he insisted on the need for personal piety,
since Yahweh required that not only the community but also
the individual be close to him. The prophet mourns the misfortunes of Jerusalem in these terms:

They oppressed the women in Sion,
    and the virgins in the cities of Juda.
The princes were hanged up by their hand:
    they did not respect the persons of the ancient.
They abused the young men indecently [young men were
                compelled to grind naked in the mill]:
    and the children fell under the wood [under the loads
          of wood].
The ancients had ceased from the gates:
    the young men from the choir of their singers [from
          their music].
The joy of our heart is ceased,
    our dancing is turned into mourning.
The crown is fallen from our head:
    woe to us because we have sinned.
Therefore is our heart sorrowful,
    therefore are our eyes become dim.
For mount Sion, because it is destroyed,
    foxes have walked upon it.
                    (Lam. 5:11-18)

But Jeremias gave grounds for hope:

But thou, O Lord, shalt remain for ever,
    thy throne from generation to generation.
Why wilt thou forget us for ever?
    Why wilt thou forsake us for a long time?
Convert us, O Lord, to thee, and we shall be converted:
    renew our days, as from the beginning.
                    (Lam. 5:19-21)

This "renewal of their days" was to come when the conquerors of the Jews were in turn vanquished by the Persians,
and Babylon was captured by Cyrus:

And Jeremias wrote in one book all the evil that was to
come upon Babylon: all these words that are written
against Babylon. And Jeremias said to Saraias: When thou
shalt come into Babylon, and shalt see, and shalt read all
these words, Thou shalt say: O Lord, thou hast spoken
against this place to destroy it: so that there should be
neither man nor beast to dwell therein, and that it should
be desolate for ever. And when thou hast made an end of
reading this book, thou shalt tie a stone to it, and shalt
throw it into the midst of the Euphrates: And thou shalt
say: Thus shall Babylon sink, and she shall not rise up
from the affliction that I will bring upon her (Jer. 51:60-4).

Ezechiel was Yahweh's great prophet among the captive
people; he received his prophetical mission at Jerusalem six
years before the capture of the city. He tells us how the word
of God was put into his mouth:

I fell upon my face, and I heard the voice of one that
spoke. And he said to me: Son of man, stand upon thy
feet, and I will speak to thee. And the spirit entered into
me after that he spoke to me, and he set me upon my feet:
And I heard him speaking to me, and saying: Son of
man, I send thee to the children of Israel, to a rebellious
people, that hath revolted from me. . . . And they to whom
I send thee are children of a hard face, and of an obstinate
heart: and thou shalt say to them: Thus saith the Lord
God: If so be they at least will hear, and if so be they will
forbear . . . they shall know that there hath been a prophet
in the midst of them. And thou, O son of man, fear not,
neither be thou afraid of their words: for thou art among
unbelievers and destroyers, and thou dwellest with scor-
pions. . . . And thou shalt speak my words to them. . . .
Open thy mouth, and eat what I give thee.
And I looked, and behold, a hand was sent to me,

wherein was a book rolled up: and he spread it before me, and it was written within and without: and there were written in it lamentations, and canticles, and woe. And he said to me: Son of man, eat all that thou shalt find: eat this book. . . . And he said to me: Son of man, thy belly shall eat, and thy bowels shall be filled with this book, which I give thee. And I did eat it: and it was sweet as honey in my mouth. And he said to me: Son of man, go to the house of Israel, and thou shalt speak my words to them (Ez. 2:1-9; 3:1-4).

When the misfortunes foretold by Ezechiel occurred, he accompanied the exiles and became their comforter. He told them, or rather God made known to them through his mouth, that a restoration would come about, that the day would dawn when Israel and Juda would mend their broken unity, and that a new Covenant would be entered into in place of the old. This time it would be an "eternal Covenant" over which a great prince would preside; around him all would gather once more, like sheep round a good shepherd:

For this saith the Lord God: Behold I myself will seek my sheep, and will visit them. . . . And I will bring them out from the peoples . . . and will bring them to their own land: and I will feed them in the mountains of Israel, by the rivers, and in all the habitations of the land. . . . I will feed my sheep: and I will cause them to lie down, saith the Lord God. I will seek that which was lost: and that which was driven away, I will bring again: and I will bind up that which was broken, and I will strengthen that which was weak (Ez. 34:11-16).

Ezechiel declared that the signs of the old Covenant, such as the Sabbath and circumcision, would be held in honor once more, but he, too, insisted that these external observances be the sincere expression of a personal religion:

And I will pour upon you clean water, and you shall be
cleansed from all your filthiness, and I will cleanse you
from all your idols. And I will give you a new heart, and
put a new spirit within you: and I will take away the
stony heart out of your flesh, and will give you a heart
of flesh. And I will put my spirit in the midst of you:
and I will cause you to walk in my commandments
(Ez. 36:25-7).

To Jeremias and Ezechiel, as prophets of the Exile, must
be added the authors of the "Book of Comfort" and the
"Poems of the Servant." These writings, of the "second
Isaias," were added to those of the prophet of that name because they seem to be a continuation of his work. The "Book
of Comfort" contains fifteen chapters (Isa. 40-65); from these
must be taken the "Poems of the Servant," which have been
combined with them and are to be found in the following
passages: Isa. 42:1-9; 49:1-7; 50:4-9; and 52:13 to 53:12.

The "Book of Comfort" seems to have been written about
542 B.C., two or three years before Cyrus captured Babylon.
The purpose of the book is stated in the first lines:

Be comforted, be comforted, my people, saith your God.
Speak ye to the heart of Jerusalem, and call to her:
    for her evil is come to an end,
    her iniquity is forgiven:
    she hath received of the hand of the Lord
    double for all her sins.
              (Isa. 40:1-2)

Yahweh, the "King of Israel," is the only true God, the
"Book of Comfort" continues. He created the world and
knows the future. The release from servitude that he promised
his people is about to take place. To effect it, he will make use
of his "servant and friend," Cyrus the Persian, who has already

vanquished Astyages of Media and Croesus of Lydia and will
soon overcome Nabonidus of Babylon (539 B.C.). The powerless idols of this proud city will then be carried off like mere
merchandise on the backs of beasts of burden, and the chosen
people will once more travel the road to Jerusalem:

Thus saith the Lord:
What is this bill of the divorce of your mother,
    with which I have put her away?
Or who is my creditor,
    to whom I sold you?
Behold you are sold for your iniquities,
    and for your wicked deeds have I put your
                mother away.
            (50:1)

And now thus saith the Lord
    that created thee, O Jacob,
    and formed thee, O Israel:
Fear not, for I have redeemed thee,
    and called thee by thy name: thou art mine.
When thou shalt pass through the waters, I will be
                with thee,
    and the rivers shall not cover thee:
When thou shalt walk in the fire, thou shalt not be burnt,
    and the flames shall not burn in thee:
For I am the Lord thy God,
    the Holy One of Israel, thy Saviour:
I have given Egypt for thy atonement,
    Ethiopia and Saba for thee.
           (43:1-3)

Thus saith the Lord, the king of Israel,
    and his redeemer the Lord of hosts:
I am the first, and I am the last,
    and besides me there is no God.

Who is like to me? let him call and declare:
>   and let him set before me the order,
>   since I appointed the ancient people.

(44:6-7)

Who hath measured the waters in the hollow of his hand,
>   and weighed the heavens with his palm?
Who hath poised with three fingers the bulk of the earth,
>   and weighed the mountains in scales,
>   and the hills in a balance?

(40:12)

Woe to him that gainsayeth his maker,
>   a sherd of the earthen pots:
Shall the clay say to him that fashioneth it:
>   What art thou making,
>   and thy work is without hands?

(45:9)

To whom then have you likened God?
>   or what image will you make for him?

(40:18)

Thus saith the Lord:
Keep ye judgment, and do justice:
>   for my salvation is near to come.

(56:1)

Throughout the "Book of Comfort" the vision goes far beyond the chosen people. The divine message is of universal application, the Covenant destined one day to encompass the whole world:

Enlarge the place of thy tent,
>   and stretch out the skins of thy tabernacles
>   [thy dwellings];
>   spare not: lengthen thy cords, and strengthen
>   thy stakes.

For thou shalt pass on [spread abroad] to the right hand,
                         and to the left:
    and thy seed shall inherit the Gentiles,
    and shall inhabit the desolate cities.

                         (54:2-3)

All you that thirst, come to the waters:
    and you that have no money, make haste, buy, and eat:
    come ye, buy wine and milk without money,
    and without any price....
And the nations that knew not thee shall run to thee,
    because of the Lord thy God,
    and for the Holy One of Israel.

                         (55:1, 5)

The four prophetical poems of the "Servant of Yahweh"
form the climax of the Old Testament. As we shall see on the
subject of the suffering Messias (Chapter 6), they foretell the
coming of a mysterious person, whose life is to be one of
gentleness and suffering, who will take upon himself the sins of
others and save sinners by substitution. Moreover, his mission
will not be confined to Israel, for, as Yahweh says of him, "I
have given thee ... for a light of the Gentiles" (Isa. 42:6).

THE RETURN FROM EXILE AND THE RESTORATION: FROM ZOROBABEL TO ESDRAS

Cyrus seized Babylon in 539 B.C. Although he was a Persian,
and therefore a worshiper of Ahuramazda, he took care, as a
matter of policy, to allow the peoples who fell into his power
to retain their own divinities. He authorized the Israelites to
return to their own land and there to worship their God.
We know the terms of the decree that he issued in 538 B.C.:

Thus saith Cyrus king of the Persians: The Lord the
God of heaven hath given to me all the kingdoms of the

earth, and he hath charged me to build him a house in Jerusalem, which is in Judea. Who is there among you of all his people? His God be with him. Let him go up to Jerusalem, which is in Judea, and build the house of the Lord the God of Israel: he is the God that is in Jerusalem. And let all the rest in all places wheresoever they dwell, help him every man from his place, with silver and gold, and goods, and cattle, besides that which they offer freely to the temple of God, which is in Jerusalem (Esd. 1:2-4).

A first party of exiles set out in the spring of 537. The departure took place amid scenes of enthusiasm. The Jews could sing the verses of the prophet foretelling their deliverance, which we have already quoted in Chapter 1:

> The voice of one crying,
>> In the desert [1] prepare ye the way of the Lord,
>> make straight in the wilderness the paths of our God.
> Every valley shall be exalted,
>> and every mountain and hill shall be made low,
>> and the crooked shall become straight,
>> and the rough ways plain.
> And the glory of the Lord shall be revealed,
>> and all flesh together shall see,
>> that the mouth of the Lord hath spoken. . . .
>
> Get thee up upon a high mountain,
>> thou that bringest good tidings to Sion:
>> lift up thy voice with strength,
>> thou that bringest good tidings to Jerusalem:
>> lift it up, fear not,
>> say to the cities of Juda: Behold your God.
>>   (Isa. 40:3-5, 9)

[1] The Douay version, following the Vulgate, has "The voice of one crying in the desert: Prepare ye," etc.—Translator's note.

For the administration of the country, twelve governors, one for each tribe, were appointed by the Persian king. The most important of them was Zorobabel, one of David's descendants, who figures in the Gospel genealogy of Christ. The high priest Josue, son of the last high priest in Jerusalem, whom Nabuchodonosor had put to death, accompanied the returning exiles.

Their first task was to set up again the altar of burnt offerings. Then they intended to start rebuilding the Temple. The Samaritans demanded to be allowed to participate, but the strict Yahwists, deeming them too paganized, refused their help. In their annoyance the Samaritans prevailed upon the Persian authorities to prevent the Jews in Jerusalem from continuing their undertaking. Not until fifteen years later was the rebuilding of the Temple again resumed. The prophets Aggeus and Zacharias were lavish with their encouragement, and the Jews still in Babylon sent substantial aid. Speaking to his fellow countrymen who lost heart in the face of all sorts of difficulties, Aggeus said:

Is it time for you
    to dwell in ceiled houses,
    and this house lie desolate? . . .

Thus saith the Lord of hosts:
Set your hearts upon your ways.
Go up to the mountain, bring timber,
    and build the house:
    and it shall be acceptable to me,
    and I shall be glorified, saith the Lord.

                    (Ag. 1:4-8)

Zacharias, for his part, shows Yahweh speaking as follows:

I will return to Jerusalem in mercies:
>   my house shall be built in it,
>   saith the Lord of hosts:
>   and the building line shall be stretched forth upon
>   Jerusalem. . . .
Sing praise, and rejoice, O daughter of Sion:
>   for behold I come, and I will dwell in the midst of thee.
>   (Zach. 1:16; 2:10)

In 515 the new Temple was finished; part of the treasures carried off by Nabuchodonosor had been brought back. For those who had known the former house of Yahweh, the new one cut a poor figure, but it was to see the days of the Messias; there Jesus was to go to pray. During a ceremony in the new Temple Aggeus spoke to the Jews:

Who is left among you,
>   that saw this house in its first glory?
>   and how do you see it now?
Is it not in comparison to that as nothing in your eyes?
Yet now take courage, O Zorobabel,
>   saith the Lord,
And take courage, O Jesus the son of Josedec the high priest,
And take courage, all ye people of the land,
>   saith the Lord of hosts: and perform
(For I am with you, saith the Lord of hosts). . . .
Great shall be the glory of this last house
>   more than of the first.
>   (Ag. 2:4-10)

For want of evidence, we know nothing of events occurring between 515 and 458; even for those of the half century following, the chronology is very uncertain. The two figures who dominate this period are Nehemias and Esdras.

Nehemias, cupbearer to Artaxerxes I, was one of the faithful followers of Yahweh whose profession had kept them in Babylon. His influence at the Persian court enabled him to secure the separation of Judea from the province of Samaria, to which it had been joined in 587, and the provision that it be administratively autonomous. He came to Jerusalem for the first time in about 445.

Equipped with ample powers, he had the walls of the city rebuilt in order to allow the Jewish community to live in peace according to the Law. He remained in Jerusalem for twelve years, endeavoring to restore observance of the Mosaic prescriptions and to root out abuses. Of the latter, there were many: beasts cast out of the herds were offered to Yahweh; religious taxes were evaded as much as possible; the priests drifted with the tide; many Jews married foreigners. Nehemias required of the priests strict fulfillment of their duties, and of the people, exact observance of the Sabbath-day rest. He would allow no further infiltration of foreign blood into the community of Israel. He writes:

> In those days also I saw Jews that married wives, women of Azotus, and of Ammon, and of Moab. . . . And I chid them, and laid my curse upon them. And I beat some of them, and shaved off their hair, and made them swear by God that they would not give their daughters to their sons, nor take their daughters for their sons, nor for themselves, saying: Did not Solomon king of Israel sin in this kind of thing? and surely among many nations, there was not a king like him, and he was beloved of his God, and God made him king over all Israel: and yet women of other countries brought even him to sin. . . .
>
> And one of the sons of Joiada the son of Eliasib the high priest, was son in law to Sanaballat the Horonite, and I drove him from me. . . .
>
> So I separated from them all strangers, and I appointed

the courses of the priests and the Levites, every man in his
ministry: And for the offering of wood at times appointed,
and for the first-fruits: remember me, O my God, unto
good. Amen (Neh. 13:23-31).

The woman whom the son of Joiada married was the
daughter of the ruler of Samaria.

It was not, however, Nehemias, a layman, but Esdras, a
priest, who was destined to carry out the great religious
reformation of Israel. In the decree of Artaxerxes charging
Esdras with the responsibility of appointing judges and scribes
and seeing that the Law of Yahweh was observed in Israel,
Esdras is described as "the most learned of the law of the God
of heaven"; this is probably an allusion to the functions of
secretary for Jewish affairs which he performed at the Persian
court. In what year did Esdras come to Jerusalem? Three
dates have been suggested—458, 428, and 398. According to
some authorities, he spent two periods in the Holy City; according to others, only one. In any case, the intervention of
this great man proved of capital importance. Owing to the
efforts of Nehemias, administrative order had been re-established in the country. It now remained to imbue this reform
with a soul. Esdras brought with him "the book of the law" as
it had been codified by the scribes during the Exile. Substan-
tially at least, it was the Pentateuch as we have it today. It was
read and explained during the solemn ceremonies that concluded with the renewal of the Covenant; this renewal was
recorded in a document signed by the priests, Levites, and
elders.

The part played by Esdras is of such importance that some
extreme critics have attributed to him authorship of the
Pentateuch. This is quite erroneous, for we have abundant
proof that the Law and Mosaic traditions were in existence
before his time. It is true, nonetheless, that Esdras can be

called "the father of Judaism" if by this term is meant that form of religion which originated in the decree of Artaxerxes at the time Esdras went to Jerusalem, and which became so firmly established that nothing could subsequently penetrate its defenses.[2]

THE RESISTANCE TO HELLENISM: THE MACHABEES

Far from Jerusalem, however, many Jews remained faithful to Yahweh or continued to claim him as their God. There were those who had not returned from exile and tarried for some time in Babylon. Among them were the painstaking scribes, whom we have already mentioned, who continued to collect the sources and documents of the history of Israel. After having assembled the books of the Law (the Pentateuch), they turned to the prophetical books, and then to the sapiential books.

Among the Samaritans, also, there remained servants of Yahweh. The grandson of the high priest Joiada, expelled by Nehemias, took refuge among them, as did other priests unable to stomach his reform. Their presence led to the building of a schismatic temple on Mount Garizim. The Samaritans possessed one of the Pentateuchs brought by Esdras from Babylon. In their eyes this was the whole of Scripture. At variance with

[2] The activities of Nehemias and Esdras are described in the books that bear their names. At the same period were written:

The Book of Malachias (c. 450): At the same time that Malachias reprimands his fellow countrymen, he foretells a time when Yahweh will receive "a pure oblation." He also foretells the Precursor of the Messias.

The Book of Jonas (c. 450) is a work of edification and of universalist tendency. In it Yahweh is shown to love the pagans of Ninive as he loves the Jews, for he is "a gracious and merciful God, patient and of much compassion, and easy to forgive" (4:2).

The Book of Joel (c. 400) is inclined to xenophobia.

The Book of Ruth (c. 450) is a historical work. Its author seems to react against the reforms of Nehemias by showing how Ruth, a Moabite, a foreigner, who had accepted the conditions of the Covenant, was incorporated into the Jewish community and became an ancestress of David.

Jerusalem, when the prophetical and sapiential books reached them, they never admitted these two collections. They gradually weaned themselves from the syncretism with which they were charged by the Jews of Jerusalem, but these persisted in regarding them as heretics and foreigners, and continued to detest them. The Samaritans felt the same way about the Jews of Jerusalem. This state of open warfare still existed in our Lord's day though it did not prevent his conversing at length with a Samaritan woman to convert her, or setting up before the Jews a Samaritan as an example of true charity.

Among the Jews of the Dispersion must be mentioned also those in Egypt. It will be remembered that a party of Jews of Jerusalem took Jeremias to Egypt after the fall of the Holy City. There he encountered many of his compatriots who had been there for a long time. Some were even serving in the Egyptian army as mercenaries. Papyri found in Egypt inform us about the life of the Jewish community at Elephantine. In 419 it possessed a temple dedicated to Yahweh in which holocausts were offered, though other divinities were also worshiped there. There was another temple at a later date at Leontopolis in the delta, founded by the heir of the high priest. This one was orthodox, although it violated the law of Deuteronomy authorizing a single place of worship.

When at the end of the fourth century Alexandria was founded, a quarter of the city was reserved for the Jews. From the Jewish colonies of Egypt came the Book of Wisdom, the Greek translation of Sirach (Ecclesiasticus), and the translation of the Old Testament known as the Septuagint. The latter owes its name to the apocryphal letter of Aristeas, written about 150, in which it is asserted that seventy-two elders, confined in seventy-two cells, came out at the end of seventy-two days, with seventy-two identical Greek translations of the Bible. The truth is that the Pentateuch had already been translated into Greek at the time of Aristeas and that the remainder of the Bible was translated during the half century that followed. This Greek translation became the official translation used in the synagogues in Egypt, and the Jews of Alexandria celebrated an annual feast in thanksgiving to God for having given it to them. From it are taken the quotations from the Old Testament contained in the New, with the result that it has enjoyed considerable prestige among Christian writers. Some Christian writers even went so far as to say that it was inspired, like the original text; because of this the rabbis came to regard it as a disaster and had other Greek translations made to take its place. The Septuagint version is valuable, in spite of its unequal nature, as it shows how Jews two hundred years before Christ understood certain passages of the Bible.

Let us return to the Jews of Jerusalem. During the two centuries of the Persian domination (538-323) they were able freely to practice their religion, and the Covenant was probably never lived with less imperfection. They came next under Greek domination; this also lasted for two centuries (323-142). Alexander of Macedonia in eight years (331-323) overcame Egypt and the Persian empire, and at his death his generals divided the conquered territory among them. Egypt fell to Ptolemy, son of Lagus, who founded the Ptolemaic dynasty; Syria to Seleucus, who founded the Seleucid dynasty. Palestine was first under the domination of the Ptolemies (323-197), then of the Seleucidae (197-142).

Following Alexander's example, the Ptolemies treated the Jews with kindness. While favoring Greek customs and ideas, they refrained from interfering with the religious organization of Israel, which had the Torah for its charter. In general they won the affection of the inhabitants, confining themselves to maintaining order by leaving garrisons where they were required. They also favored the Jewish colonies in Egypt, particularly that at Alexandria.

The battle of Paneas (198), in which Syria defeated Egypt, caused Palestine to pass under the dominion of the Seleucidae. At first they showed themselves tolerant in matters of religion, but under Antiochus IV (Epiphanes) the situation changed. Not content with trying to Hellenize the Jews completely, he did his best to destroy their religion. In 169, with the collusion of the peculiar high priest Menelas, he sacked the Temple and took away the seven-branched candlestick and the altar of incense. In 167 he caused an idol of Jupiter Olympus to be set up on the altar of holocausts—this was the "abomination of desolation." He forbade observance of the Sabbath day, the possession of copies of the Law, and the practice of circumcision. Finally he ordered the worship of pagan gods under pain of death. Wholesale apostasy occurred, especially in the towns, among the priests and notables. There were also a number of martyrs who, having fled to the desert, allowed themselves be killed, making no effort to defend themselves when they were attacked on the Sabbath.

Then began the period of armed resistance. It was supported by the religious society of the Hasidim, and had at its head the Machabees (the "hammers"), as the Mathathias family were known. The father of the family was a priest of Jerusalem who had taken refuge at Modin:

> And they that were sent from king Antiochus came thither, to compel them that were fled into the city of Modin, to sacrifice, and to burn incense, and to depart from the law of God. And many of the people of Israel consented, and came to them: but Mathathias and his sons stood firm.
>
> And they that were sent from Antiochus, answering, said to Mathathias: Thou art a ruler, and an honourable and great man in this city, and adorned with sons, and brethren. Therefore come thou first, and obey the king's

commandment, as all nations have done, and the men of
Juda and they that remain in Jerusalem: and thou, and thy
sons, shall be in the number of the king's friends, and enriched with gold, and silver, and many presents.

Then Mathathias answered, and said with a loud voice:
Although all nations obey king Antiochus, so as to depart
every man from the service of the law of his fathers, and
consent to his commandments: I and my sons, and my
brethren will obey the law of our fathers. God be merciful
unto us: it is not profitable for us to forsake the law, and
the justices of God. We will not hearken to the words of
king Antiochus, neither will we sacrifice, and transgress
the commandments of our law, to go another way.

Now as he left off speaking these words, there came a
certain Jew in the sight of all to sacrifice to the idols upon
the altar in the city of Modin, according to the king's
commandment. And Mathathias saw and was grieved, and
his reins trembled, and his wrath was kindled according
to the judgment of the law, and running upon him he slew
him upon the altar. Moreover the man whom king Antiochus had sent, who compelled them to sacrifice, he slew
at the same time, and pulled down the altar, and showed
zeal for the law, as Phinees did by Zamri, the son of Salomi.

And Mathathias cried out in the city with a loud voice,
saying: Every one that hath zeal for the law, and main-
taineth the testament, let him follow me. So he, and his sons
fled into the mountains, and left all that they had in the
city (1 Mac. 2:15-28).

On the death of Mathathias his son Judas took command of
the army and won a series of victories. These took him right
up to Jerusalem, which, in 164, was almost completed liber-
ated. Judas died valiantly at the battle of Beerzeth in 160. His
brother Jonathan succeeded him and in 152 assumed the title

of high priest. Jonathan having fallen in his turn, Simon, the youngest of the Machabee brothers, took his place as military and religious leader. He brought the liberation of the nation to a successful conclusion, and after 142 the Seleucidae no longer dominated the country. Simon was succeeded by his son John Hircanus, who took the title of king and founded the Hasmonean dynasty. John Hircanus, or Hircanus I (134-104), became as powerful as David. He succeeded in obtaining possession of Sichem and Samaria, razed the schismatic temple on Garizim to the ground, and subdued the Idumeans and obliged them to accept circumcision.

The Hasmonean dynasty, in spite of its religious leanings, did not enjoy peace for long. Since it was not of Judean origin and was exercising both royal and pontifical power, which had been kept separate since the time of Saul, it encountered the opposition of the Pharisees and other Yahwists who desired to maintain the religion of the Covenant in all its integrity. Under Alexander Jannaeus (103-76), son of Hircanus I, the Pharisees revolted, causing the death of 50,000 Jews. The king ordered the crucifixion of 800 prisoners and had their wives and children put to death before their eyes. After the death of Alexander, his widow Alexandra made peace with the Pharisees. The influence the Pharisees acquired at this time was to predominate among the Jews thereafter. The disaster that led to the downfall of the Hasmonean dynasty came as a direct result of the rivalry between Alexander's two sons, Aristobulus and Hircanus II. The latter, who had inherited the kingdom and the high-priesthood, was dispossessed by his brother. Both were imprudent enough to appeal to Rome to arbitrate in the dispute between them. Rome dispatched Pompey, who had recently annexed Syria. He lost no time in laying siege to Jerusalem and captured the city in the autumn of 63, Cicero being at this time first consul.

Henceforth the Jews paid tribute to the Romans, who gave

them a king of their own, the Idumean Herod, known as "the Great," who reigned from 37 to 4 B.C. To gain the good will of the nation, Herod married a Hasmonean, a granddaughter of Hircanus II, and in the place of the Temple built after the Exile constructed a better one. In order to assert Roman (and his own) domination, he put to death a great number of the aristocracy, all the members of the Sanhedrin except one, two of his sons, two of his brothers-in-law, his wife, his wife's grandfather (Hircanus II), and, in general, all the Jews whose opposition he feared. Herod Archelaus—he it was that Saint Joseph feared would put the child Jesus to death—and the three other Herods mentioned in the Gospels are the grandsons of Herod the Great. In order to ensure the obedience of these kings, Rome appointed a Roman procurator as the final authority in both governmental and judicial matters. In this capacity Pilate, the procurator at the time, was induced to condemn our Lord to death. In A.D. 66 there was a Jewish rebellion, and Titus was instructed to quell it. He captured Jerusalem in A.D. 70, and the Temple was burned to the ground. Another uprising took place in A.D. 132, only to be repressed by Emperor Hadrian. Tens of thousands of Jews were put to death or deported, the Jewish state was abolished, and the Jewish religion proscribed throughout the Roman empire.

PARTIES AND SECTS

The Pharisees and Sadducees did not appear as organized parties until the time of the Hasmoneans, although the ideas for which they stood were evident earlier. From then onward they exerted considerable influence in the life of Israel.

The tendencies of the Sadducees were those characteristic of the important priestly families; they were frequently involved in public affairs and were opportunists. They set great store by the Law, but only by the written Law. They did not consider themselves bound to accept the beliefs and observances added to it by oral tradition. Thus on the ground that they were not in the Torah, they did not hold the doctrines of the immortality of the soul and the resurrection of the body, though these were held by the majority of the Jews at this time.

The Pharisees were the spiritual heirs of the Hasidim (the "devout"), this name deriving from their zeal for the complete observance of the Law. This zeal caused the Hasidim to side with the Machabees at the beginning of the struggle against the Seleucidae. It also prompted their opposition to the Hasmonean dynasty when it took to ungodly and warlike ways. The Pharisees adopted the scrupulous legalism of the Hasidim. Their excessive regard for the "doctors" and casuists led the Pharisees to place their interpretations on the same footing as the Law, to see in them an oral Law that carried the same weight as the written one. They were proudly self-satisfied in their alleged knowledge and "purity," holding themselves aloof not only from the heathens, but also from the less educated Jews, whose ignorance, in their view, caused them constantly to sin. They called these Jews the *'am-ha-ares,* or "people of the land," while they themselves were the *perishim,* or "those apart." They were extremely sensitive in matters of orthodoxy. They believed in the immortality of the soul, reward and punishment after death, and the resurrection of the body; and professed a developed system of angelology.

The favor of Queen Alexandra (76-67), and later of Herod the Great, gained for the Pharisees a position of influence in the Sanhedrin, in which the priestly and Sadducean aristocracy was predominant. The Sanhedrin regarded itself as the successor to the Council of Elders of the Mosaic period. In reality it was a continuation of the *gerousia* of the Hellenistic period.

Under the presidency of the high priest it always exercised authority in religious matters, even after the Romans had withdrawn from it the right of pronouncing the death sentence.

The Essenes were ascetics living in community. A period of trial, a noviciate, and the reception of baptism were necessary preliminaries to entry among them. Although they carried the concern for legal purity to even greater lengths than the Pharisees, the Essenes held their own peculiar doctrines, which were not in conformity with Jewish orthodoxy. They did not see, for example, the necessity of sacrifices. Josephus and Philo bear witness to the great reputation they acquired by their rigorous asceticism.

In 1910 was discovered in Cairo the Sadocite document, and in 1947, among the manuscripts of the Dead Sea, hymns of thanksgiving and a Manual of Discipline. These documents have revealed the existence of another sect, that of the New Covenant, which drew its inspiration and example from the "Master of Justice." There is, of course, some kinship between this sect and the Essenes, but too much should not be made of the relationship, for the members of the New Covenant did not hold all the doctrines of the Essenes. In particular, it would be wrong to regard the Master of Justice as a first "incarnation" of the Master of Galilee, our Lord Jesus Christ. The Master of Justice appears as having been persecuted by a Hasmonean high priest, just as Jesus was persecuted by the high priest and Sanhedrin of his time; but nowhere is the Master of Justice depicted as an incarnate God who "rose from among the dead." It would be wrong, too, to seek too close an analogy between the charity that was practiced by the followers of the New Covenant and that which was urged by Jesus. The Manual of Discipline lays down that "all those chosen of God must be loved and all those whom he has cast out must be hated," or, again, "the Sons of Light must be loved and the Sons of Darkness must be hated." In fact, in

the New Covenant, love of one's neighbor was practiced
when he belonged to the sect.

THE SCRIBES—THE SAPIENTIAL LITERATURE

In the Jewish community, in which civil and religious life
was regulated by the Law, the study of Scripture was essential, and the scribe, who devoted himself to it professionally,
finally came to occupy a place of extreme importance. Not
only did he recopy the Hebrew text, which almost no one
understood since the Aramaic of Babylon had become the
vernacular, but he translated it and commented on it in the
rabbinical schools and interpreted it in order to adapt its legal
prescriptions to changing conditions. Moreover, he occupied
a place of honor in the synagogue on the Sabbath day and
was held in higher consideration than even the priest. The
Book of Sirach (Ecclesiasticus) says of the ideal scribe:

> He explores the wisdom of the men of old
>   and occupies himself with the prophecies;
> He treasures the discourses of famous men,
>   and goes to the heart of involved sayings;
> He studies obscure parables,
>   and is busied with the hidden meanings of the sages.
> He is in attendance on the great,
>   and has entrance to the ruler. . . .
> His care is to seek the Lord, his Maker,
>   to petition the Most High,
> To open his lips in prayer,
>   to ask pardon for his sins.
> Then, if it pleases the Lord Almighty,
>   he will be filled with the spirit of understanding;
> He will pour forth his words of wisdom
>   and in prayer give thanks to the Lord. . . .

Many will praise his understanding;
    his fame can never be effaced;
Unfading will be his memory,
    through all generations his name will live.
(Sir. 39: 1-9)

We have already seen that at the time of the Exile the scribes set down in writing and codified the legal traditions and the accounts of the history of Israel (in the Pentateuch). They next gathered together the *corpus* of prophetical writings. Then they composed a third and last *corpus*, the sapiential *corpus*, so called because of the predominant place occupied in it by "wisdom" literature; for the most part this literature was written by scribes, but in this case by "inspired scribes."

There is only a vague link between the Book of Psalms and the sapiential cycle, in which it is included. Many of the Psalms go back to David, some were composed during the Exile, but most of them belong to the fifth century. Some are hymns or prayers; others are of a didactic nature; still others, which we shall examine later, are of a definitely Messianic character.

The Book of Job, one of the finest poems in all literature, was written in about 450. It deals with the problem of suffering and of evil. Job exclaims:

Perish the day on which I was born,
    the night when they said, "The child is a boy!"
May that day be darkness:
    let not God above call for it,
    nor light shine upon it!
May darkness and gloom claim it,
    clouds settle upon it,
    the blackness of the night affright it!

May obscurity seize that day;
> let it not occur among the days of the year,
> nor enter into the count of the months!
>> (Job 3:3-6)

It is not in human wisdom but in divine that lies the explanation of why the just man is condemned to suffer:

Whence, then, comes wisdom,
> and where is the place of understanding?
It is hid from the eyes of any beast;
> from the birds of the air it is concealed. . . .
Abaddon and Death say,
> "Only by rumor have we heard of it."

God knows the way to it;
> it is he who is familiar with its place.
For he beholds the ends of the earth
> and sees all that is under the heavens. . . .

He has weighed out the wind,
> and fixed the scope of the waters; . . .
When he made rules for the rain
> and a path for the thunderbolts,
Then he saw wisdom and appraised it,
> gave it its setting, knew it through and through.
And to man he said:
> Behold, the fear of the Lord is wisdom;
> and avoiding evil is understanding.
>> (Job 28:2-28)

And Job, renouncing his own personal notion of justice in order to throw himself on the justice and holiness of Yahweh, concludes in humble submission to the mysteries of divine guidance:

I know that you can do all things,
> and that no purpose of yours can be hindered.

I have dealt with great things that I do not understand;
    things too wonderful for me, which I cannot know.
I had heard of you by word of mouth,
    but now my eye has seen you.
Therefore I disown what I have said,
    and repent in dust and ashes.

(Job 42:2-6)

The sapiential cycle, in the proper sense of the term,[3] begins
with the Book of Proverbs. This is a collection of anthologies,
of which the oldest writings (25-9) are traditionally ascribed
to Solomon; the most recent (1-9) were composed after the
return from exile, as an introduction to the whole work.
Proverbs (or *mashal*) were familiar to the scribes, who used
them to express, in a concise manner, a maxim, an aphorism, a
comparison, or even an epigram. Certain of the proverbs be-
tray a human wisdom couched in language that mingles
shrewdness with a touch of malice; others bring out clearly the
superiority of the righteous over the wicked. In the first nine
chapters of the work the wise man, speaking to his son, sometimes calls upon Wisdom in person; the emphasis placed by
the latter on the reprobation of adultery recalls particularly
the language of the Prophets, in which the Covenant is represented as a marriage, and participation in the worship of other
nations is shown as conjugal infidelity on the part of Israel.

[3] It is more because of their date of composition, than because of their
literary form, that the books of Daniel, Judith, and Esther were included
among the sapiential books. All three appear to have been written in about
the middle of the second century.
    The greater part of the Book of Daniel is an apocalypse, that is, a revela-
tion of things to come. The author declares that the kingdom of the righteous which Yahweh is soon to establish will be universal and without end.
    In the same apocalyptic manner Judith speaks of the war between Yahweh
and the powers of evil, and shows how Yahweh, employing poor human
means, manages without trouble to gain the victory.
    The teaching of the Book of Esther is likewise that Israel can place un-
limited confidence in Yahweh and that the powers of evil will not prevail
against him.

The Book of Ecclesiastes or Coheleth ("the teacher") appeared during the third century under the pseudonym of
Solomon. Two authors are believed to have collaborated on it.
One is disillusioned, and to him the seeking of happiness here
below is mere foolishness:

> What has been, that will be; what has been done, that
> will be done. Nothing is new under the sun. Even the
> thing of which we say, "See this is new!" has already
> existed in the ages that preceded us. . . .
> When I applied my mind to know wisdom and knowl-
> edge, madness and folly, I learned that this also is a chase
> after wind. For in much wisdom there is much sorrow,
> and he who stores up knowledge stores up grief. . . .
> I said to myself, "Come, now, let me try you with
> pleasure and the enjoyment of good things." But behold,
> this too was vanity. Of laughter I said: "Mad!" and of
> mirth: "What good does this do?". . .
> Therefore I loathed life, since for me the work that is
> done under the sun is evil; for all is vanity and a chase
> after wind (Eccles. 1:9-18; 2:1-17).

The other collaborator is a devout scribe who accepts what
happens as allowed or desired by Yahweh. Hence for him,
whether we understand it or not, all is good for Yahweh cannot desire evil.

The Canticle of Canticles (meaning "the greatest of Songs")
was written between the return from exile and Esdras' mission.
Jewish exegetes have seen these love songs as an allegory ex-
tolling the marriage between Yahweh and Israel. Christian
exegetes see the Canticle of Canticles as the portrayal and
praise of the union of Christ with the human soul or even with
the whole of humanity.

The author of the Book of Sirach (Ecclesiasticus), Jesus of
Sirach, was a devout scribe of Jerusalem. This book, written

in Hebrew in about 190 and translated into Greek in about 125 by a grandson of the author, was written too late to be inserted in the Jewish canon. It was held in such great esteem, however, that the custom grew up of quoting it on a par with the Scriptures. In it Wisdom is defined out of her own mouth— "Wisdom sings her own praises" (24:1)—as a personified attribute of God. The following passage seems to be a prophecy of the revelation of the Word and a prologue to the prologue of Saint John's Gospel:

> From the mouth of the Most High I came forth,
>   and mistlike covered the earth.
> In the highest heavens did I dwell,
>   my throne on a pillar of cloud.
> The vault of heaven I compassed alone,
>   through the deep abyss I wandered. . . .
>
> Before all ages, in the beginning, he created me,
>   and through all ages I shall not cease to be. . . .
> I spread out my branches like a terebinth,
>   my branches so bright and so graceful. . . .
> Come to me, all you that yearn for me,
>   and be filled with my fruits; . . .
> He who obeys me will not be put to shame,
>   he who serves me will never fail.
>
> (Sir. 24:3-21)

The Book of Wisdom, the last in date of the books of the Old Testament, was written in Greek in about the year 80 at Alexandria. The author, familiar with Greek thought, which he turns to account, makes use of the Scriptures in accordance with the Septuagint version and opposes the surrounding Egyptian polytheism. For him, the problem occupying Job and Ecclesiastes is fully solved: present life is a preparation for the life to come; the reign of justice will be re-established, and happiness will be found once more after our time of early disillusion. This writer's views on Wisdom are more profound than those of his predecessors. He prepares us in some sort to regard it as a divine hypostasis and to see in it the Christ of Saint Paul and Saint John.

> But the souls of the just are in the hands of God,
>> and no torment shall touch them.
> They seemed, in the view of the foolish, to be dead;
>> and their passing away was judged an affliction
>> and their going forth from us, utter destruction.
> But they are in peace.
> For if before men, indeed, they be punished,
>> yet is their hope full of immortality;
> Chastised a little, they shall be greatly blessed,
>> because God tried them
>> and found them worthy of himself.
> As gold in the furnace, he proved them,
>> and as sacrificial offerings he took them to himself.
> In the time of their visitation they shall shine,
>> and shall dart about as sparks through stubble;
> They shall judge nations and rule over peoples,
>> and the Lord shall be their King forever.
> Those who trust in him shall understand truth,
>> and the faithful shall abide with him in love:
>> because grace and mercy are with his chosen ones.
>
> (Wis. 3:1-9)

Thus, right up to the end, divine inspiration was elaborating that teaching which would predispose the chosen people to receive the transcendent message of the Messias.

CHAPTER 5

Yahweh Our God

THE ONE GOD

THE RELIGION of the Old Testament is that of one God revealing himself to humanity. In this it is entirely different from the religions and philosophies of the past. Ancient religions, in fact, abounded in pantheons and gods. Although some philosophers of antiquity did conclude that there existed one supreme divinity, this divinity in no way resembled the God of the Bible, who, without losing anything of his transcendence, speaks to men.

This God bears a name that he himself revealed to Moses: "I am who am"; in other words, "My name is 'I am.'" He desired that in contrast to the idols "who are not" the Jews should call him "He is" (Exod. 3:13-15). In Hebrew this is translated *Yahweh.*

Ineffable name of God! Name that cannot be spoken, not because of the respect that made the doctors of the Law forbid its utterance; nor because of any magical power that, so the ancients supposed, is given to him who succeeds in pronouncing exactly the name of a god. It is the ineffable name because no human utterance, no metaphysics, no theodicy can express the whole reality intimated by this name and revelation.

THE GOD OF THE PATRIARCHS

Was this name known before Moses? Was it used by the patriarchs to designate their God? Three traditions are to be found in the Pentateuch on this subject.

According to the "Elohist" tradition, which seems to have been current in the kingdom of Israel, the patriarchs called God *'Elohim*. *'Elohim* is the plural of *'El*, but it is the royal plural, for the Elohist writer is generally careful to use a singular verb with it, thus showing that it is not several but one God that is mentioned.

According to the Yahwist tradition, which seems to have been current in the kingdom of Juda, God was called *Yahweh* from the beginning of the world. In this case it would appear that the word had subsequently been lost, for it was no longer used by the Israelites who followed Moses into the desert.

In those passages of the Pentateuch in which the sacerdotal tradition finds expression God is sometimes called *'El 'Olam*, "the Eternal God," sometimes *'El 'Elyon*, "the Most High God," and sometimes *'El Shaddai*, of which the origin is not known—it is translated in the Vulgate as "the Almighty God."

Whatever name the patriarchs used for their God, this God already possessed the attributes and characteristics that subsequent revelations only emphasized more clearly.

He is a "jealous" God. Since the whole universe belongs to him, he requires that men acknowledge his exclusive sovereignty, and he desires for himself all their sacrifices and worship. Not only has he no equal, but he has no rival, not even of a secondary nature; as a consequence, the teraphim, for example, to which Laban (Abraham's nephew) and Rachel (Jacob's wife) remained attached were in his eyes idols to which he would not allow the slightest homage to be paid.

He is an almighty and eternal God. Eternal: he was at the beginning and before the beginning, before matter, before the void. Almighty: nothing escapes his power, neither stars, plants, animals, nor man, whom he has "fashioned" with special care, in whom he "breathed the breath of life," endowing him with intelligence and free will, "in his own image and likeness." The two varying accounts of creation in chapters 1 and 2 of Genesis, based on two different Hebrew traditions, portray admirably this almighty power creating effortlessly: "God said, 'Let there be light,' and there was light." Directly he speaks, it is created, and well created; it is as he desired it: "God saw that the light was good."

The God of the patriarchs is a merciful God. His benevolence and mercy lead him to hearken to prayer and to forgive. He did not abandon Adam after the Fall but continued to speak to him. He offered his Covenant to Noe and all mankind after the Flood. He took Abraham from idolatrous surroundings and made him his friend. He was willing to spare Sodom if ten just men could be found in the city. He caused Joseph's trial to turn to his advantage and that of many others.

Yet he is a God of justice and holiness, as is proved by the punishments he inflicted on transgressors of the moral law. He punished the pride of Adam and Eve when they dared to encroach on his privileges and desired to become "like God"; he brought to naught the plans of the builders of Babel when they endeavored to reach up to the heavens; he made Cain, the slayer of his brother, a fugitive on the earth; and drowned in the Flood a race among whom evil prevailed. Again, because of his holiness he reproved and rejected human sacrifice; destroyed Sodom, in which unnatural vice was rife; and gave to Abraham as his watchword, "Walk in my presence and be perfect."

The God whom the patriarchs worshiped is a transcendent God. Even when he condescends "to walk and converse" with his creatures, the distance between him and them remains infinite. Man, unable to endure the dazzling brightness of the divinity, would fall thunderstruck if placed in his presence. Angels, therefore, serve as intermediaries, like screens, and on the most important occasions, it is the mysterious "Angel

of Yahweh" who comes. When Agar, ill-treated by Sarai,
Abraham's wife, fled to the desert,

> . . . an angel of the Lord found her beside a spring of water
> in the desert, the spring on the road to Sur. He said, "Agar,
> maid of Sarai, where have you come from and where are
> you going?" She answered, "I am fleeing from my mis-
> tress Sarai." The angel of the Lord said to her, "Return to
> your mistress and submit to her authority." The angel of
> the Lord added, "I will so multiply your posterity that it
> shall be too many to count." The angel of the Lord also
> said to her:

> "You are with child,
>   and shall bear a son;
> You shall call him Ismael,
>   because the Lord has heard of your humiliation.

> "He shall be a wild ass of a man,
>   his hand against everyone,
> And everyone's hand against him;
>   he shall dwell apart, opposing all his kinsmen."

> She named the Lord, who spoke to her: "You are the
> God of vision" for she said, "Have I really seen God . . ?"
> (Gen. 16:7-13).

When Abraham made ready to sacrifice his son Isaac, he
was stopped by the Angel of Yahweh, who said to him, "Do
not lay a hand on the boy; do nothing to him. I know now
that you fear God."

> The angel of the Lord called from heaven to Abraham
> and said, I swear by myself, says the Lord, since you have
> done this and have not withheld your only son, I will
> indeed bless you, and will surely multiply your descend-
> ants as the stars of the heavens, as the sands on the seashore.

Your descendants shall possess the gates of their enemies. In your descendants all the nations of the earth shall be blessed, because you have obeyed me (Gen. 22:15-19).

The transcendence of the God of the patriarchs is clearly shown by the role played by angels in the various "theophanies," or divine appearances. These beings, so superior to man, are seen as simple servants, always ready to obey Yahweh, hastening to carry out his will.

THE GOD OF MOSES

The God of the Book of Exodus, who indeed affirms that he is "the God of Abraham, Isaac and Jacob," gives to Moses a fuller revelation of his attributes and nature.

The name of "Yahweh" by which he desires to be designated testifies that he alone possesses "being": "You shall not have other gods besides me," because I alone *am*. Those divinities that man conceives in his own likeness—the forces of nature which he deifies, the ancestors whom he raises to divine rank—are only idols, devoid of all save outward appearance. Yahweh is the great living God, on whom all creatures depend, who can require of them obedience to his law. He states that he is jealous: jealous, because he desires to be the only one to receive their worship; jealous, because he loves and desires to be loved:

"Hear, O Israel! . . . You shall love the Lord, your God, with all your heart, and with all your soul, and with all your strength. . . ."

"You shall not carve idols for yourselves in the shape of anything in the sky above or on the earth below or in the waters beneath the earth; you shall not bow down before them or worship them. For I, the Lord, your God, am a jealous God, inflicting punishments for their fathers' wickedness on the children of those who hate me, down to the third and fourth generation, but bestowing mercy, down to the thousandth generation, on the children of those who love me and keep my commandments" (Deut. 6:4-6; 5:8-10).

The God of the Covenant is a spiritual being who cannot be limited by any image or localization. Although he manifests himself on occasion in a precise place and allows himself to be spoken of in anthropomorphic terms, he remains hidden, invisible, and untouchable—in the cloud going before the Hebrews, in the lightning acompanying the promulgation of the Law, and in the Ark of the Covenant which is a sign of his invisible presence. To avoid all danger of a materialist conception, carved images as representations of him are entirely forbidden.

Although he is beyond the reach of the senses, he nonetheless exercises absolute power over material things and over man. The greatest of prodigies is no effort to him: he performed wonders of a terrifying nature in Egypt to secure his recognition by Pharao and the elders of Israel; he stretched out his hand and the waters of Jordan fell apart; the manna that he caused to rain down and many other miracles bear witness to this almighty power.

The finest of his attributes is his holiness. It is manifest in his words and his demands. "Be holy, for I, the Lord, your God, am holy"—this is the message that the leader and legislator of the Hebrews is charged to bear not only to the priests and Levites, but to all the members of the community of Israel (Lev. 19:2). Then follows the Decalogue and a whole code of laws whose prescriptions are far superior to those found in the legislation of the Egyptians, Assyrians, and Hittites, although these peoples were much more advanced in material matters:

"You shall not defraud your neighbor. You shall not withhold overnight the wages of your day laborer.... You shall not act dishonestly in rendering judgment. Show neither partiality to the weak nor deference to the mighty. ... You shall not go about spreading slander among your kinsmen.... You shall not bear hatred for your brother in your heart.... You shall love your neighbor as yourself. ... When an alien resides with you in your land... have the same love for him as for yourself; for you too were once aliens in the land of Egypt....

"Anyone who curses his father or mother shall be put to death.... If a man commits adultery with his neighbor's wife, both the adulterer and the adultress shall be put to death... If a man lies with a male as with a woman, both of them shall be put to death for their abominable deed" (Lev. 19:13-18, 33-4; 20:9-14).

If all that we owed to Israel were the transmission of the Decalogue, our debt of gratitude would still be incalculable. As Moses said to his people:

For what great nation is there that has gods so close to it as the Lord, our God, is to us whenever we call upon him? Or what great nation has statutes and decrees that are as just as this whole Law which I am setting before you today? (Deut. 4:7-8).

THE GOD OF THE PROPHETS

To read Jewish history from Josue to the Exile is to be filled with admiration at the way the message of monotheism, instead of becoming lost amid idolatry and corruption, not only remains intact but is marvelously amplified and enriched. This wonderful development is largely due to the prophets. Some of them, in exquisite phrase, extol the divine attributes revealed in former times.

The expression "Lord of hosts" (*Sabaoth*), first used in connection with the victories providentially won by Israel (1 Sam. 4:4), is applied by Amos to show in Yahweh the one and only master of creation. Possibly he borrowed the term from the vocabulary of the Assyro-Babylonians, who regarded the planets and stars as "the army of Anou," god of the heavens:

> He that formeth the mountains
> > and createth the wind,
> > and declareth his word to man,
> > he that maketh the morning mist,
> > and walketh upon the high places of the earth:
> The Lord the God of hosts is his name. . . .

> Seek him that maketh Arcturus and Orion,
> > and that turneth darkness into morning,
> > and that changeth day into night:
> > that calleth the waters of the sea,
> > and poureth them out upon the face of the earth:
> The Lord is his name.
> He that with a smile bringeth destruction upon the strong,
> > and waste upon the mighty. . . .

> And the Lord God of hosts
> > is he who toucheth the earth, and it shall melt;
> > and all that dwell therein shall mourn:
> > and it shall rise up as a river,
> > and shall run down as the river of Egypt.

He that buildeth his ascension in heaven,
    and hath founded his bundle upon the earth: [1]
    who calleth the waters of the sea,
    and poureth them out upon the face of the earth,
The Lord is his name.

(Amos 4:13; 5:8; 9:5-6)

Lord of the stars and of the angels, of the fruitfulness of the earth and its infertility, he is also Lord of the kingdoms of this world, whose destinies he controls and which, though they know it not, carry out his plans:

> I will call together all the families of the kingdoms of the north, saith the Lord: and they shall come, and shall set every one his throne in the entrance of the gates of Jerusalem, and upon all the walls thereof round about, and upon all the cities of Juda. . . .
>
> Cannot I do with you as this potter, O house of Israel, saith the Lord? Behold as clay is in the hand of the potter, so are you in my hand, O house of Israel. I will suddenly speak against a nation, and against a kingdom, to root out, and to pull down, and to destroy it. If that nation against which I have spoken, shall repent of their evil, I also will repent of the evil that I have thought to do to them. And I will suddenly speak of a nation and of a kingdom, to build up and plant it. If it shall do evil in my sight, that it obey not my voice; I will repent of the good that I have spoken to do unto it (Jer. 1:15; 18:6-10).

In opposition to the one God whose almighty power they extol, the prophets make the powerless idols the target of their sarcasm:

---

[1] Thus the Douay version following the Vulgate. A more accurate reading would probably be, "who builds his upper chambers in the heavens, and founds his vault upon the earth"—Translator's note.

Thus saith the Lord the king of Israel, and his redeemer the Lord of hosts: ... Who hath formed a god, and made a graven thing that is profitable for nothing? Behold, all the partakers [worshipers] thereof shall be confounded: for the makers are men: they shall all assemble together, they shall stand and fear, and shall be confounded together. The smith hath wrought with his file, with coals, and with hammers he hath formed it, and hath wrought with the strength of his arm: he shall hunger and faint, he shall drink no water, and shall be weary. The carpenter hath stretched out his rule, he hath formed it with a plane: he hath made it with corners, and hath fashioned it round with the compass: and he hath made the image of a man, ... a beautiful man, dwelling in a house. He hath cut down cedars, taken the holm, and the oak that stood among the trees of the forest: he hath planted the pine tree, which the rain hath nourished. And it hath served men for fuel: and he took thereof, and warmed himself; and he kindled it and baked bread: but of the rest he made a god, and adored it: he made a graven thing, and bowed down before it. Part of it he burnt with fire, and with part of it he dressed his meat: he boiled pottage, and was filled, and was warmed, and said: Aha, I am warm, I have seen the fire. But the residue thereof he made a god, and a graven thing for himself: he boweth down before it, and adoreth it, and prayeth unto it saying: Deliver me, for thou art my God (Isa. 44:6, 10-17).

Although the oneness of God, his almighty power, justice, holiness, and goodness are mentioned and proclaimed by all the prophets, each of them, in accordance with his own temperament and the inspiration he has received, emphasizes particularly one or other of the divine attributes.

No one has spoken more vehemently than Amos of

Yahweh's justice and of what it holds in store for the stubborn
transgressors of the moral law.

Israel has been particularly privileged. For that reason it
will be dealt with the more severely:

> You only have I known
> of all the families of the earth:
> Therefore will I visit upon you
> all your iniquities.
>
> (Amos 3:2)

Amos goes on to say that the people are always talking of
the "day of Yahweh"; that day shall come indeed, but not
with the blessings on which they are counting. He tells them
what the day of the Lord will be:

> The day of the Lord is darkness, and not light;
> As if a man should flee from the face of a lion,
> and a bear should meet him:
> or enter into the house, and lean with his hand upon
> the wall,
> and a serpent should bite him.
> Shall not the day of the Lord be darkness, and not light?
> and obscurity and no brightness in it?
>
> (Amos 5:18-20)

He warns the rich who pursue their pleasures, enjoying an
easy life in Israel:

> You that sleep upon beds of ivory,
> and are wanton on your couches: ...
> You that sing to the sound of the psaltery: ...
> [They] drink wine in bowls,
> and anoint themselves with the best ointments.
>
> (Amos 6:4-6)

It is by bribing judges, weighing corn with false weights, grinding the face of the poor, whom they treat as merchandise, that they obtain the money required for their pleasures; but

> The end is come upon my people Israel:
> I will not again pass by them any more.
>
> (Amos 8:2)

The fate of the women who behave like beasts will be no better than that of the men:

> Hear this word, ye fat kine of Basan
> that are in the mountains of Samaria:
> you that oppress the needy,
> and crush the poor:
> that say to your masters: Bring and we will drink!
>
> The Lord God hath sworn by his holiness
> That lo, the days shall come upon you,
> when they shall lift you up on pikes
> and what shall remain of you in boiling pots.
> And you shall go out at the breaches
> one over against the other,
> and you shall be cast forth into Armon,
> saith the Lord.
>
> (Amos 4:1-3)

The passages quoted in Chapters 3 and 4 showed in what terms the prophets speak of the love that fills God's heart. Yahweh, in the words of Osee, loves like a husband, who, even after the woman he loves has betrayed him, cannot live without her and does everything possible to win her back.

> Because Israel was a child, and I loved him:
> and I called my son out of Egypt....

How shall I deal with thee, O Ephraim,
  shall I protect thee, O Israel?
  [shall I deliver thee to the enemies of Israel?] ...
I will not execute the fierceness of my wrath,
  I will not return to destroy Ephraim:
Because I am God, and not man. ...

Return, O Israel. ...

And it shall be in that day ...
  that she shall call me: My husband,
  and she shall call me no more Baali. ...
And I will espouse thee to me for ever. ...
  in mercy and in commiserations.
And I will espouse thee to me in faith:
  and thou shalt know that I am the Lord.
                    (Osee 11:1-9; 14:2; 2:16-20)

God also loves as a father; he calls Israel his "son." But this fatherhood, in the utterances of the prophets, seldom extends beyond the chosen people. It is from the Gospels that each of us learns that he can say to God, "Our Father, who art in heaven."

All the prophets were at pains to proclaim and bring out forcibly the holiness of God. In their utterances they keep returning to this divine attribute. Some of them underwent personal experiences in this connection. Isaias continually refers to Yahweh by the name of "the holy one of Israel," in all probability because there remained with him a deep impression of his vision of the year 740. We may recall his terror on seeing Yahweh "sitting upon a throne high and elevated," and hearing the seraphim crying one to another "Holy, holy, holy, the Lord God of hosts" (Isa. 6). He cried out, "Woe is me . . . because I am a man of unclean lips." Thereupon an angel touched his mouth with a live coal to purify it.

All those who drew near to Yahweh were afraid. So great is his purity, beauty, and divine perfection in comparison with the wretchedness of man that the latter cannot bear the brilliance of the divine presence. When Yahweh approached, Elias, like Moses, covered his face with his cloak; Ezechiel, like Abraham, fell face downward on the ground, half dead.

It is clear that so pure and holy a God must require that man, created in his likeness, tend to holiness. According to the prophets, this comprises humility, faith, and purity.

Nothing is more abhorrent to God than to see man, "whose breath is in his nostrils," trusting in himself. Isaias declares that

The lofty eyes of man are humbled,
    and the haughtiness of men shall be made to stoop:
    and the Lord alone shall be exalted in that day.

Because the day of the Lord of hosts shall be
    upon every one that is proud and highminded,
    and upon every one that is arrogant, and he shall be
        humbled,
    and upon all the tall and lofty cedars of Libanus,
    and upon all the oaks of Basan,
    and upon all the high mountains,
    and upon all the elevated hills,
    and upon every high tower, and every fenced wall,
    and upon all the ships of Tharsis,
    and upon all that is fair to behold.

And the loftiness of men shall be bowed down,
    and the haughtiness of men shall be humbled,
    and the Lord alone shall be exalted in that day. . . .

Cease ye therefore from the man
    whose breath is in his nostrils,
    for he is reputed high.
    [in whose nostrils there is but one breath,
    for what worth is he?]
                   (Isa. 2:11-17, 22)

The faith God required of the Jews is shown by their
history to have been reasonable and justified:

You are my witnesses, saith the Lord,
    and my servant whom I have chosen:
    that you may know, and believe me,
    and understand that I myself am.
Before me there was no God formed,
    and after me there shall be none.

I am, I am the Lord,
    and there is no Saviour besides me.
                   (Isa. 43:10-11)

Quotations from Isaias given in the preceding chapters
show clearly that, for the purity which will make Israel a holy
people, Yahweh will not accept a merely external and legal
purity. He demands interior purification and a good conscience:

If you return and be quiet, you shall be saved;
    in silence and in hope shall your strength be.
And you would not:
    but have said: No,
    but we will flee to horses:
    therefore shall you flee.
And we will mount upon swift ones:
    therefore shall they be swifter that shall pursue
                  after you.

A thousand men shall flee for fear of one . . .
    till you be left as the mast of a ship on the top of a
                        mountain,
and as an ensign upon a hill.
                            (Isa. 30:15-17)

To those who are "left," Yahweh will give "a new heart,"
and he will "put a new spirit within" them (Ez. 36:25-7);
among them he will find souls that are "poor and little, and of
a contrite spirit," on whom his glance may rest (Isa. 66:1-2)
and with whom he will enter into a new "covenant of peace"
which "shall be an everlasting covenant" (Ez. 37:26). These
promises were not fulfilled until Jesus came, and Saint Paul
was able to write to the Corinthians: "Know you not, that you
are the temple of God, and that the spirit of God dwelleth in
you? . . . For the temple of God is holy, which you are"
(1 Cor. 3:16-17).

GOD IN THE RELIGIOUS TEACHING OF JUDAISM

During the years between the return from exile and the
coming of our Lord considerable doctrinal progress was made.
It was fostered by the piety of an elite who, remaining faithful
to the spirit of the Law and to the prophets' teachings on
holiness, practiced a religion that was increasingly spiritual.
God came to be ever better known and better loved. As in the
following verses, the prayers of some devout souls gave evidence of a more lofty and loving spirit:

Bless the Lord, O my soul;
    and all my being, bless his holy name. . . .

The Lord secures justice
    and the rights of all the oppressed.
He has made known his ways to Moses,
    and his deeds to the children of Israel.

Merciful and gracious is the Lord,
  slow to anger and abounding in kindness.
He will not always chide,
  nor does he keep his wrath forever.
Not according to our sins does he deal with us,
  nor does he requite us according to our crimes.

For as the heavens are high above the earth,
  so surpassing is his kindness toward those who fear him.
As far as the east is from the west,
  so far has he put our transgressions from us.
As a father has compassion on his children,
  so the Lord has compassion on those who fear him,
For he knows how we are formed;
  he remembers that we are dust.
                              (Ps. 102:1-14)

Among the best of the people there is a widening of heart:
a genuine love of neighbor enters their souls; hatred of the
"foreigner" disappears, and the conversion of "idolaters" is
desired.

For all men were by nature foolish who were in ignorance
                                of God,
        and who from the good things seen did not succeed in
                                knowing him who is,
        and from studying the works did not discern the
                                artisan;
But either fire, or wind, or the swift air,
        or the circuit of the stars, or the mighty water,
        or the luminaries of heaven, the governors of the
                                world, they considered gods.
Now if out of joy in their beauty they thought them gods,
        let them know how far more excellent is the Lord than
                                these;

for the original source of beauty fashioned them.
Or if they were struck by their might and energy,
    let them from these things realize how much more
                        powerful is he who made them.
For from the greatness and beauty of created things
    their original author, by analogy, is seen.
                                (Wis. 13:1-5)

There were in those days wonderful examples of holiness
in Israel. Could a saint be found who was more heroic than the
mother of the martyrs mentioned by the Book of Macchabees?

> [She] beheld her seven sons slain in the space of one
> day, and bore it with a good courage, for the hope that
> she had in God: And she bravely exhorted every one of
> them in her own language, being filled with wisdom: and
> joining a man's heart to a woman's thought, She said to
> them: I know not how you were formed in my womb:
> for I neither gave you breath, nor souls, nor life, neither
> did I frame the limbs of every one of you. But the Creator
> of the world, that formed the nativity of man, and that
> found out the origin of all, he will restore to you again in
> his mercy, both breath and life, as now you despise your-
> selves for the sake of his laws. . . .
> [When the turn of the youngest came] bending herself
> towards him, mocking the cruel tyrant, she said in her own
> language: My son, have pity upon me, that bore thee nine
> months in my womb, and gave thee suck three years, and
> nourished thee, and brought thee up unto this age. I be-
> seech thee, my son, look upon heaven and earth, and all
> that is in them: and consider that God made them out of
> nothing, and mankind also. So thou shalt not fear this
> tormentor, but being made a worthy partner with thy
> brethren, receive death, that in that mercy I may receive
> thee again with thy brethren. . . .

Then the king being incensed with anger, raged against him more cruelly than all the rest, taking it grievously that he was mocked. So this man also died undefiled, wholly trusting in the Lord (2 Mac. 7:20-40).

The victims of the Seleucid persecution believed, then, in the immortality of the soul. At this period such a belief was widespread in Israel. But had the problem of the suffering of the righteous been solved thereby? In ancient times it had been solved by saying that suffering came to the innocent because his ancestors had merited it—"The fathers have eaten a sour grape, and the teeth of the children are set on edge." But after Jeremias and Ezechiel few were satisfied with explanations of this kind. At all events, the author of the Book of Job no longer found them to his taste.

Then Job answered and said:..
Know then that God has dealt unfairly with me,
    and compassed me round with his net. ...

He has barred my way and I cannot pass;
    he has veiled my path in darkness;
He breaks me down on every side, and I am gone;
    my hope he has uprooted like a tree.
His wrath he has kindled against me;
    he counts me among his enemies...
My brethren have withdrawn from me,
    and my friends are wholly estranged. ...
I call my servant, but he gives no answer,
    though in my speech I plead with him.
My breath is abhorred by my wife;
    I am loathsome to the men of my family.

The young children, too, despise me;
    when I appear, they speak against me.
                    (Job 19:1-18)

Smitten by Satan with "severe boils from the soles of his feet to the crown of his head," Job "took a potsherd to scrape himself, as he sat among the ashes." His wife called on him to blaspheme: "Curse God and die." But Job did not despair; he told his friend Baldad:

> ... as for me, I know that my Vindicator lives,
>   and that he will at last stand forth upon the dust
> Whom I myself shall see, and not another—
>   and from my flesh I shall see God;
>   my inmost being is consumed with longing.
> But you who say, "How shall we persecute him,
>   seeing that the root of the matter is found in him?"
> Be afraid of the sword for yourselves,
>   for these crimes deserve the sword;
>   that you may know that there is a judgment.
>   (Job 19:25-9)

Does that mean that already in the fifth century Job believed in the resurrection of the body? It does not seem so, for otherwise the writer would not have felt obliged to reward his patience and faith even here below:

> Thus the Lord blessed the latter days of Job more than his earlier ones. For he had fourteen thousand sheep, six thousand camels, a thousand yoke of oxen, and a thousand she-asses. And he had seven sons and three daughters, of whom he called the first Jemima, the second Cassia, and the third Ceren-happuch. In all the land no other women were as beautiful as the daughters of Job; and their father gave them an inheritance among their brethren. After this, Job lived a hundred and forty years; and he saw his children, his grandchildren, and even his great grandchildren. Then Job died, old and full of years (Job 42:12-17).

Indeed, the majority of the Jews always believed that the righteous man would find his reward here on earth. Once again we have to wait until Jesus solves the problem by his promise of recompense beyond the tomb: "Blessed are the poor in spirit: for theirs is the kingdom of heaven. . . . Blessed are they that mourn for they shall be comforted."

In the religious teaching of this period an increasingly important place is occupied by angels. There are good and bad angels; they are at war with one another, but all obey God when he commands. The good angels desire man's welfare, the bad seek to harm him. Among the former some are of a higher rank, as one informed Tobias:

> When thou didst pray with tears, and didst bury the dead, and didst leave thy dinner, and hide the dead by day in thy house, and bury them by night, I offered thy prayer to the Lord. And because thou was acceptable to God, it was necessary that temptation should prove thee. And now the Lord hath sent me to heal thee, and to deliver Sara thy son's wife from the devil. For I am the angel Raphael, one of the seven who stand before the Lord (Tob. 12:12-15).

The names of the other two higher spirits, to whom Christian tradition has assigned the title of archangel, are revealed to us by Daniel as Michael and Gabriel.

The chief of the bad angels is Satan. The Book of Wisdom identifies him with the tempter of Genesis (Wis. 2:24), by whom death came into the world. The author of the Book of Job shows him taking pleasure in torturing an innocent man. Nevertheless, in the Old Testament he is still only the enemy of humanity; it is after the coming of our Saviour that he appears also as the personal enemy of the Most High, fighting desperately to impede the coming of the kingdom of God.

The Prelude to the Doctrine of the Trinity

Prophecies and promises are always easier to understand after their fulfillment than before. That is why Christians find in Scriptures things that the Jews did not see. They are especially fond of discovering in the Old Testament the prelude to the mystery of the Trinity, which was entirely unknown to Israel and which only the New Testament revealed to us.

When, for example, in the narrative of the creation we read of the Spirit of God moving over the waters and the Word of Yahweh infallibly creating what it expresses, when we find the Psalmist praising the Word of Yahweh by which the heavens were made and the Breath of his mouth by which the heavenly army was formed (Ps. 32), we naturally think of the Holy Spirit and the Word "by whom all things were made."

When God created man, he said, "Let us make man in our image and likeness" (Gen. 1:26); when he drove Adam out of Eden, he said, "Indeed! the man has become like one of us" (Gen. 3-22); and before stopping the builders of Babel from continuing their tower, he said, "Let us go down, and there confuse their language" (Gen. 11:7). Although in the literal sense these uses of the plural indicate merely use of the plural of majesty or a deliberation between God and his angels, the Fathers saw them as the first intimations of the revelation of the doctrine of the Trinity, and in the "Angel of Yahweh" they discerned our Lord himself; the threefold *Sanctus* of Isaias' vision they regarded as an acclamation addressed to each person of the Trinity.

The Creed of Nicea-Constantinople asserts that the Holy Spirit "spoke by the prophets." The Fathers related the third Person of the Trinity with the "Spirit of God" who imbued Joseph with wisdom, who helped Josue guide the people of the Hebrews, who gave the judges and Saul the strength that enabled them to win victories, who bestowed on David the gift of composing prayers and psalms (2 Sam. 22:2) and on the prophets their inspiration and their prophetic utterance. Ezechiel indeed asserted, "the spirit entered into me," "the spirit also lifted me," "the spirit of the Lord fell upon me" (Ez. 2:2; 3:14, 24; 11:5, 24). Isaias declared that this same Spirit will be given to the King of Justice who will issue from the root of Jesse and begin the Messianic age: "And the spirit of the Lord shall rest upon him: the spirit of wisdom, and of understanding, . . . the spirit of knowledge . . . of the fear of the Lord" (Isa. 11:2-3); this Spirit will be given especially to the Servant of Yahweh, as is stated in this passage, which Jesus was to apply to himself:

> The spirit of the Lord is upon me,
> > because the Lord hath anointed me:
> He hath sent me to preach to the meek,
> > to heal the contrite of heart,
> > and to preach a release to the captives,
> > and deliverance to them that are shut up.
> > > (Isa. 61:1)

On the morning of Pentecost, Saint Peter alluded to verses from Joel, in connection with the coming down of the Holy Spirit:

> . . . I will pour out my spirit upon all flesh:
> And your sons and your daughters shall prophesy:
> > your old men shall dream dreams,
> > and your young men shall see visions.
> Moreover upon my servants and handmaids
> [Even upon the menservants and maidservants]
> > in those days I will pour forth my spirit.
> > > (Joel 2:28-9)

The second Person of the Trinity seems to be foretold and
prefigured in the Old Testament by two words, which in it
are frequently endowed with a special significance, namely,
"Word" or *Logos,* and "Wisdom." It cannot of course be said
that they are used in the sense of a divine hypostasis, but the
impression is given that they are a prelude to it.

In the following passage the bold personification of the
Word is particularly striking:

> For when peaceful stillness compassed everything
>   and the night in its swift course was half spent,
> Your all-powerful word from heaven's royal throne
>   bounded, a fierce warrior, into the doomed land,
>   bearing the sharp sword of your inexorable decree.
> And as he alighted, he filled every place with death.
>
> (Wis. 18:14-16)

Wisdom, the name of a divine attribute, assumes, particularly in the sapiential books, a personified form that approxi-
mates a hypostasis. In the Book of Proverbs we read:

> "The Lord begot me, the firstborn of his ways,
>   the forerunner of his prodigies of long ago; . . .
> Before the mountains were settled into place,
>   before the hills, I was brought forth; . . .
>
> When he established the heavens I was there,
>   when he marked out the vault over the face of the
>   deep; . . .
> When he set for the sea its limit,
>   so that the waters should not transgress his command;
> Then was I beside him as his craftsman,
>   and I was his delight day by day,
> Playing before him all the while,

playing on the surface of his earth
[and I found delight in the sons of men.]"

(Prov. 8:22-31)

The same impression is given by these verses from Sirach
(Ecclesiasticus):

"From the mouth of the Most High I came forth,
    and mistlike covered the earth.
In the highest heavens did I dwell,
    my throne on a pillar of cloud.
The vault of heaven I compassed alone,
    through the deep abyss I wandered.
Over the waves of the sea, over all the land,
    over every people and nation I held sway.
Among all these I sought a resting place;
    in whose inheritance should I abide?

"Then the Creator of all gave me his command,
    and he who formed me chose the spot for my tent,
Saying, 'In Jacob make your dwelling,
    In Israel your inheritance.'
Before all ages, in the beginning, he created me,
    and through all ages I shall not cease to be.
In the holy Tent I ministered before him,
    and in Sion I fixed my abode...."

(Sir. 24:3-10)

Of all the passages in which Wisdom tends to be personified,
the most characteristic is the following:

For she is an aura of the might of God
    and a pure effusion of the glory of the Almighty;
    therefore nought that is sullied enters into her.

For she is the refulgence of eternal light,
　　the spotless mirror of the power of God,
　　the image of his goodness.
(Wis. 7:25-6)

Saint Paul no doubt had these passages in mind when he
spoke of our Lord as "the image of the invisible God" (Col.
1:15), and when he said that the Son, by whom God spoke
to us, is "the brightness of his glory, and the figure of his
substance, and upholding all things by the word of his power"
(Heb. 1:3). It is true that an event of immense importance
had occurred in the meantime: the Word had come to dwell
among us and reveal the mystery of the most holy Trinity.

On this article of our faith, as on many others, the revelation contained in the Old Testament was only partial and had
to await the completion God was to give it in the New Testament. However, in adding new light to the partial revelation
already given, God withdrew nothing of what he had revealed about himself. That is why, in our faith and in our
prayers, we can still continue to turn to the great God of
Moses, the merciful God of Osee, the holy God of Isaias; for
us, as for the Jews, he is always "Yahweh, our God."

CHAPTER 6

The Messias

THE MESSIANIC PROMISES UP TO THE TIME OF DAVID

IN ADDITION to monotheism, Israel gave to the world the hope of a Messias. We shall see now what this implied in the course of centuries and how the Jews carried out this second mission.

God made the promise of a Saviour in a mysterious way at the very moment when our first parents were driven out of the Garden of Eden. Speaking to the serpent, the tempter, he said: "I will put enmity between you and the woman, between your seed and her seed; he shall crush your head" (Gen. 3:15).

Through the children of Abraham, who himself was a descendant of Sem, Eve's posterity was to be victorious over the devil. On several occasions Yahweh told Abraham, "I will bless you, and make your name great. . . . In your descendants all the nations of the earth shall be blessed" (Gen. 12:2-3; 18:18; 22:18).

The victor was to be born, in the line of Abraham from Jacob-Israel, Abraham's grandson; and in the line of Jacob, from Juda, Jacob's son. It was Juda who was designated by his dying father as heir to the promise.

The sceptre shall not depart from Juda,
    nor the staff from between his feet,
Until he [the Peacemaker] comes to whom it belongs.
    To him shall be the obedience of all nations.
                (Gen. 49:10)

That is the first passage in which universal royalty is promised to the King-Messias.

God renewed his undertaking by Moses when Jacob's descendants, the Israelites, had gone out of Egypt:

> "A prophet like me [Moses] will the Lord, your God, raise up for you from among your own kinsmen; to him you shall listen. This is exactly what you requested of the Lord, your God, at Horeb on the day of the assembly, when you said, 'Let us not again hear the voice of the Lord, our God, nor see this great fire any more, lest we die.' And the Lord said to me, 'This was well said. I will raise up for them a prophet like you from among their kinsmen, and I will put my words into his mouth; he shall tell them all that I command him. If any man will not listen to my words which he speaks in my name, I myself will make answer for it' " (Deut. 18:16-19).

Proof that it is indeed the Messias that is intended here is found in the fact that Jesus applied this prophecy to himself:

> Think not that I will accuse you to the Father. There is one that accuseth you, Moses, in whom you trust. For if you did believe Moses, you would perhaps believe me also; for he wrote of me. But if you do not believe his writings, how will you believe my words? (John 5:45-7).

In the account of the Exodus there is another, very curious, Messianic prophecy, that of Balaam. Balaam was a professional soothsayer who prophesied, blessed, and cursed as he was told, sometimes in the name of one god and sometimes in the name of another. When Moses, to insure free passage of the Jordan, attacked and defeated the Amorrites of Transjordan, Balac, king of the Moabites, fearing a like fate, sent messengers to Balaam saying:

"A people has come here from Egypt who now cover the face of the earth and are settling down opposite us! Please come and curse this people for us; they are stronger than we are. We may then be able to defeat them and drive them out of the country. For I know that whoever you bless is blessed and whoever you curse is cursed" (Num. 22:5-6).

Balaam, who set a high price on his services, at first gave every appearance of refusing: "Even if Balac gave me his house full of silver and gold, I could not do anything, small or great, contrary to the command of the Lord." In the end he decided to go.

So the next morning when Balaam arose, he saddled his ass, and went off with the princes of Moab. . . .

When Balac heard that Balaam was coming, he went out to meet him at the boundary city Ir-Moab on the Arnon at the end of the Moabite territory. . . . Then Balaam went with Balac, and they came to Cariath-Husoth. Here Balac slaughtered oxen and sheep, and sent portions to Balaam and to the princes who were with him.

The next morning Balac took Balaam up on Bamoth-Baal, and from there he saw some of the clans [Hebrews] (Num. 22:21, 36-41).

To secure Yahweh's agreement to placing curses on the lips of the prophet, the king of Moab offered in sacrifice seven bullocks and seven rams. On the first occasion Balaam prophesied as follows:

How can I curse whom God has not cursed?
How denounce whom the Lord has not denounced?
For from the top of the crags I see him,
from the heights I behold him.

> Here is a people that lives apart
>> and does not reckon itself among the nations.
>>> (Num. 23:8-9)

On two further occasions Balac sacrificed seven bullocks and seven rams to the God of Israel, and Balaam attempted to curse in order to satisfy his royal client, but again only blessings issued from his mouth. He tried for a fourth and last time and then it was that God placed on his lips this Messianic prophecy:

> The utterance of one who hears what God says, . . .
> I see him, though not now;
>> I behold him, though not near:
> A star shall advance from Jacob,
>> and a staff shall rise from Israel,
> That shall smite the brows of Moab . .
> Till Edom is dispossessed . .
> Israel shall do valiantly. . .
>> (Num. 24:16-18)

In Mesopotamia and Egypt deified kings were commonly known as "stars."

Previous to the Fathers of the Church, Jewish tradition already acknowledged that this oracle referred to the Messias. That is why, for example, Bar-Cocheba, wishing to be hailed as the long-awaited Messias, took the name of "Son of the Star" when, in 132, he endeavored to stir up his Jewish fellow countrymen against the Romans. Is it to be supposed that the Magi who came to worship the child Jesus held Balaam's prophecy as Messianic? At our Saviour's birth, at all events, a star indeed rose over Israel, and on the last page of the Apocalypse our Lord declares, "I, Jesus, have sent my Angel to testify to you these things in the churches. I am the root and stock of David, the bright and morning star" (Ap. 22:16).

The writer of the books of Samuel placed on the lips of Anna, Samuel's mother, a psalm written at a later period, the last verses of which also foretell the Messias. Anna thanks the Lord for having brought her barrenness to an end and for bestowing on her a son:

There is none holy as the Lord is:
>for there is no other beside thee,
>and there is none strong like our God. . . .

The Lord killeth and maketh alive,
>he bringeth down to hell [Sheol] and bringeth
>>back again.

The Lord maketh poor and maketh rich,
>he humbleth and he exalteth.

He raiseth up the needy from the dust,
>and lifteth up the poor from the dunghill: . . .

For the poles of the earth are the Lord's,
>and upon them he hath set the world.

He will keep the feet of the saints,
>and the wicked shall be silent in darkness,
>because no man shall prevail by his own strength.

The adversaries of the Lord shall fear him:
>and upon them shall be thunder in the heavens.

The Lord shall judge the ends of the earth,
>and he shall give empire to his king,
>and shall exalt the horn of his Christ.

>(1 Sam. 2:2-10)

In the Bible the "horn" is always a symbol of power. The words "his Christ" [his anointed one] here refer not only to a person who, like the kings and the priests, has been anointed with holy oil, but to one who is alone of his kind, "the anointed one" in the highest sense of the word, whose power will extend to the judgment at the end of time. It was

in this way, moreover, that Zachary, "filled with the Holy
Ghost," prophesied saying:

> Blessed be the Lord God of Israel;
> > because he hath visited and wrought the redemption of
> > > his people;
> > and hath raised up a horn of salvation to us . . .
> > salvation from our enemies,
> > and from the hand of all that hate us: . . .
> To perform mercy to our fathers,
> > and to remember his holy testament [covenant],
> > the oath which he swore to Abraham our father. . . .
> The Orient from on high hath visited us:
> > to enlighten them that sit in darkness,
> > and in the shadow of death.
> > > > (Luke 1:68-79)

Even more exactly the Blessed Virgin in the *Magnificat* recalled the Canticle of Anna and the prophecy that it contained:

> He hath showed might in his arm;
> > he hath scattered the proud in the conceit of their heart.
> He hath put down the mighty from their seat,
> > he hath exalted the humble.
> He hath filled the hungry with good things;
> > and the rich he hath sent empty away.
> He hath received Israel his servant,
> > being mindful of his mercy:
> As he spoke to our fathers,
> > to Abraham and his seed for ever.
> > > > (Luke 1:51-5)

DAVID AND THE PSALMS

Before considering the Psalms and the prophetical books,
mention must be made of the Messianic message that Yahweh

caused to be brought to David after his installation in Jerusalem. Having built for himself a house of cedar, David desired to build one also for Yahweh, whose Ark ought not to
remain indefinitely in the tent. Now the Lord looked not to
David but to Solomon for the construction of the Temple.
He ordered the prophet Nathan to dissuade David from carrying out his plan, to tell him that Yahweh did not desire David
to build him a house, rather "the Lord will make thee a house"
by founding a dynasty. The message to be delivered to David
continued:

> I [The Lord] will give thee rest from all thy enemies.
> ... And when thy days shall be fulfilled, and thou shalt
> sleep with thy fathers, I will raise up thy seed after thee ...
> and I will establish his kingdom. ... I will be to him a
> father, and he shall be to me a son: and if he commit any
> iniquity, I will correct him with the rod of men, and with
> the stripes of the children of men. But my mercy I will
> not take away from him. ... And thy house shall be
> faithful, and thy kingdom for ever before thy face, and
> thy throne shall be firm for ever (2 Sam. 7:11-16).

It is clear that certain terms of this promise do not apply to
the Messias-King, but to the kings who succeeded David and
who deserved only too well the rod and the stripes. It is an
example of what is frequently encountered in the Messianic
and eschatological prophecies: they lack the normal ordering
of events, placing on the same level and at the same time
events separated by years and often by centuries. No doubt
in this case the immediate application of the prophecy is to
Solomon; still, in the person of Solomon is comprised his
whole posterity (14-16). Thus Saint Peter is quite right
(Acts 2:30) in applying it to Jesus Christ, David's descendant,
and to his eternal kingdom. The title "Son of David" given to
the Messias in the rabbinical writings, as well as its particular

application to Jesus in the New Testament, implies that the Messianic interpretation of this passage was widely acknowledged by the Jews.

This prophecy is therefore one of the most important in the whole of the Old Testament. It indicates a considerable advance in the history of the Messianic revelation. Not only is the Redeemer to belong to the seed of the woman (Gen. 3:15), to the seed of Sem (Gen. 9:26), to the posterity of Abraham (Gen. 12:3 ff), and to the tribe of Juda (Gen. 49:10); his family, too, is designated. The family of David is proclaimed by Yahweh as the depositary of the Messianic kingship through which is to be accomplished the promise made to Abraham: "In your descendants all the nations of the earth shall be blessed."

The promise made to David through Nathan recurs in Psalm 131:

> The Lord swore to David
>> a firm promise which he will not withdraw:
> "Your own offspring
>> I will set upon your throne;
> If your sons keep my covenant
>> and the decrees which I shall teach them,
> Their sons, too, forever
>> shall sit upon your throne."
> For the Lord has chosen Sion;
>> he prefers her for his dwelling.
> "Sion is my resting place forever;
>> in her will I dwell, for I prefer her. ..."
>> (Ps. 131:11-14)

The same prophecy forms the theme of Psalm 88, which, like Psalm 131, belongs to a relatively recent period. The Psalmist is careful to show that although political power has lately been taken away from David's descendants, there will

yet arise one from among them whose sovereignty will be
eternal:

"I have made a covenant with my chosen one,
        I have sworn to David my servant:
    Forever will I confirm your posterity
        and establish your throne for all generations. . . .

"My faithfulness and my kindness shall be with him
        and through my name shall his horn be exalted.
    I will set his hand upon the sea,
        and his right hand upon the rivers.

"He shall say of me, 'You are my father,
        my God, the Rock, my savior.'
    And I will make him the first-born,
        highest of the kings of the earth.
    Forever I will maintain my kindness toward him,
        and my covenant with him stands firm.
    I will make his posterity endure forever
        and his throne as the days of heaven.

"If his sons forsake my law
        and walk not according to my ordinances,
    If they violate my statutes
        and keep not my commands,
    I will punish their crime with a rod
        and their guilt with stripes.
    Yet my kindness I will not take from him,
        nor will I belie my faithfulness.

"I will not violate my covenant;
        the promise of my lips I will not alter.
    Once, by my holiness, have I sworn;
        I will not be false to David.

His posterity shall continue forever,
    and his throne shall be like the sun before me;
Like the moon which remains forever—
    a faithful witness in the sky."

                                   (Ps. 88:4-5, 25-38)

Many of these emphatic expressions go far beyond anything that can be said of the most glorious sovereigns of Israel. They assume however their full significance when they are considered in the context of the universal kingdom of the Messias, who, in truth, will have dominion over the sea, the rivers, and all the king of the earth.

Psalms 109 and 2 are of a clearly Messianic nature.

In accordance with rabbinical tradition, Jesus declared that Psalm 109, which was written by David, refers to the Messias and is inspired by the Holy Ghost (Matt. 22:41-6; Mark 12: 35-7; Luke 20:41-4):

The Lord said to my Lord: "Sit at my right hand
    till I make your enemies your footstool."
The scepter of your power the Lord will stretch forth
                  from Sion:
    "Rule in the midst of your enemies.
Yours is princely power in the day of your birth, in holy
                  splendor;
    before the daystar, like the dew, I have begotten you."

The Lord has sworn, and he will not repent:
    "You are a priest forever, according to the order of
                Melchisedec."

The Lord is at your right hand;
    he will crush kings on the day of his wrath.
He will do judgment on the nations. . . .

                               (Ps. 109:1-6)

David's "Lord," therefore, will possess all the prerogatives of prince, priest, and judge. The scepter of sovereignty will be his by right of birth, and his enemies will be brought to naught. He will be a priest, not like Aaron but like Melchisedec, that mysterious figure whom Abraham regarded as far superior to himself (Heb. 7:1-19). Indeed, he will be seated at the right hand of the Father, the place that he took on the day of the Ascension (Mark 16:19, Acts 7:55-6) and from which he will come on the Day of Judgment, appearing in the clouds of heaven (Matt. 26:64).

It is Psalm 2, also held as Messianic in the New Testament (Acts 4:25-7; Hebrews and Apocalypse), that for the first time bestows on the promised Saviour the name of Messias, which he was thenceforth to bear: *Mashiah* in Hebrew, *Christos* in Greek, both meaning "anointed."

> Why do the nations rage
>> and the peoples utter folly?
> The kings of the earth rise up
>> and the princes conspire together
>> against the Lord and against his anointed: ...
>
> He who is throned in heaven laughs;
>> the Lord derides them.
> Then in anger he speaks to them;
>> he terrifies them in his wrath:
> "I myself have set up my king
>> on Sion; my holy mountain."
>
> I will proclaim the decree of the Lord:
>> The Lord said to me, "You are my son;
>> this day I have begotten you.
> Ask of me and I will give you
>> the nations for an inheritance
>> and the ends of the earth for your possession

You shall rule them with an iron rod;
  you shall shatter them like an earthen dish."

And now, O kings, give heed;
  take warning, you rulers of the earth.
Serve the Lord with fear and rejoice before him;
  with trembling pay homage to him,
Lest he be angry and you perish from the way,
  when his anger blazes suddenly.

(Ps. 2:1-12)

The culminating point of this poem is of course the verse
in which God gives the Messias the title of Son, begotten
by him. It is by reason of this sonship that Christ received
power over kings and peoples. The whole universe is his
natural inheritance.

Psalm 71, which was composed either by Solomon or on his
behalf, is almost entirely concerned with the Messias and his
reign:

May he endure as long as the sun,
  and like the moon through all generations. . . .
Justice shall flower in his days,
  and profound peace, till the moon be no more.

May he rule from sea to sea,
  and from the River to the ends of the earth. . . .
All kings shall pay him homage,
  all nations shall serve him. . .

May he live to be given the gold of Arabia,
  and to be prayed for continually;
    day by day shall they bless him. . .
May his name be blessed forever
  as long as the sun his name shall remain.

(Ps. 71:5-17)

As in the preceding verses of Psalm 71, Rabbinic exegesis regarded the following verses of Psalm 44 as a Messianic prophecy:

Fairer in beauty are you than the sons of men;
    grace is poured out upon your lips;
    thus God has blessed you forever. . . .
Your throne, O God, stands forever and ever;
    a tempered rod is your royal scepter.
You love justice and hate wickedness;
    therefore God, your God, has anointed you
    with the oil of gladness above your fellow kings.
               (Ps. 44:3-8)

Saint Paul applied this passage to the Messias, with the purpose of proving that he is above the angels. He wrote, "And to the angels indeed he saith: 'He that maketh his angels Spirits, and his ministers a flame of fire.' But to the Son: 'Thy throne, O God, is for ever and ever: a sceptre of justice is the sceptre of thy kingdom. Thou hast loved justice, and hated iniquity: therefore, God, thy God, hath anointed thee with the oil of gladness above thy fellows' " (Heb. 1:7-9).[1]

Many other psalms, as we are told by Jesus and the authors of the New Testament, contain passages referring to the Messias. From Psalm 117, for example, to give but one quotation, our Lord cited verses 22 and 23 to confound the doctors of the Law:

Jesus saith to them: "Have you never read in the Scriptures: 'The stone which the builders rejected, the same is become the head of the corner? By the Lord this has been done; and it is wonderful in our eyes.' Therefore I say to you, that the kingdom of God shall be taken from you,

---

[1] This is the Douay translation of the Epistle to the Hebrews and the two translations, Douay and Confraternity (quoted above), of Psalm 44 are not identical; but it will be seen that the sense is the same—Translator's note.

and shall be given to a nation yielding the fruits thereof. And whosoever shall fall on this stone, shall be broken: but on whomsoever it shall fall, it shall grind him to powder" (Matt. 21:42-4).

THE MESSIAS IN THE PROPHETS

Of the utterances of the prophets, some concern the Messias while others refer to the Messianic era. We deal here with the former, leaving study of the latter to Chapter 7 in which we come to consideration of the Church.

At the head of all the seers of Israel stands the great Isaias, whom Saint Jerome termed "the prophet evangelist," so closely does the Messias foretold by him resemble the Messias of the Gospels.

The prophecy that opens what is called his "Emmanuel cycle" was uttered during the time when Achaz was king of Juda (736-716). Achaz, finding himself at war with the kings of Syria and Samaria, decided to call on the Assyrians for help. Isaias went to him to dissuade him from carrying out this plan. There was nothing to be feared, he told him, from these petty kings. "See thou be quiet," he went on, "fear not, and let not thy heart be afraid of the two tails of these firebrands smoking with . . . wrath"; the powerful Assyrians would be far more dangerous because they would introduce idolatry. Achaz was to put his trust in Yahweh, his God, and if he doubted, let him ask for a sign, "either unto the depth of hell, or unto the height above." Achaz, an idolater at heart, refused on the pretext of not "tempting the Lord" (7:4-12). Whereupon the prophet uttered these words:

Hear ye, therefore, O house of David:
Is it a small thing for you to be grievous to men,
     that you are grievous to my God also?
Therefore the Lord himself shall give you a sign.

Behold a virgin [2] shall conceive, and bear a son,
   and his name shall be called Emmanuel.
He shall eat butter and honey,
   that he may know to refuse evil, and to choose good.
For before the child know to refuse the evil, and to choose
        the good,
   the land which thou abhorrest
   shall be forsaken of the face of her two kings.
                (Isa. 7:13-16)

Here, as in almost all the prophecies, two periods encroach
on each other, and there is some confusion. Nevertheless, it is
clear that the "sign" is not principally concerned with the
son (Ezechias) about to be born to the king nor to the one
that Isaias was soon to have (Shear-Yashub). In the first place,
neither the queen nor the prophet's wife were "virgins," and,
secondly—and chiefly—neither of these children were to de-
serve that the following passage be applied to them:

The people that walked in darkness,
   have seen a great light:
      to them that dwelt in the region of the shadow of
               death,[3]
   light is risen. . . .

For a child is born to us,
   and a son is given to us,
   and the government is upon his shoulder:
   and his name shall be called,

[2] The Hebrew text reads "the maiden," which the Septuagint translates
"the virgin." In any case the meaning is the same and this prophecy is
rightly considered as referring to her who is "blessed among women," to the
blessed Virgin Mary, mother of our Saviour.

[3] To "them that sit in darkness, and in the shadow of death," as Zachary
was to say in the *Benedictus* canticle (Luke 1:79).

> Wonderful, Counsellor, God the Mighty,
>> the Father of the world to come,[4] the Prince of Peace.
> His empire shall be multiplied,
>> and there shall be no end of peace:
> He shall sit upon the throne of David, and upon his
>> kingdom;
>> to establish it and strengthen it
>> with judgment and with justice
>> for henceforth and for ever:
>> the zeal of the Lord of hosts will perform this.
>>   (Isa. 9:2, 6-7)

Whence shall arise this Emmanuel, whose name means "God with us"? From the line of Jesse, the father of David:

> There shall come forth a rod out of the root of Jesse [a
>> branch from the trunk of Jesse],
>> and a flower shall rise up out of his root.
> And the spirit of the Lord shall rest upon him:
>> the spirit of wisdom, and of understanding,
>> the spirit of counsel, and of fortitude,
>> the spirit of knowledge, and of godliness.
> And he shall be filled with the spirit of the fear of the Lord.[5]
> He shall not judge according to the sight of the eyes,
>> nor reprove according to the hearing of the ears.
> But he shall judge the poor with justice,
>> and shall reprove with equity for the meek of the earth;
> And he shall strike the earth with the rod of his mouth,
>> and with the breath of his lips he shall slay the wicked.
> And justice shall be the girdle of his loins:
>> and faith the girdle of his reins.
>>   (Isa. 11:1-5)

[4] Instead of "Father of the world to come" (father of the new Israel), the Septuagint has "eternal Father."

[5] This passage has given rise to the doctrine of the "gifts of the Holy Spirit."

Thus the world in which Emmanuel will reign is to be a world made new, an idyllic world, where all creatures will live in peace:

> The wolf shall dwell with the lamb:
> > and the leopard shall lie down with the kid:
> > the calf and the lion and the sheep shall abide together,
> > and a little child shall lead them. . . .

> They shall not hurt, nor shall they kill
> > in all my holy mountain,
> > for the earth is filled with knowledge of the Lord,
> > as the covering waters of the sea.

> In that day the root of Jesse,
> > who standeth for an ensign of peoples,
> > him the Gentiles shall beseech,
> > and his sepulchre [dwelling] shall be glorious.

> And it shall come to pass in that day,
> > that the Lord shall set his hand the second time
> > to possess the remnant of his people.
> > > (Isa. 11:6-11)

Having thus foretold that this "rod of Jesse" on whom rests the "spirit of Yahweh" will be a universal king, restoring justice everywhere and putting an end to the oppression of the poor, Isaias closes the Emmanuel cycle with a canticle of thanksgiving:

> Sing ye to the Lord, for he hath done great things;
> > show this forth in all the earth.
> Rejoice, and praise, O thou habitation of Sion:
> > for great is he that is in the midst of thee,
> > the Holy One of Israel.
> > > (Isa. 12:5-6)

We have just encountered (Isa. 11:11) the expression "the
remnant of his people." The "remnant," the "remnant of
Israel," the "remnant of Yahweh," are terms frequently found
in the prophets. The prophets used the expression "the remnant" in foretelling events that would take place either in
the near future or in far-off times to come. On this occasion
in Isaias the event was in both the near and remote future.
Isaias had called his second son Shear-Yashub (meaning "a
remnant shall return"); and concerning the king of Assyria,
who had mastered the kingdom of Israel and was about to try
to seize the kingdom of Juda, he said, "And it shall come to
pass in that day, that the remnant of Israel, and they that shall
escape of the house of Jacob, shall lean no more upon him
that striketh them" (the Assyrian, held in esteem by Achaz),
"but they shall lean upon the Lord, the holy One of Israel, in
truth. The remnant shall be converted, the remnant, I say, of
Jacob, to the mighty God" (10:20-2). He said also:

> And that which shall be saved of the house of Juda, and
> which is left, shall take root downward, and shall bear
> fruit upward: For out of Jerusalem shall go forth a rem-
> nant, and salvation from mount Sion: the zeal of the Lord
> of hosts shall do this (Isa. 37:31-2).

What was foretold for the near future was not long in
coming to pass, for the "Angel of Yahweh" inflicted a deadly
disease on the Assyrian army, compelling it hastily to raise the
siege of Jerusalem.

Isaias is never at a loss for wonderful expressions with which
to refer to the Messias and the blessed era over which he will
reign:

> The Lord of hosts shall make
>   unto all people in this mountain,
>   a feast of fat things,

> a feast of wine,
>> of fat things full of marrow,
>> of wine purified from the lees.
> And he shall destroy in this mountain
>> the face of the bond with which all people were tied,
>> and the web that he began over all nations.
> He shall cast death down headlong for ever.
>
> And the Lord God shall wipe away
>> tears from every face,
>> and the reproach of his people
>> he shall take away from off the whole earth.
>>>>> (Isa. 25:6-8)

The Messias himself is "the key of the house of David...
he shall open, and none shall shut: and he shall shut, and none
shall open" (22:22). He is "a stone in the foundation of Sion,
a tried stone, a corner stone, a precious stone, founded in the
foundation" and laid by the Lord (28:16). Jesus said that *he*
was this stone. He referred to the following prophecy when
the disciples of John the Baptist came to ask him if he was
"he who should come":

> The land that was desolate and impassable shall be glad,
>> and the wilderness shall rejoice,
>> and shall flourish like the lily...
> The glory of Libanus is given to it:
>> the beauty of Carmel, and Saron;
>
> They shall see the glory of the Lord,
>> and the beauty of our God.
> Strengthen ye the feeble hands,
>> and confirm the weak knees,
> Say to the fainthearted:
>> Take courage, and fear not:

Behold your God will bring
the revenge of recompense:
God himself will come and will save you.

Then shall the eyes of the blind be opened,
and the ears of the deaf shall be unstopped.
Then shall the lame man leap as a hart,
and the tongue of the dumb shall be free.
(Isa. 35:1-6)

At the very time when the Jews were driven into exile and
all seemed lost to them forever, Jeremias foretold the restoration of Israel and the coming of the new Jerusalem. He refers
to the Messias as a branch, using the same term as Isaias:

Behold the days come, saith the Lord,
and I will raise up to David a just branch:
and a king shall reign, and shall be wise:
and shall execute judgment and justice in the earth.

In those days shall Juda be saved,
and Israel shall dwell confidently:
and this is the name that they shall call him:
The Lord our Just one.
(Jer. 23:5-6)

In the new Jerusalem, God will enter into a new Covenant,
and it will include the whole of humanity:

For there shall be a day, in which the watchmen of Mount
Ephraim shall cry:
Arise, and let us go up to Sion to the Lord our God . . .

Hear the word of the Lord, O ye nations,
and declare it in the islands that are afar off,
and say: He that scattered Israel will gather him:
and will keep him as the shepherd doth his flock. . . .

They shall come, and shall give praise in mount Sion:
>   and they shall flow together to the good things of
>   the Lord....

Return, O virgin of Israel, return to these thy holy cities ...
>   for the Lord hath created a new thing upon the earth.
>   (Jer. 31:6, 10-12, 21-2)

These verses recall those of Isaias which are quoted by Saint
Paul (Gal. 4:27) in support of his statement that the new
order has already come to pass:

Give praise, O thou barren, that bearest not:
>   sing forth praise, and make a joyful noise, thou that
>   didst not travail with child:
>   for many are the children of the desolate,
>   more than of her that hath a husband, saith the Lord.

Enlarge the place of thy tent,
>   and stretch out the skins of thy tabernacles
>   [thy dwellings] ...
For thou shalt pass on [spread abroad] to the right hand,
>   and to the left:
>   and thy seed shall inherit the Gentiles,
>   and shall inhabit the desolate cities.
>   (Isa. 54: 1-3, 5)

In Ezechiel we find that the hope of the Messias remains
inseparably bound up with the house of David. But he no
longer promises it a temporal reign. Indeed, he informs King
Sedecias that there will be no more kings in Juda: The crown
will be taken away, he says, the diadem removed; there will
be desolation and iniquity until he comes "to whom judgment
belongeth, and I will give it to him" (21:27). In fact, politically speaking, there was subsequently no king of the line of

David. Zorobabel, a descendant of Joakim who governed Jerusalem after the return from exile, was only a high commissioner and did not have the royal title. The phrase "until he comes" is a reference to the Messianic blessing given by Jacob to Juda. It infers that the reign of him who is to come, that the kingdom of the branch which is to sprout from the tree of David, will not be a political one:

> Thus saith the Lord God: I myself will take of the marrow of high cedar, and will set it: I will crop off a tender twig from the top of the branches thereof, and I will plant it on a mountain high and eminent. On the high mountains of Israel will I plant it, and it shall shoot forth into branches, and shall bear fruit, and it shall become a great cedar: and all birds shall dwell under it, and every fowl shall make its nest under the shadow of the branches thereof (Ez. 17:22-4).

Ezechiel no longer calls the David who is to come "king"; he gives him the title of "prince." And before the Gospel, he shows him as the Good Shepherd feeding his sheep:

> And I will set up one shepherd over them, and he shall feed them, even my servant David: he shall feed them, and he shall be their shepherd. And I, the Lord, will be their God: and my servant David the prince in the midst of them. . . .
>
> And they shall have one shepherd. . . . and David my servant shall be their prince for ever. And I will make a covenant of peace with them, it shall be an everlasting covenant with them (Ez. 34:23-5; 37:24-6).

The "second Isaias" even calls on God to leave heaven for a time in order to come and inaugurate the Messianic era:

> O that thou wouldst rend the heavens,
>   and wouldst come down . . .

that thy name might be made known to thy enemies:
that the nations might tremble at thy presence.
When thou shalt do wonderful things, we shall not bear
them:
thou didst come down, and at thy presence the mountains melted away.
From the beginning of the world they have not heard, nor
perceived with the ears:
the eye hath not seen,
O God, besides thee, what things thou hast prepared
for them that wait for thee.
(Isa. 64: 1-4)

It can be said that this prayer came to be heard even better
than its author could have expected, for the God who came
down from heaven was meek and humble of heart, and he
endeavored to win men's hearts rather than melt mountains.

Zacharias' mission was to announce that he would be mani-
fested in lowliness, that he would be an unpretentious and
peaceful king:

Rejoice greatly, O daughter of Sion.
Shout for joy, O daughter of Jerusalem.
Behold thy King will come to thee,
the just and saviour:
he is poor, and riding upon an ass,
and upon a colt, the foal of an ass.
And I will destroy the chariot out of Ephraim [he says],
and the horse out of Jerusalem,
and the bow for war shall be broken:
And he shall speak peace to the Gentiles,
and his power shall be from sea to sea,
and from the rivers [river, i.e., Euphrates] even to the
end of the earth.
(Zach. 9:9-10)

Saint Matthew emphasized the fulfillment of this prophecy
in his account of the triumphal entry into Jerusalem (Matt.
21:4-5).

The prophet Micheas, Isaias' compatriot and contemporary,
speaks of the Good Shepherd uniting under his crook the
sheep of the whole world; and six centuries before the event,
he points to the little village in which Emmanuel was to be
born:

And thou, Bethlehem, Ephrata,
    art a little one among the thousands of Juda: [5]
    out of thee shall he come forth unto me
    that is to be the ruler of Israel:
    and his going forth *is* from the beginning,
    from the days of eternity.
Therefore will he [Yahweh] give them up [to their
               enemies]
    even till the time wherein she that travaileth shall
               bring forth:
    and the remnant of his brethren shall be converted to
             the children of Israel.
He [the awaited ruler] shall stand,
    and feed [govern] in the strength of the Lord,
    in the height of the name of the Lord his God:
    and they shall be converted,
    for now shall he be magnified
    even to the ends of the earth.
And this man shall be our peace.
                    (Mic. 5:2-5)

When the Wise Men came to worship the newly born Child
and inquire where he was to be found, the scribes of Jeru-

---

[5] [Too little to be included among the thousands of Juda.] A "thousand"
or "*chiliad*" was an administrative division of the tribe, comprising at least
a thousand families (Num. 1:16). "*'Ephratah*" means fertile.

salem were able to tell them at once, so great had been the impression made by this prophecy.

Of the two Messianic prophecies of Malachias, the first is a counterpart of the divine curse addressed to the bad priests of those times:

> I will send poverty [the curse] upon you, and will curse your blessings, yea, I will curse them, because you have not laid it to heart. . . . I will scatter upon your face the dung of your solemnities, and it shall take you away with it. . . . For the lips of the priest shall keep knowledge, and they shall seek the law at his mouth: because he is the angel of the Lord of hosts. But you have departed out of the way, and have caused many to stumble at the law: you have made void the covenant of Levi, saith the Lord of hosts (Mal. 2:2-3, 7-8).

Fortunately other times are to come. The Messianic era is to dawn, in which God will receive sacrifices worthy of him: "From the rising of the sun even to the going down, my name is great among the Gentiles, and in every place there is sacrifice, and there is offered to my name a clean oblation" (1:11).

This prophecy is followed by another referring to the Precursor:

> Behold I send my angel [messenger], and he shall prepare the way before my face. . . . Behold I will send you Elias the prophet, before the coming of the great and dreadful day of the Lord. And he shall turn the heart of the fathers to the children, and the heart of the children to their fathers (Mal. 3:1; 4:5-6).

It was in these very words that Gabriel informed Zachary of the birth of John the Baptist. And Jesus himself declared to his disciples that John "is Elias that is to come" (Luke 1:17; 7:27; Matt. 11:13-14).

Daniel, who can be regarded as the last of the prophets, uttered two Messianic prophecies of the highest importance.

The first was occasioned by a dream that Nabuchodonosor, king of Babylon, experienced. In his dream he had seen an extraordinary statue, which had greatly frightened him. Daniel, obliged under pain of death to explain the dream to the king, spoke as follows:

> This statue, which was great and high, tall of stature, stood before thee, and the look thereof was terrible. The head of this statue was of fine gold, but the breast and the arms of silver, and the belly and the thighs of brass: And the legs of iron, the feet part of iron and part of clay. Thus thou sawest, till a stone was cut out of a mountain without hands: and it struck the statue upon the feet thereof that were of iron and of clay, and broke them in pieces. Then was the iron, the clay, the brass, the silver, and the gold broken to pieces together, and became like the chaff of a summer's thrashingfloor, and they were carried away by the wind: and there was no place found for them: but the stone that struck the statue became a great mountain, and filled the whole earth.
>
> This is the dream: we will also tell the interpretation thereof (Dan. 2:31-6).

Daniel explained to the king that this statue represented the unstable empires of the earth, whose place was to be taken by an indestructible kingdom not of this earth.

> In the days of those kingdoms the God of heaven will set up a kingdom that shall never be destroyed, and his kingdom shall not be delivered up to another people; and it shall break in pieces and shall consume all these kingdoms, and itself shall stand for ever. According as thou sawest that the stone was cut out of the mountain without

hands, and broke in pieces the clay, and the iron, and the brass and the silver, and the gold . . . (Dan. 2:44-5).

The second prophecy is that of the four beasts of the sea. The first was like a lion, the second like a bear, the third like a leopard, but the fourth was

> . . . terrible and wonderful, and exceeding strong, it had great iron teeth, eating and breaking in pieces, and treading down the rest with its feet: and it was unlike to the other beasts which I had seen before it, and had ten horns. I considered the horns, and behold another little horn sprung out of the midst of them: and three of the first horns were plucked up at the presence thereof: and behold eyes like the eyes of a man were in this horn, and a mouth speaking great things. I beheld till thrones were placed, and the Ancient of days sat: his garments were white as snow, and the hair of his head like clean wool: his throne like flames of fire: the wheels of it like a burning fire. A swift stream of fire issued forth from before him: thousands of thousands ministered to him, and ten thousand times a hundred thousand stood before him: the judgment sat and the books were opened. . . . I beheld therefore in the vision of the night, and lo, one like the Son of man came with the clouds of heaven, and he came even to the Ancient of days: and they presented him before him. And he gave him power, and glory, and a kingdom: and all peoples and tribes and tongues shall serve him: his power is an everlasting power that shall not be taken away: and his kingdom that shall not be destroyed (Dan. 7:7-14).

"The Son of man." Daniel here gives the head of the Messianic kingdom a new title. It is one that Jesus himself liked to use: "The Son of man is not come to be ministered

unto, but to minister, and to give his life a redemption for
many" (Matt. 20:28). "The Son of man is Lord even of the
sabbath" (Matt. 12:8, Mark 9:6; Mark 2:10; Luke 5:24). "So
must the Son of man be lifted up" (John 3:14). On one of the
most solemn occasions of his earthly life, when before the
Sanhedrin the high priest said to him, "I adjure thee by the
living God, that thou tell us if thou be the Christ the Son
of God," Jesus answered, "Thou hast said *it*. Nevertheless
I say to you, hereafter you shall see the Son of man sitting on
the right hand of the power of God, and coming in the clouds
of heaven" (Matt. 26:63-4; Mark 14:61-2; Luke 22:67-70).

THE SUFFERING MESSIAS

This aspect of the Messias, on which the Jews did not
readily dwell, is brought out clearly by several prophecies,
whose fulfillment our Lord and the evangelists were at pains
to emphasize (Ps. 15:9-11; 21:1; Zach. 11:12-13; 12:10, etc.).

Rather than examine all of them briefly, let us consider at
some length the most striking among them, that known as the
"Poems of the Servant," which finds a place at the end of the
Book of Isaias. There appears here a person who says of
himself:

> The Lord formed me from the womb to be his servant,
>   that I may bring back Jacob unto him,
>   [and that Israel may be gathered to him].
> (Isa. 49:5)

He will surpass Moses in virtue, and the greatest of the
prophets in his teaching. He will be the light of nations and
will spread the kingdom of Yahweh to the ends of the world.
For the redemption of all, he will undergo pains untold and
the death of a criminal. His spiritual posterity will be faithful

to him unto the end of time, and he himself will not be destroyed by death.

> Behold my servant, I will uphold him:
>> my elect, my soul delighteth in him:
> I have given my spirit upon him,
>> he shall bring forth judgment to the Gentiles.

> He shall not cry . . .
>> neither shall his voice be heard abroad.
> The bruised reed he shall not break,
>> and the smoking flax he shall not quench.

> He shall bring forth judgment unto truth:
>> he shall not be sad, nor troublesome
>> [he will not fail nor be discouraged],
> till he set judgment in the earth:
>> and the islands shall wait for his law.
>>>> (Isa. 42:1-4)

The tone of this passage recalls the utterance of God the
Father giving testimony to his Son at his baptism and at his
transfiguration. And the whole passage is quoted by Saint
Matthew when he desires to show the character of our Lord's
preaching and his gentleness (Matt. 12:17-21).

Next the Servant himself speaks in order to say how great
will be his patience and faithfulness:

> The Lord hath given me a learned tongue,
>> that I should know how to uphold by word him that
>>> is weary:
> He wakeneth in the morning, in the morning he wakeneth
>>> my ear,
>> that I may hear him as a master.
> The Lord God hath opened my ear,
>> and I do not resist: I have not gone back.

I have given my body to the strikers,
    and my cheeks to them that plucked them:
    I have not turned away my face from them that rebuke
            me, and spit upon me.

The Lord God is my helper,
    therefore am I not confounded:
    therefore have I set my face as a most hard rock,
    and I know that I shall not be confounded.
                                        (Isa. 50:4-7)

The Servant goes on to declare that as a faithful disciple of
Yahweh he is worthy to be heard by all, and that those who
reject what he has to say and take part against him will be
burned in the fire that they themselves have lighted. Then
comes the remarkable poem that has rightly been called "the
Passion according to Isaias," so faithfully does it depict the
merits and the sufferings of our Saviour:

He shall grow up as a tender plant . . .
    and as a root out of a thirsty ground:
    there is no beauty in him, nor comeliness: and we have
            seen him,
    and there was no sightliness, that we should be desirous
            of him:
Despised, and the most abject of men,
    a man of sorrows, and acquainted with infirmity:
    and his look was as it were hidden and despised
    [like one from whom men hide their faces],
    whereupon we esteemed him not.

Surely he hath borne our infirmities
    and carried our sorrows:
    and we have thought him as it were a leper,
    and as one struck by God and afflicted.

But he was wounded for our iniquities,
 he was bruised for our sins:
 the chastisement of our peace was upon him,
 and by his bruises we are healed.

All we like sheep have gone astray,
 every one hath turned aside into his own way:
 and the Lord hath laid on him the iniquity of us all.

He was offered because it was his own will
[He was ill-treated and afflicted],
 and he opened not his mouth:
 he shall be led as a sheep to the slaughter,
 and shall be dumb as a lamb before his shearer,
 and he shall not open his mouth.

He was taken away from distress, and from judgment
[By an oppressive judgment he was taken away]:
 Who shall declare his generation?
 Because he is cut off out of the land of the living:
 for the wickedness of my people have I struck him.

And he shall give the ungodly for his burial,
 and the rich for his death
[And his tomb shall be with the ungodly and evildoers]
 because he hath done no iniquity,
 neither was there deceit in his mouth.

The Lord was pleased to bruise him in infirmity:
 if [when] he shall lay down his life for sin,
 he shall see a long-lived seed,
 and the will of the Lord shall be prosperous in his hand.
Because his soul hath laboured,
 he shall see and be filled:

By his knowledge [by his sufferings]
    shall this my just servant justify many,
    and he shall bear their iniquities,
Therefore will I distribute to him very many,
    and he shall divide the spoils of the strong.

Because he hath delivered his soul unto death,
    and was reputed with the wicked:
    and he hath borne the sins of many,
    and hath prayed for the transgressors.
                                        (Isa. 53)

These last features complete the portrait of the Messias as
the prophets have painted it. Sprung from Juda and David,
born of a virgin Mother, he will be both the most perfect of
men and the only Son of God. Preceded by another Elias, he
will be a wonder-worker whom nature will obey and the
master of all truth. Meek and humble of heart, he will bear
with our weakness, yet he will not refrain from reproving us
for our sins. The King of the whole world, he will refuse all
temporal crowns and will ride mounted on an ass. Free
of any stain of sin, he will take upon himself all the sins
of the world, and in expiation for them he will endure the
cruelest of tortures. Sentenced to death as a criminal, he will
foretell that it is he who will come to judge all humanity. He
will triumph over death and receive all nations as his inheritance. The spiritual Kingdom that he will found, and
whose Priest and King he will remain, will last forever.

Who would ever have thought that a living man could in
all particulars fit so rich, so strange, so heterogeneous a portrait? Yet this person exists. He is our Lord Jesus Christ, who
has not only accomplished all that the Old Testament foretold
of him, but has so added to it that these prophecies are mere
sketches when compared with the masterpiece revealed to us
by the New Testament.

CHAPTER 7

From the Jewish Community to the Christian Church

THE concept of a universal church is of Christian origin. The idea of an organization of men in spiritual union, independent of frontiers and other temporal divisions, was entirely foreign to the whole of antiquity. For such a society to be possible, it was necessary for Christ to proclaim the great principle of the separation of the two powers: "Render therefore to Caesar the things that are Caesar's; and to God, the things that are God's" (Matt. 22:21; Mark 12:17; Luke 20:25). Yet the Christian Church, as a society open to all the souls of the whole world, was foretold, proclaimed, and, in some sort, prepared by Israel; it can therefore be said that it has its roots in the former Covenant and that here again the Old Testament finds its fulfillment in the New.

THE JEWISH COMMUNITY

The very word for "church" in Greek (the language of the New Testament) is taken from the Jewish sacred books. As long as they were in Egypt, the descendants of Jacob-Israel were only a "people," and this term is used by the Pentateuch to designate the Hebrews of those times. After Moses, they formed a "community" that owed its cohesion to the Law; this community the Scriptures refer to sometimes under the name of "synagogue" (in Hebrew, 'edah; in Greek, in the Septuagint, synagōgē) and sometimes under that of ekklēsia (the Greek word; the Hebrew is *qahal*). Etymologically, the two terms are synonymous and mean "assembly." In practice, the Bible uses them indiscriminately to designate either the community of Israel, whose members are united by a religious bond, or a meeting at which those present have been called together for a religious motive. During the Exile the Jews acquired the habit of meeting for prayer in common; the Jews in Egypt and elsewhere were also accustomed to do so. The words "synagogue" and *ekklēsia* [1] thereupon came to bear a third meaning, as they still do today, of the building in which the assembly took place.

Synagogues (or churches) became numerous in Palestine after the Exile. No sacrifice took place in them, since sacrifice could be offered only in the Temple at Jerusalem. The services were confined to a commentary on the Scriptures and the recital of private prayers. If a priest was present, he read some formula of blessing; the remainder of the proceedings was in the hands of lay officers. There was a layman, an "elder," a "presbyter," at the head of the synagogue; he was called the "archisynagogue." Among the officers was the targumist or translator, who was entrusted with the translation of the Hebrew text into Aramaic or Greek, and the "servant" or "minister," whose functions resembled those of our sacristans.

Saint Luke tells of a stormy meeting when Jesus took part in the synagogue service of his village:

> And he came to Nazareth, where he was brought up: and he went into the synagogue, according to his custom, on the sabbath day; and he rose up to read. And the book of Isaias the prophet was delivered unto him. And as he unfolded the book, he found the place where it was written:

---

[1] This Greek word for "church" became in Latin *ecclesia* and in French *église* (also in other romance languages the similarity is obvious). The English word "church" is of different origin, though it is also from the Greek, coming from *kyriakon*—Translator's note.

"The Spirit of the Lord is upon me. Wherefore he hath anointed me to preach the Gospel to the poor, he hath sent me to heal the contrite of heart, to preach deliverance to the captives, and sight to the blind, to set at liberty them that are bruised, to preach the acceptable year of the Lord, and the day of reward." And when he had folded the book, he restored it to the minister, and sat down.

And the eyes of all in the synagogue were fixed on him. And he began to say to them: This day is fulfilled this scripture in your ears. . . . And all they in the synagogue, hearing these things, were filled with anger.

And they rose up and thrust him out of the city; and they brought him to the brow of the hill, whereon their city was built, that they might cast him down headlong. But he passing through the midst of them, went his way (Luke 4:16-30).

Many of the usages and institutions of the Israel of old have been passed on to, or left traces in, the Christian Church, especially the priesthood. To the priests, the Lawgiver on Sinai entrusted the office of teaching:

When Moses had written down this law, he entrusted it to the Levitical priests who carry the Ark of the Covenant of the Lord, and to all the elders of Israel, giving them this order: "On the feast of booths . . . you shall read this law aloud in the presence of all Israel. Assemble the people —men, women and children, as well as the aliens who live in your communities—that they may hear it and learn it, and so fear the Lord, your God, and carefully observe all the words of this law" (Deut. 31:9-12).

Their office of offering sacrifice placed on the priests special obligations. They were required to abstain from strong drink when they were to exercise their ministry:

The Lord said to Aaron, "When you are to go to the
Meeting Tent, you and your sons are forbidden under pain
of death, by a perpetual ordinance throughout your generations, to drink any wine or strong drink. You must be
able to distinguish between what is sacred and what is
profane, between what is clean and what is unclean; you
must teach these Israelites all the laws that the Lord has
given them through Moses" (Lev. 10:8-11).

During the reign of King Josaphat (870-848) some priests
and Levites took up missionary work and went from place to
place giving religious instruction to the people.

After the Exile the importance of the priestly caste increased; this occurred when with the disappearance of royalty
all powers passed under the authority of the high priest. Under
the Hasmoneans the high priest presided over the Sanhedrin,
or High Council, which was composed of seventy members.
There belonged to it the chiefs of the people, the scribes, and
the leading doctors of the Law. These last, in spite of their
literalist and casuistic propensities, exerted a healthy influence
at the meetings, counteracting that of the skeptical and self-
seeking priests dominated by the Sadducees.

Under the Romans the Sanhedrin lost some of its judicial
and political functions, including the right of pronouncing the
death sentence. However, it retained complete authority in the
religious sphere. For serious sins, as already in the time of
Esdras (Esd. 10:8), it could decree exclusion from the synagogue. This was the sanction that was threatened against our
Saviour's disciples. Saint John recounts that after the cure of
the man born blind the Jews asked his parents:

Is this your son, who you say was born blind? How
then doth he now see?

His parents answered them, and said: We know that
this is our son, and that he was born blind: But how he

now seeth, we know not; or who hath opened his eyes, we know not: ask himself: he is of age, let him speak for himself.

These things his parents said, because they feared the Jews: for the Jews had already agreed among themselves, that if any man should confess him to be Christ, he should be put out of the synagogue (John 9:19-22).

The same Gospel suggests that in the exercise of his office the high priest was sometimes endowed with the gift of prophecy. When Jesus appeared before the members of the Sanhedrin,

... one of them, named Caiphas, being the high priest that year, said to them: You know nothing. Neither do you consider that it is expedient for you that one man should die for the people, and that the whole nation perish not. And this he spoke not of himself: but being the high priest of that year, he prophesied that Jesus should die for the nation. And not only for the nation, but to gather together in one the children of God, that were dispersed (John 11:49-52).

FOREIGNERS ADMITTED AMONG THE ISRAELITES

In order to preserve intact the revelation and worship of the one living God, the Law raised considerable barriers between Israel and other nations. The Hebrews had much to learn from the Egyptians, Chanaanites, Phoenicians, Assyrians, and Babylonians, who were far more advanced than they in all that concerned material civilization. If they had mixed with these nations, they would also have learned from them their idolatry. For this reason the prophets called every alliance entered into with neighboring nations treason and "fornication."

Orthodox Jews, therefore, were inclined to regard foreigners as the enemies of their God. Yet throughout the Old

Testament it is seen that Yahweh often does good to these enemies, and that he has many friends outside the chosen people. The only conclusion to be drawn is that God's heart is larger than men may think, that the Israel of God is wider than the "Israel according to the flesh," and that Yahweh was not always to reserve the benefit of the Covenant to the descendants of Sem and Abraham alone.

Already in the time of Abraham the divine mercy was shown to Abimelech, king of the Philistines:

> Abraham journeyed from there toward the land of the Negeb, and dwelt between Cades and Sur. While he lived in Gerara, Abraham said of Sara his wife, "She is my sister." So Abimelech, king of Gerara, sent and took Sara. But God came to Abimelech in a dream by night and said to him, "You shall die because of the woman you have taken; for she is married." Now Abimelech had not approached her; so he said, "Lord, will you slay the innocent? Did not he himself say to me, 'She is my sister'? and did not she herself say, 'He is my brother'? With a sincere heart and clean hands I have done this." . . .
>
> Abimelech called Abraham, and said to him, "What have you done to us? And how have I offended you that you should bring down on me and my kingdom a great sin? No one should be treated as you have treated me.". . . Abraham answered, "I thought, 'Surely there is no fear of God in this place; and they will kill me on account of my wife!' Besides, she is indeed my sister, my father's daughter but not my mother's; and she became my wife.". . .
>
> Then Abimelech took flocks and herds and cattle, men and women servants, and gave them to Abraham, and restored Sara his wife to him, and said, "My land is before you; settle wherever it pleases you.". . .

Then Abraham prayed to God; and God cured Abimelech and his wife and maidservants, and they bore children. For the Lord had closed the wombs of Abimelech's household because of Sara, the wife of Abraham (Gen. 20:1-18).

The example of Melchisedec, who was not a Jew, is also evidence that there were worshipers of Yahweh outside the tribe of Abraham. As Abraham was returning from victory over Chodorlahomor and his allies, Melchisedec, the king-priest of Salem (where Jerusalem was subsequently built), went out to meet him, bearing bread and wine, for he was "priest of the Most High God" (Gen. 14:19-20).

When the Hebrews established themselves in Chanaan, they were given orders to exterminate the population of this territory. Consequently, the holy war that ensued was fought with extreme savagery against the Chanaanites, Ammonites, Madianites, Moabites, and other idolaters whose easy form of religion and seductive women would have led the children of Israel into polytheism. Even then, however, exceptions were made in favor of some of these foreigners when they showed their faith in Yahweh. This happened in the case of the harlot Rahab who hid the spies of the Jewish army, because "the Lord, your God, is God in heaven above and on earth below" (Jos. 2:11).

The city itself they burned with all that was in it, except the silver, gold, and articles of bronze and iron, which were placed in the treasury of the house of the Lord. Because Rahab the harlot had hidden the messengers whom Josue had sent to reconnoiter Jericho, Josue spared her with her family and all her kin, who continue in the midst of Israel to this day.

On that occasion Josue imposed the oath: Cursed before the Lord be the man who attempts to rebuild this city, Jericho. He shall lose his first-born when he lays its foundation, and he shall lose his youngest son when he sets up its gates (Jos. 6:24-6).

Rahab was integrated into the community of Israel. From Saint Matthew (1:5) we know that she married Salmon, of the tribe of Juda, and was the mother of Booz.

Another example of this kind of adoption is that of Ruth, the Moabite. She married a man from Bethlehem, the son of Noemi, who had emigrated with his father and mother to the plateau of Moab to avoid the famine that prevailed in Bethlehem. Both father and son died. Learning that "the Lord had visited his people and given them food," Noemi decided to return to the land of Juda but she did not want Ruth, her daughter-in-law, to go with her:

> But Ruth said, "Do not ask me to abandon or forsake you! for wherever you go I will go, wherever you lodge I will lodge, your people shall be my people, and your God my God. Wherever you die I will die, and there be buried. May the Lord do so and so to me, and more besides, if aught but death separates me from you!"
>
> Noemi then ceased to urge her, for she saw she was determined to go with her (Ruth 1:16-18).

The two women went to live in Bethlehem. It was there that Booz noticed Ruth among the gleaners who followed his harvesters, and fell in love with her:

> Booz took Ruth. When they came together as man and wife, the Lord enabled her to conceive and she bore a son.
>
> Then the women said to Noemi, "Blessed is the Lord who has not failed to provide you today with an heir! May he become famous in Israel! He will be your comfort and the support of your old age, for his mother is the daughter-in-law who loves you. She is worth more to you than seven sons!"

Noemi took the child, placed him on her lap, and became his nurse. And the neighbor women gave him his name, at the news that a grandson had been born to Noemi. They called him Obed. He was the father of Jesse, the father of David (Ruth 4:13-17).

Even certain foreign groups were admitted to the Jewish community. The Gabaonites, for example, who on the arrival of the conquerors told them a story that deceived them:

On learning what Josue had done to Jericho and Hai, the inhabitants of Gabaon put into effect a device of their own. They chose provisions for a journey, making use of old sacks for their asses, and old wineskins, torn and mended. They wore old, patched sandals and shabby garments; and all the bread they took was dry and crumbly. Thus they journeyed to Josue in the camp at Galgal, where they said to him and to the men of Israel, "We have come from a distant land to propose that you make an alliance with us. . . . This bread of ours was still warm when we brought it from home as provisions the day we left to come to you, but now it is dry and crumbled. Here are our wineskins, which were new when we filled them, but now they are torn. Look at our garments and sandals, which are worn out from the very long journey."

. . . So Josue made an alliance with them and entered into an agreement to spare them, which the princes of the community sealed with an oath (Jos. 9:3-15).

As a consequence, the Jews felt themselves under a certain obligation to the Gabaonites. In their defense Josue undertook the campaign during which he commanded the sun to stand still. In atonement for an act of cruelty toward them, perpetrated by Saul, David put seven of Saul's descendants to death. After the return from exile the Gabaonites appeared on the official record on which Nehemias listed the repatriated

Israelites, an indication that they too had become Yahweh's servants.

During the next period we find the Ark of the Covenant carried provisionally to the house of Abinadab, and then to that of Obededom, who, though not Israelites, were nonetheless adorers of the God of Israel (1 Sam. 7:1; 2 Sam. 8:10-12; 1 Par. 13:9-14).

Urias, whom David had killed in order to take his wife, was a Hittite officer serving in the Jewish army. The reverence that he showed for the Ark seems to indicate that he believed in the true God (2 Sam. 11:11). The widow of Sarephta from whom Elias received hospitality was a Sidonian. She said to the prophet, "I know that thou art a man of God, and the word of the Lord in thy mouth is true" (3 Kings 17:24). Naaman, a general in the service of the king of Syria, was cured of his leprosy by Eliseus; he desired to carry some of the earth of Israel with him when he returned to Damascus, in order there to set up an altar to Yahweh, whom he had taken for his God:

> And returning to the man of God with all his train, he [Naaman] came, and stood before him, and said: In truth, I know there is no other God in all the earth, but only in Israel: I beseech thee therefore take a blessing of thy servant.
>
> But he answered: As the Lord liveth, before whom I stand, I will receive none. And when he pressed him he still refused.
>
> And Naaman said: As thou wilt: but I beseech thee, grant to me thy servant, to take from hence two mules' burden of earth: for thy servant will not henceforth offer holocaust, or victim, to other gods, but to the Lord. But there is only this, for which thou shalt entreat the Lord for thy servant, when my master goeth into the temple of

Remmon, to worship: and he leaneth upon my hand, if I bow down in the temple of Remmon, when he boweth down in the same place, that the Lord pardon me thy servant for this thing.

And he said to him: Go in peace. So he departed from him in the springtime of the earth (4 Kings 5:15-19).

In the days when he was a man of virtue and wisdom Solomon also was one of those who believed that the God of Israel conferred blessings on other peoples. The prayer that he recited after the dedication of the Temple shows this clearly.

Moreover also the stranger, who is not of thy people Israel, when he shall come out of a far country for thy name's sake (for they shall hear every where of thy great name and thy mighty hand, and thy stretched out arm) so when he shall come, and shall pray in this place, then hear thou in heaven, in the firmament of thy dwelling place, and do all those things, for which that stranger shall call upon thee: that all the people of the earth may learn to fear thy name, as do thy people Israel (3 Kings 8:41-3).

The devout King Josias (640-609) did not believe that God could make himself known to foreigners, but the inspired author of Paralipomenon seems to reprove him for this and attribute his death to this mistake. He tells us how Nechao, king of Egypt, urged by God to go to war against the Assyrians,

... came up to fight in Charcamis by the Euphrates: and Josias went out to meet him. But he sent messengers to him, saying: What have I to do with thee, O king of Juda? I come not against thee this day, but I fight against another house, to which God hath commanded me to go in haste: forbear to do against God, who is with me, lest he kill thee.

Josias would not return, but prepared to fight against him, and hearkened not to the words of Nechao from the mouth of God, but went to fight in the field of Mageddo. And there he was wounded by the archers, and he said to his servants, Carry me out of the battle, for I am grievously wounded. And they removed him from the chariot into another, that followed him after the manner of kings, and they carried him away to Jerusalem, and he died, and was buried in the monument of his fathers, and all Juda and Jerusalem mourned for him (2 Par. 35:20-4).

Aside from the writings of the prophets, which we will discuss presently, the books of the Old Testament contain a number of other passages foreshadowing and even asserting the doctrine of universal salvation which the Gospels and Saint Paul were to set forth with such clarity. The Book of Daniel has many passages like the following:

Then Nabuchodonosor breaking forth, said: Blessed be the God of them, to wit, of Sidrach, Misach, and Abdenago, who hath sent his angel, and delivered his servants that believed in him: and they changed the king's word and delivered up their bodies that they might not serve, nor adore any god, except their own God. By me therefore this decree is made, that every people, tribe and tongue, which shall speak blasphemy against the God of Sidrach, Misach, and Abdenago, shall be destroyed, and their houses laid waste: for there is no other God that can save in this manner (Dan. 3:95-6).

The whole Book of Jonas is devoted to showing how God compelled a recalcitrant prophet to go and preach to the inhabitants of Ninive, thus proving that divine mercy did not exclude these pagans.

The hero of the Book of Job and his friends are also non-Jews; yet Yahweh on two occasions says of Job that "there is no one on earth like him, blameless and upright" (Job 1:8; 2:3).

Toward a Universal Religion: The Prophets

The prophets in particular foretold that the religion of the Messianic era would be endowed with that character of universality which is a feature of the Christian Church. It is true that they make Jerusalem the religious center of the world to come, but it was from Jerusalem that the preaching of Jesus, and after Pentecost that of the Apostles whom he sent to teach all nations, became known abroad.

In the Book of Amos, the first of the so-called writing prophets, we read:

> In that day I will raise up the tabernacle of David, that is
> fallen:
>   and I will close up the breaches of the world thereof:
>   and repair what is fallen:
>   and I will rebuild it as in the days of old.
> That they may possess the *remnant of Edom*,[2]
>   and all nations because my name is invoked upon them:
>   saith the Lord that doth these things.
>   (Amos 9:11-12)

At the Council of Jerusalem, Saint James founded on this passage his argument in favor of dispensing Gentiles who had become Christians from observance of the Mosaic Law. He quotes it from the Septuagint version which, endowing the prophecy with an even stronger universalist sense, does not say "Edom" but "I will set it up, that *the residue of men* [2] may seek after the Lord, and all nations upon whom my name is invoked" (Acts 15:16-18).

[2] Italics ours.

On occasion, God endows prophecies with a meaning and a bearing unrealized by the prophet who utters them. The following passage would seem to be an instance of this:

> ... I will pour out my spirit upon all flesh:
> And your sons and your daughters shall prophesy:
> > your old men shall dream dreams,
> > and your young men shall see visions.
> Moreover upon my servants and handmaids
> [Even upon the menservants and maidservants]
> > in those days I will pour forth my spirit. . . .
>
> And it shall come to pass,
> > that every one that shall call upon the name of the
> > Lord shall be saved.
> > > (Joel 2:28-32)

It seems clear that Joel envisaged only those who found salvation on Mount Sion and those who survived in Jerusalem (2:32); but in fact this passage refers to the salvation of all men. Saint Peter was to quote it on the day of Pentecost to summon all his hearers to be converted (Acts 2:16-21), and Saint Paul used it to prove that "there is no distinction of the Jew and the Greek; for the same is Lord over all, rich unto all that call upon him" (Rom. 10:12-13).

Jeremias asserts that he has been made a prophet "over the nations, and over kingdoms, to root up, and to pull down, and to waste, and to destroy, and to build, and to plant" (Jer. 1:10). He foretells, therefore, great devastation, showing Yahweh plucking out of their land "all my wicked neighbours" that attack Israel. Yet once these pagans have been punished, the prophet is glad to show that they will be "built up" again and that divine mercy will be shown in their behalf:

> And when I shall have plucked them out, I will return,
> and have mercy on them: and I will bring them back,

every man to his inheritance, and every man into his land.
And it shall come to pass, if they will be taught, and will
learn the ways of my people, to swear by my name
[saying], The Lord liveth, as they have taught my people
to swear by Baal: [then] they shall be built up in the midst
of my people (Jer. 12:14-16).

The time will come, therefore, when "Jerusalem shall be
called the throne of the Lord: and all the nations shall be
gathered together to it, in the name of [Yahweh] to Jerusalem,
and they shall not walk after the perversity of their most
wicked heart" (Jer. 3:17). Acknowledging the nothingness of
their idols, they will form but one body with the chosen
people:

> O Lord, my might, and my strength,
>   and my refuge in the day of tribulation:
>   to thee the Gentiles shall come from the ends of the
>   earth, and shall say:
> Surely our fathers have possessed lies,
>   a vanity which hath not profited them.
> Shall a man make gods unto himself, and they are no gods?
>
> Therefore I will this once cause them to know,
>   I will show them my hand and my power:
>   and they shall know that my name is [Yahweh].
>   (Jer. 16:19-21)

That is, "He who Is," the only God who exists.
In Ezechiel (1:15-28) Yahweh's chariot which, carried on
the wings of the cherubim, goes hither and thither covering
great distances and crossing frontiers, stands for the preaching
of Christ, for its efficacy is universal. The same theme forms
the inspiration of the following allegory, in which are seen all
peoples coming to seek religious truth of the Messianic king,
who has sprung from Israel:

Thus saith the Lord God: I myself will take of the
marrow of the high cedar, and will set it: I will crop off a
tender twig from the top of the branches thereof, and I
will plant it on a mountain high and eminent. On the
high mountains of Israel will I plant it, and it shall shoot
forth into branches, and shall bear fruit, and it shall become
a great cedar: and all the birds shall dwell under it, and
every fowl shall make its nest under the shadow of the
branches thereof. And all the trees of the country shall
know that I the Lord have brought down the high tree,
and exalted the low tree: and have dried up the green tree,
and have caused the dry tree to flourish (Ez. 17:22-4).

Jesus used almost the same figure to define the kingdom that
he was founding: "The kingdom of heaven is like to a grain
of mustard seed, which a man took and sowed in his field.
Which is the least indeed of all seeds; but when it is grown
up, it is greater than all herbs, and becometh a tree, so that
the birds of the air come, and dwell in the branches thereof"
(Matt. 13:31-2).

It is in Isaias especially that there are innumerable instances
of prophecy foretelling the universality of salvation brought
by the Messias. The prophet sees Jerusalem becoming the religious capital of the world:

And in the last days
        the mountain of the house of the Lord
        shall be prepared on the top of mountains, . . .
        and all nations shall flow unto it.

And many people shall go, and say:
        Come and let us go up . . .
        and [Yahweh] will teach us his ways,
        and we will walk in his paths:

For the law shall come forth from Sion,
  and the word of the Lord from Jerusalem.

                                        (Isa. 2:3)
Again:

My just one is near at hand, my saviour is gone forth,
  the islands shall look for me,
  and shall patiently wait for my arm. . . .

And the children of the stranger that adhere to the Lord,
  to worship him, and to love his name, to be his
                        servants: . . .
  I will bring them into my holy mount,
  and will make them joyful in my house of prayer:
  their holocausts, and their victims shall please me upon
                        my altar:
  for my house shall be called the house of prayer, for
                        all nations.

                                (Isa. 51:5; 56:6-7)
The Ethiopians will come:

At that time shall a present be brought to the Lord of hosts,
  from a people rent and torn in pieces:
  from a terrible people, after which there hath been no
                        other:
  from a nation expecting, expecting and trodden
                        underfoot,
  whose land the rivers have spoiled,
  to the place of the name of the Lord of hosts,
  to mount Sion.

                                  (Isa. 18:7) [3]

[3] The above is the Douay version, a translation from the Vulgate. The French version, which is translated from the original, conveys the meaning more clearly.

  At that time gifts will be brought to the Lord of hosts,
     from a tall people with shining skins,
     from a people feared from afar off,

Yahweh will go to save the Egyptians, whom he had
formerly dealt with so harshly:

In that day there shall be an altar of the Lord in the midst
of the land of Egypt,
and a monument of the Lord at the borders thereof:
It shall be for a sign,
and for a testimony to the Lord of hosts in the land
Egypt.
For they shall cry to the Lord because of the oppressor,
and he shall send them a Saviour and a defender to
deliver them.

And the Lord shall be known by Egypt,
and the Egyptians shall know the Lord in that day,
and shall worship him with sacrifices and offerings:
and they shall make vows to the Lord, and perform
them.
And the Lord shall strike Egypt with a scourge,
and shall heal it.
And they shall return to the Lord,
and he shall be pacified towards them, and heal them.
(Isa. 19:19-22)

All will be invited to the great banquet and will be able to
eat their fill:

And the Lord of hosts shall make
unto all people in this mountain,
a feast of fat things,
a feast of wine,

---

from an imperious and conquering people
whose land is divided by rivers,
to the dwelling of the name of the Lord of hosts,
to Mount Sion.
                                   —Translator's note

of fat things full of marrow,
of wine purified from the lees.
And he shall destroy in this mountain
the face of the bond with which all people were tied,
and the web that he began over all nations.
He shall cast death down headlong for ever.

And the Lord God shall wipe away
tears from every face,
and the reproach of his people
he shall take away from off the whole earth:
for the Lord hath spoken it.

And they shall say in that day: Lo, this is our God,
we have waited for him, and he will save us:
this is the Lord, we have patiently waited for him,
we shall rejoice and be joyful in his salvation.
                            (Isa. 25:6-9)

No one will be excluded from the benefit of redemption,
and all will find happiness in coming at last to "Him who Is":

Assemble yourselves, and come, and draw near together,
ye that are saved of the Gentiles. . . .

There is no God else besides me,
a just God and a saviour, there is none besides me.
Be converted to me, and you shall be saved,
all ye ends of the earth:
for I am God, and there is no other.
                            (Isa. 45:20-2)

Let Israel rejoice at being increased to include all the earth.

Give praise, O thou barren, that bearest not:
sing forth praise, and make a joyful noise, thou that
                            didst not travail with child:

for many are the children of the desolate,
more than of her that hath a husband, saith the Lord.

Enlarge the place of thy tent,
        and stretch out the skins of thy tabernacles
                            [thy dwellings];
        spare not: lengthen thy cords, and strengthen
                            thy stakes.
For thou shalt pass on [spread abroad] to the right hand,
                            and to the left....

Lift up thy eyes round about, and see:
All these are gathered together, they are come to thee...
        showing forth praise to the Lord.
                            (Isa. 54: 1-3; 60:4, 6)

Zacharias, one of the last of the prophets, also declared to
Israel that it was to be the apostle and especially the witness
of this conversion of the world to monotheism:

Thus saith the Lord of hosts: In those days, wherein ten
men of all languages of the Gentiles shall take hold, and
shall hold fast the skirt of one that is a Jew, saying: We
will go with you, for we have heard that God is with you
(Zach. 8:23).

"God with us," or Emmanuel, is the "Servant of Yahweh"
whose mission is thus defined:

It is a small thing that thou shouldst be my Servant
        to raise up the tribes of Jacob,
        and to convert the dregs of Israel:
Behold I have given thee to be the light of the Gentiles,
        that thou mayest be my salvation
        even to the farthest part of the earth.
                            (Isa. 49:6)

Jesus carried out this mission by founding the universal Church, which is bound no longer by limitations of time or of space, for he has promised to be present to help her "even to the consummation of the world" and that "the gates of hell shall not prevail against" her.

CHAPTER 8

The Future Life

WHAT BOSSUET wrote nearly three centuries ago remains true: "Although the Jews possessed in their Scriptures certain promises of eternal happiness, and at about the time of the Messias used frequently to speak of it, . . . this truth was so far from being a formal and universal belief of the people of God under the old Law that the Sadducees, who did not hold it, were not only allowed in the synagogue but were even raised to the priesthood. . . . One of the characteristics of the new people is that their religion is founded on belief in the future life, and this was the consequence of the coming of the Messias" (*Discours sur l'histoire universelle*, 2nd part, 19).

THE SOUL AFTER DEATH: SHEOL

According to Genesis, death is the punishment of sin. When our first parent broke the divine commandment, God said to him:

"Because you have listened to your wife, and have eaten of the tree of which I commanded you not to eat:

"Cursed be the ground because of you;
    in toil shall you eat of it all the days of your life;
Thorns and thistles shall it bring forth to you,
    and you shall eat the plants of the field.

In the sweat of your brow you shall eat bread,
   till you return to the ground,
Since out of it you were taken;
   for dust you are and unto dust you shall return."
                                          (Gen. 3:17-19)

After Adam, the account of each of the patriarchs concludes with the same words, "then he died." The only exception is the account of Henoch; the Bible says that he was
better than the rest and "walked with God; and he was seen
no more because God took him" (Gen. 5:24). Henoch and
Elias are the only persons whom the Old Testament mentions
as having left this world without experiencing death.

Genesis does not tell us what becomes of the soul when the
body returns to dust. Only much later, in Ecclesiastes, do we
learn that "the dust returns into its earth, from whence it was,
and the spirit returns to God who gave it" (12:7). Mean-
while, to the upright of the patriarchal period, to die meant
"going to their fathers in peace." That was the expression
used by Yahweh himself: "You shall go to your fathers in
peace, and be buried at a good old age" (Gen. 15:15). The
place of rest where the dead were to be joined to their fathers
was thought to be situated under the earth and called Sheol
(*Hades* in the Greek of the Septuagint, *Infernum* in the Latin
of the Vulgate). It must be noted that Sheol and the tomb are
not one and the same thing. Whereas, it was believed, the
body went to the tomb, the soul went to Sheol. The destiny
of the soul was not linked with that of the body; the nature
of the tomb had no importance in relation to the destiny of the
soul.

An excellent proof of this belief of the patriarchs is found
in the words of Jacob when he heard of the disappearance of
Joseph:

"It is my son's tunic. A wild beast has devoured him;
Joseph has been torn to pieces!" Then Jacob rent his
garments, girded himself with sackcloth and mourned his
son many days. Though all his sons and daughters tried
to comfort him, he refused to be consoled, and said: "I
will go down mourning, to my son in the nether world"
[Sheol] (Gen. 37:33-5).

Jacob was well aware that Joseph had not preceded him into
the tomb, since he believed that Joseph had been devoured by
a wild beast and had not received the accustomed burial. To
him, therefore, Sheol did not mean the tomb. Sheol was a
place where the souls of the dead continued to exist, the tomb
a place where their bodies returned to dust.

Although the Law forbade necromancy in any form and
punished it by stoning (Lev. 19:31; 20:6, 27; Deut. 18:11),
the Book of Samuel shows us Saul in desperate straits going
to consult the witch of Endor:

The Philistines were gathered together, and came and
camped in Sunam: and Saul also gathered together all
Israel, and came to Gelboe. And Saul saw the army of the
Philistines, and was afraid . . . and said to his servants: Seek
me a woman that hath a divining spirit, and I will go to
her, and inquire by her. And his servants said to him:
There is a woman that hath a divining spirit at Endor.
Then he disguised himself: and put on other clothes, and
he went, and two men with him, and they came to the
woman by night, and he said to her: Divine to me by thy
divining spirit, and bring me up him whom I shall tell
thee. . . . And the woman said to him: Whom shall I
bring up to thee? And he said, Bring me up Samuel.

And when the woman saw Samuel, she cried out with a
loud voice, and said to Saul: Why hast thou deceived me?
for thou art Saul. And the king said to her: Fear not, what

hast thou seen? And the woman said to Saul: I saw gods ascending out of the earth. And he said to her: What form is he of? And she said: An old man cometh up, and he is covered with a mantle. And Saul understood that it was Samuel, and he bowed himself with his face to the ground, and adored.

And Samuel said to Saul: Why hast thou disturbed my rest, that I should be brought up? And Saul said, I am in great distress: for the Philistines fight against me, and God is departed from me, and would not hear me, neither by the hand of prophets, nor by dreams: therefore I have called thee that thou mayest show me what I shall do.

And Samuel said: Why askest thou me, seeing the Lord has departed from thee, and is gone over to thy rival: For the Lord will do to thee as he spoke by me, and he will rend thy kingdom out of thy hand, and will give it to thy neighbour David. . . . And the Lord also will deliver Israel with thee into the hands of the Philistines; and to morrow thou and thy sons shall be with me: and the Lord will also deliver the army of Israel into the hands of the Philistines. And forthwith Saul fell all along on the ground, for he was frightened with the words of Samuel, and there was no strength in him, for he had eaten no bread all that day (1 Sam. 28:4-20).

According to this account, we see that Saul, a sinner, and Samuel, a holy prophet, were to meet in Sheol. This is proof that in the eleventh century the Jews still did not know that after death every man would be rewarded according to his conduct in life.

The Psalms contain frequent allusions to Sheol. Some of them are extremely pessimistic. Psalm 87, for example, goes so far as to imagine that even the innocent who have suffered are abandoned by God after death:

For my soul is surfeited with troubles
    and my life draws near to the nether world [Sheol];
I am numbered with those who go down into the pit;
    I am a man without strength.
My couch is among the dead,
    like the slain who lie in the grave,
Whom you remember no longer
    and who are cut off from your care. . . .

Will you work wonders for the dead?
    Will the shades arise to give you thanks?
Do they declare your kindness in the grave,
    your faithfulness among those who have perished? . .
                  (Ps. 87:4-6, 11-12)

As time went on, other psalms gave expression to the assurance that the fate of the upright will not be the same as that of
the wicked:

This is the way of those whose trust is folly,
    the end of those contented with their lot:
Like sheep they are herded into the nether world [Sheol];
    death is their shepherd, and the upright rule over
                 them. . . .
But God will redeem me
    from the power of the nether world by receiving me.
                  (Ps. 48:14-16)

At least one psalm of David, if interpreted literally, would
seem to show that the royal poet believed in the resurrection
of the body:

Therefore my heart is glad and my soul rejoices,
    my body, too, abides in confidence;

Because you will not abandon my soul to the nether
world [Sheol],
nor will you suffer your faithful one to undergo
corruption.
You will show me the path to life,
fullness of joys in your presence,
the delights at your right hand forever.
(Ps. 15:9-11)

Saint Paul, like Saint Peter (Acts 2:24-32), applied this
passage to the risen Christ: "And we declare unto you that the
promise which was made to our fathers, this same God hath
fulfilled to our children, raising up Jesus, in the second psalm
also as is written: . . . 'Thou shalt not suffer thy holy one to see
corruption.' For David, when he had served in his generation,
according to the will of God, slept and was laid unto his
fathers, and saw corruption. But he whom God hath raised
from the dead, saw no corruption" (Acts 13:32-7).

RESURRECTION OF THE BODY

When the prophets speak of resurrection, they refer to that
of Israel. Isaias shows Yahweh with his mind made up to
finish with the guilty nation:

Let not the dead live, let not the giants rise again
[The dead will not live, the shades will not rise]:
therefore hast thou visited and destroyed them,
and hast destroyed all their memory.
(Isa. 26:14)

Then, on the nation's repentance, the prophet shows it
brought back to life by God's mercy:

Thy dead men shall live, my slain shall rise again:
awake, and give praise, ye that dwell in the dust:

for thy dew (O Lord) is the dew of light:
and the land of the giants thou shalt pull down into ruin
[and thou wilt let it fall on the land of the shades].

(Isa. 26: 19-20)

Ezechiel's vision of the dead bones restored to life also refers
to the resurrection of the chosen people.

The hand of the Lord was upon me, and brought me
forth in the spirit of the Lord: and set me down in the
midst of a plain that was full of bones. And he led me
about through them on every side: now they were very
many upon the face of the plain, and they were exceeding
dry. And he said to me: Son of man, dost thou think these
bones shall live? And I answered: O Lord God, thou
knowest.

And he said to me: Prophesy concerning these bones;
and say to them: Ye dry bones, hear the word of the Lord.
Thus saith the Lord God to these bones: Behold I will send
spirit into you, and you shall live. And I will lay sinews
upon you, and will cause flesh to grow over you, and will
cover you with skin: and I will give you spirit, and you
shall live, and you shall know that I am the Lord. And I
prophesied as he had commanded me: and as I prophesied
there was a noise, and behold a commotion: and the
bones came together, each one to its joint. And I saw, and
behold the sinews, and the flesh came up upon them: and
the skin was stretched out over them, but there was no
spirit in them.

And he said to me: Prophesy to the spirit, prophesy, O
son of man, and say to the spirit: Thus saith the Lord God:
Come, spirit, from the four winds, and blow upon these
slain, and let them live again. And I prophesied as he had
commanded me: and the spirit came into them, and they
lived: and they stood up upon their feet, an exceeding

great army. And he said to me: Son of man: All these
bones are the house of Israel (Ez. 37:1-11).

Although symbols of this kind do not refer to the resurrection of the body, nonetheless they disposed certain minds to
belief in this dogma, which was subsequently to be revealed.

Was this belief held by the author of the Book of Job, who
lived a century and a half later? Sometimes he causes his hero
to speak like one in despair:

My days are swifter than a weaver's shuttle;
 they come to an end without hope. . . .
As a cloud dissolves and vanishes,
 so he who goes down to the nether world [Sheol]
   shall come up no more.
    (Job 7:6, 9)

Sometimes, on the other hand, Job imagines that in the end,
like an absent-minded officer who suddenly recalls the un-
fortunate sentry whom he has left too long on duty, God will
remember him:

Oh, that you would hide me in the nether world [Sheol]
 and keep me sheltered till your wrath is past;
 would fix a time for me, and then remember me!
When a man has died, were he to live again,
 all the days of my drudgery I would wait,
 until my relief should come.
You would call, and I would answer you;
 you would esteem the work of your hands.
    (Job 14:13-15)

Job goes even further. He evolves the idea that his much
tried body will perhaps one day rise again and that he will experience happiness after this life. Was this a utopian dream? At

all events he desired that it be recorded with some solemnity
by being cut in stone:

> Oh, would that my words were written down!
>   Would that they were inscribed in a record:
> That with an iron chisel and with lead
>   they were cut in the rock forever!
> But as for me, I know that my Vindicator lives,
>   and that he will at last stand forth upon the dust,
> Whom I myself shall see, and not another—
>   and from my flesh I shall see God;
>   my inmost being is consumed with longing.
>   (Job 19:23-6)

Not until the second century is there to be found in Israel
a profession of faith in the resurrection like that related in the
second book of Machabees. We have already mentioned the
seven brothers and their mother who were victims under the
persecution of Antiochus Epiphanes:

> So when the first [of the brothers] was dead after this
> manner,[1] they brought the next to make him a mocking
> stock: and when they had pulled off the skin of his head
> with the hair, they asked him if he would eat, before he
> were punished throughout the whole body in every limb.
> But he answered in his own language, and said: I will not
> do it. Wherefore he also, in the next place, received the
> torments of the first: And when he was at last gasp, he
> said thus: Thou indeed, O most wicked man, destroyest
> us out of this present life: but the King of the world will
> raise us up, who die for his laws, in the resurrection of
> eternal life.
>   After him the third was made a mocking stock, and

[1] His tongue was torn out, his scalp drawn off, the extremities of his
hands and feet were chopped off, and he was "fried in the frying pan."

when he was required, he quickly put forth his tongue, and courageously stretched out his hands, And said with confidence: These I have from heaven, but for the laws of God I now despise them: because I hope to receive them again from him. So that the king, and they that were with him, wondered at the young man's courage, because he esteemed the torments as nothing.

And after he was thus dead, they tormented the fourth in the like manner. And when he was now ready to die, he spoke thus: It is better, being put to death by men, to look for hope from God, to be raised up again by him: for, as to thee, thou shalt have no resurrection unto life. . . .

Now the mother was to be admired above measure, and worthy to be remembered by good men, who beheld her seven sons slain in the space of one day, and bore it with a good courage, for the hope that she had in God. And she bravely exhorted every one of them in her own language, being filled with wisdom: and joining a man's heart to a woman's thoughts, she said to them: I know not how you were formed in my womb: for I neither gave you breath, nor soul, nor life, neither did I frame the limbs of every one of you. But the Creator of the world, that formed the nativity of man, and that found out the origin of all, he will restore to you again in his mercy, both breath and life, as now you despise yourselves for the sake of his laws (2 Mac. 7:7-23).

Another passage from the same book shows that the problem of sanctions after death was also resolved for a number of the Jews of this period. These knew that after death the just would be rewarded and the wicked punished. They even had the idea, for certain persons who had died, of an intermediate place between that of the rewards and that of the punishments. They believed, finally, that the prayer of the living was

useful to these deceased persons. Judas Machabee had just returned from victory over the armies of Gorgias, the governor
of Idumea:

> So Judas having gathered together his army, came into
> the city Odollam: and when the seventh day came, they
> purified themselves according to the custom, and kept the
> sabbath in the same place. And the day following Judas
> came with his company, to take away the bodies of them
> that were slain, and to bury them with their kinsmen, in
> the sepulchres of their fathers. And they found under the
> coats of the slain some of the donaries of the idols of
> Jamnia, which the law forbiddeth to the Jews: so that all
> plainly saw, that for this cause they were slain. Then they
> all blessed the just judgment of the Lord, who had
> discovered the things that were hidden. And so betak-
> ing themselves to prayers, they besought him, that the
> sin which had been committed might be forgotten.
>
> But the most valiant Judas exhorted the people to keep
> themselves from sin, forasmuch as they saw before their
> eyes what had happened, because of the sins of those that
> were slain. And making a gathering, he sent twelve thou-
> sand drachms of silver to Jerusalem for sacrifice to be
> offered for the sins of the dead, thinking well and re-
> ligiously concerning the resurrection. (For if he had not
> hoped that they that were slain should rise again, it would
> have seemed superfluous and vain to pray for the dead.)
> And because he considered that they who had fallen asleep
> with godliness, had great grace laid up for them. It is
> therefore a holy and wholesome thought to pray for the
> dead that they may be loosed from sins (2 Mac. 12:38-46).

This passage is a far cry from Sirach (Ecclesiasticus) which
fifty years earlier still held that the dead were to be left to
their fate as nothing could be done for them:

My son, shed tears for one who is dead
  with wailing and bitter lament; . . .
Weeping bitterly, mourning fully,
  pay your tribute of sorrow, as he deserves,
One or two days, to prevent gossip;
  then compose yourself after your grief,
For grief can bring on an extremity
  and heartache destroy one's health. . . .
Recall him not, for there is no hope of his return;
  it will not help him, but will do you harm.

(Sir. 38:16-21)

THE JUDGMENT

The Alexandrian author of the Book of Wisdom has far
more knowledge about the future life than is found in Sirach.
He makes no mention of the resurrection of the body, and
in this he lags behind the seven brothers and their mother. But
he calmly asserts with some emphasis that "God formed man
to be imperishable; the image of his own nature he made him"
(Wis. 2:23). If in spite of this he adds, "death entered the
world," it was "by the envy of the devil," and "they who are
in his possession experience it" (2:24). The upright can be
sure that even after death they will live with God and be
happy:

The souls of the just are in the hand of God,
  and no torment shall touch them.
They seemed, in the view of the foolish, to be dead;
  and their passing away was judged an affliction
  and their going forth from us utter destruction.
But they are in peace.
For if before men, indeed, they be punished,
  yet is their hope full of immortality;

Chastised a little, they shall be greatly blessed,
   because God tried them
   and found them worthy of himself.
                                            (Wis. 3:1-5)

The wicked, on the other hand, who hold the wise man
in contempt, "shall receive a punishment to match their
thoughts" (3:10):

   . . . the Lord laughs them to scorn.
And they shall afterward become dishonored corpses
   and unceasing mockery among the dead.
For he shall strike them down speechless and prostrate
   and rock them to their foundations;
They shall be utterly laid waste
   and shall be in grief
And their memory shall perish.
                                            (Wis. 4:18-19)

We have come a long way from the time of the Judges,
when Sheol was the place of repose for both good and wicked,
who enjoyed under the ground a vague, somnolent existence.

As a result of a judgment the lot of each individual will be
fixed for eternity. Since the time of the prophets, the Jews
had known of the "day of Yahweh," that day when God
would show his power and justice by breaking the resistance
of the peoples and causing his glory to triumph. This expression, quoted by Saint Paul (1 Thess. 5:2; 2 Thess. 2:2), is
found for the first time in Amos, who says clearly that despite
the convictions of many in Israel, it too will figure among the
nations to be judged:

   Woe to them that desire the day of the Lord:
   To what end is it for you?
   Shall not the day of the Lord be darkness, and not light:
      and obscurity and no brightness in it?
                                            (Amos 5:18-20)

Joel, on the other hand, sees the "day of Yahweh" accompanied by manifestations of cosmic upheaval:

The day of the Lord is at hand,
    and it shall come like destruction from the mighty. . . .

Blow ye the trumpet in Sion,
    sound an alarm in my holy mountain,
Let all the inhabitants of the land tremble:
    because the day of the Lord cometh, because it is
                                nigh at hand!
A day of darkness, and of gloominess,
    a day of clouds and whirlwinds: . . .

For the day of the Lord is great
    and very terrible, and who can stand it?
                                (Joel 1:15; 2:1-11)

The same prophet summons all nations to the valley of Josaphat. This is a symbolic valley, as its name indicates, since "Josaphat" means "Yahweh who judges":

Let the nations arise, and let the nations come
    up into the valley of Josaphat:
For there I will sit to judge
    all nations round about. . . .

Nations, nations, in the valley of destruction:
    for the day of the Lord is near
    in the valley of destruction.
                                (Joel 3:12-14)

Sophonias is no less gloomy:

The great day of the Lord is near,
    it is near and exceeding swift:
The voice of the day of the Lord is bitter.
The mighty man shall there meet with tribulation.

That day is a day of wrath,
  a day of tribulation and distress,
  a day of calamity and misery,
  a day of darkness and obscurity,
  a day of clouds and whirlwinds,
  a day of the trumpet and alarm
  against the fenced cities, and against the high bulwarks.
And I will distress men,
  and they shall walk like blind men,
  because they have sinned against the Lord:
  and their blood shall be poured out as earth,
  and their bodies as dung.

Neither shall their silver and their gold be able to
                              deliver them
  in the day of the wrath of the Lord:
  all the lands shall be devoured by the fire of his
                              jealousy,
  for he shall make even a speedy destruction
  of all them that dwell in the land.
                              (Soph. 1:14-18)

Zacharias locates the "valley of Josaphat" near Jerusalem and, like the other prophets, foretells that all these misfortunes are to be followed by an era of happiness. The prophets' eschatology is two-sided. Their picture is a diptych: one panel represents the terrors of the Judgment and the other the heavenly happiness of the Messianic era.

Then the Lord shall go forth, and shall fight against those nations, as when he fought in the day of battle. And his feet shall stand in that day upon the mount of Olives, which is over against Jerusalem toward the east, and the mount of Olives shall be divided in the midst thereof to the east, and to the west with a very great opening, and

half of the mountain shall be separated to the north, and
half thereof to the south. . . . And the Lord shall be king
over all the earth: in that day there shall be one Lord, and
his name shall be one.

And [Jerusalem] shall be exalted, and shall dwell in her
own place, from the gate of Benjamin even to the place of
the former gate, and even to the gate of the corners: and
from the tower of Hananeel even to the king's winepresses.
And the people shall dwell in it, and there shall be no
more an anathema: but Jerusalem shall sit secure (Zach.
14:3-11).

It is Daniel who completes the painting of the Judgment in
all its details. Its colors and features all recur in the New
Testament; the eschatological descriptions in the Gospels, the
Apocalypse, and the Epistles were to add nothing to the picture produced by the last of the prophets:

Thrones were placed, and the Ancient of days sat: his
garment was white as snow, and the hair of his head like
clean wool. . . . A swift stream of fire issued forth from
before him. . . . The judgment sat, and the books were
opened. . . . I beheld therefore in the vision of the night,
and lo, one like the Son of man came with the clouds of
heaven, and he came even to the Ancient of days. . . .
And he gave him power, and glory, and a kingdom: and
all peoples, tribes and tongues shall serve him (Dan.
7:9-14).

The "Ancient of days" is Yahweh; the "Son of man,"
Jesus. The open books are a symbol of the knowledge that the
Judge will have of each one's actions; *liber scriptus proferetur*
(the written book will be brought forth), as the *Dies irae*
puts it. Our Lord changed nothing of the highly colored
description of the cosmic upheavals to come, but added to it,

as an essential element of the judgment to be pronounced, the reasons governing the sentence. Our works, our charity to our neighbor, and the faith with which we confess him before men will dictate its nature.

According to Daniel, on this solemn occasion not only nations but all men will be judged. The judgment he describes is both general and particular. He foretells also the resurrection of the elect, in what theology was later to term their "glorious bodies." And although he introduces Michael, it is more in the capacity of a high provost supervising arrangements than of a judge with power to pronounce sentence.

> At that time shall Michael rise up, the great prince, who standeth for the children of thy people: and a time shall come such as never was from the time that nations began even until that time. And at that time shall thy people be saved, every one that shall be found written in the book. And many of those that sleep in the dust of the earth, shall awake: some unto life everlasting, and others unto reproach, to see *it* always. But they that are learned [2] shall shine as the brightness of the firmament: and they that instruct many to justice, as stars for all eternity (Dan. 12:1-3).

The use of the word "many" ("many of those that sleep") should not be misunderstood. In Scripture "many" is often synonymous with "all." The "Servant of Yahweh" is to suffer for "many" (Isa. 53:11-12). For "many" will the Son of man give his life as the price of their redemption (Matt. 20:28), and shed his blood (Mark 14:24).

When our Lord said, "If thy eye scandalize thee, pluck it out. It is better for thee with one eye to enter into the king-

---

[2] Those who know the Law of God and whose knowledge has been reflected in their lives.

dom of God, than having two eyes to be cast into the hell
of fire, where their worm dieth not, and the fire is not ex-
tinguished," he was quoting once more from Isaias, a prophet
six centuries before Daniel:

> They shall go out, and see the carcasses of the men that
> have transgressed against me: their worm shall not die, and
> their fire shall not be quenched: and they shall be a loath-
> some sight to all flesh (Isa. 66:24).

It was some centuries before belief in the immortality of the
soul and the resurrection of the body gained the acceptance
of Israel. It was not yet held by all at the time of Jesus, though
the powerful party of the Pharisees and a large proportion of
the people had adopted it. The Messias did not introduce new
tenets on these points; he confined himself to confirming, by
his divine authority, the teaching that the Jews had received
from the Old Testament.

CHAPTER 9

The Moral Law

THE TORAH

To the Law, or Torah, the Jews owed everything that they became. It gave them that cohesion, strength, and indestructibility necessary to the accomplishment of the mission imposed on them by Providence. It governed all the actions of their civil and religious life. They went so far as to say that God had made it even before creating the world.

Their writings and prayers are testimony to the love and devotion in which they hold it. The Psalms praise it continually. God made the heavens and the earth; in the heavens, nothing is more splendid than the sun; on earth, nothing is superior to the Law:

> The heavens declare the glory of God,
>   and the firmament proclaims his handiwork.
> Day pours out the word to day,
>   and night to night imparts knowledge;
> Not a word nor a discourse
>   whose voice is not heard;
> Through all the earth their voice resounds,
>   and to the ends of the world, their message.
>
> He has pitched a tent there for the sun,
>   which comes forth like the groom from his bridal
>   chamber
>   and, like a giant, joyfully runs its course.

At one end of the heavens it comes forth,
>and its course is to the other end;
>nothing escapes its heat.

The law of the Lord is perfect,
>refreshing the soul;
The decree of the Lord is trustworthy,
>giving wisdom to the simple.
The precepts of the Lord are right,
>rejoicing the heart;
The command of the Lord is clear,
>enlightening the eye;
The fear of the Lord is pure,
>enduring for ever;
The ordinances of the Lord are true,
>all of them just;
They are more precious than gold,
>than a heap of purest gold;
Sweeter also than syrup,
>or honey from the comb.

>>>>>(Ps. 18:2-11)

Psalm 118, the longest and most frequently recited psalm in the Psalter—the one in which Pascal found so many wonderful things that he always experienced renewed joy in reciting it—is devoted entirely to praise of the Law: the word, or its synonyms, recurs nearly two hundred times.

"Happy is he who keeps the Law" says the Book of Proverbs (29:18). "The prudent man trusts in the word of the Lord, and the Law is dependable for him as a divine oracle," adds Sirach (Ecclesiasticus 33:3).

The Book of Wisdom links together the following axioms:

For the first step toward discipline is a very earnest desire
>>>>for [Wisdom]
>then, care for discipline is love of her;

> Love means the keeping of her laws;
> to observe her laws is the basis for incorruptibility;
> And incorruptibility makes one close to God;
> thus the desire for Wisdom leads up to a kingdom.
> (Wis. 6:17-19)

It was out of zeal for the Law that the Pharisees had hedged it round with a multiplicity of precepts, overlaying it with what the Gospels call the "traditions." Certain requirements of the written Law were severe. Saint Peter called them "a yoke ... which neither our fathers nor we have been able to bear" (Acts 15:10). The Pharisees added to it the "oral law." The "oral law" consisted of ordinances invented by the casuists and rabbis, which in the end amounted to six hundred and thirteen. Jesus termed them "insupportable burdens" that "shut the kingdom of heaven against men" (Matt. 23:4, 13). An example of the way they originated is seen in the following passage from Deuteronomy:

> Hear, O Israel! ... You shall love the Lord, your God, with all your heart, and with all your soul, and with all your strength. Take to heart these words which I enjoin on you today. Drill them into your children. Speak of them at home and abroad, whether you are busy or at rest. Bind them at your wrist as a sign and let them be as a pendant on your forehead (Deut. 6:4-8).

The meaning of the last injunction was that these laws should never be lost sight of, that they should always be kept in mind as enduring rules of thought and behavior. Hence the rabbis ordered that they be written on strips of parchment and tied on the wrist and forehead in small boxes, or "phylacteries."

It is clear that some hundreds of the precepts of the "oral law" could be disregarded by Christians, since Jesus himself

repudiated them. At first sight it seems more difficult to recon-
cile the Church's giving up a great part of the written Law
in face of Christ's statement: "One jot or one tittle shall not
pass from the Law" (Matt. 5:18; Luke 16:17).

A distinction must be made between the various kinds of
Mosaic laws. In reality, there were three codes: a civil and
penal code, a liturgical and ritual code, a moral and religious
code.

The civil and penal code regulated the relationship between masters and slaves; the periods when fields were to lie
fallow and could be gleaned; the compensation for wounds
and blows, for stealing livestock and clothes, etc. "Instructed
in all the wisdom of the Egyptians" (Acts 7:22) and, moreover, carrying out the will of God, Moses borrowed some of
these ordinances from the Egyptian code, the Babylonian
code of Hammurabi, the Sumerian code of Lipit-Ishtar, and
the Hittite code. But, borrowed or original, they could not be
valid for all peoples and all periods. Enacted in view of particular circumstances, they were bound to be changed or to
disappear once other forms of civilization appeared. The
Christians of Rome or Antioch were not, therefore, unfaithful
to the word of God by disregarding laws made for a pastoral,
nomadic people and not for them.

The same is true of the liturgical and ritual laws regarding
circumcision, animal sacrifice, clean and unclean meat, etc.
These things belong, of course, to the religious sphere, but to
that part of it which is not unchangeable; they are part of
positive law, and in this, properly constituted authority may
be legitimately exercised.

Before the Christian era the leaders of the synagogue never
required submission to all points of the liturgical and ritual
code on the part of the Gentiles who "adhered" to Yahweh
(Isa. 56:1-7). Among them a distinction was made between

"proselytes of the door," whose only obligations were to pro-
fess belief in the one true God and to observe the Sabbath,
and "proselytes of justice," who were bound to circumcision
and other observances of the Law.

Thus when the question arose whether Christians had to be
circumcised, abstain from the flesh of certain animals, etc.,
the Apostles decided in the negative. They had the right to
do so since they had been constituted heads of the Church
by her Founder, who had instructed them and was continuing
to assist them. The Twelve, together with Saint Paul, declared
that by the will of Christ, the Master and supreme Lawgiver,
the place of circumcision, animal sacrifices, and suchlike had
been taken by baptism, the Eucharist, and the other far
superior institutions of the new Covenant.

The Acts of the Apostles tells us how Saint Peter received
Cornelius into the Christian community without imposing on
him circumcision, and how he decided to abolish the distinction between clean and unclean animals:

> There was a certain man in Caesarea, named Cornelius,
> a centurion of that which is called the Italian band; A
> religious man, and fearing God with all his house, giving
> much alms to the people, and always praying to God.
> This man saw in a vision manifestly, about the ninth hour
> of the day, an angel of God coming in unto him, and say-
> ing to him: Cornelius. And he, beholding him, being
> seized with fear, said: What is it, Lord?
>
> And he said to him: Thy prayers and thy alms are
> ascended for a memorial in the sight of God. And now
> send men to Joppe, and call hither one Simon, who is sur-
> named Peter: He lodgeth with one Simon a tanner, whose
> house is by the sea side. He will tell thee what thou must
> do. And when the angel who spoke to him was departed,
> he called two of his household servants, and a soldier who

feared the Lord, of them that were under him. To whom when he had related all, he sent them to Joppe. . . .

Then Peter, going down to the men, said: Behold, I am he whom you seek; what is the cause for which you are come? Who said: Cornelius, a centurion, a just man, and one that feareth God, and having good testimony from all the nation of the Jews, received an answer of a holy angel, to send for thee into his house, and to hear words of thee. Then bringing them in, he lodged them. And the day following he arose, and went with them: and some of the brethren from Joppe accompanied him.

And the morrow after, he entered into Caesarea. And Cornelius waited for them, having called together his kinsmen and special friends. And it came to pass, that when Peter was come in, Cornelius came to meet him, and falling at his feet adored. But Peter lifted him up, saying: Arise, I myself also am a man. And talking with him, he went in, and found many that were come together. . . .

While Peter was yet speaking these words, the Holy Ghost fell on all them that heard the word. And the faithful of the circumcision, who came with Peter, were astonished, for that the grace of the Holy Ghost was poured out upon the Gentiles also. For they heard them speaking with tongues, and magnifying God. Then Peter answered: Can any man forbid water, that these should not be baptized, who have received the Holy Ghost as well as we? And he commanded them to be baptized in the name of the Lord Jesus Christ. Then they desired him to tarry with them some days.

And the apostles and brethren, who were in Judea, heard that the Gentiles also had received the word of God. And when Peter was come up to Jerusalem, they that were of the circumcision contended with him, saying: Why didst thou go in to men uncircumcised, and didst eat with them? But Peter began and declared to them the matter in order, saying:

I was in the city of Joppe praying, and I saw in an ecstasy of mind a vision, a certain vessel descending, as it were a great sheet let down from heaven by four corners, and it came even unto me. Into which looking, I considered, and saw fourfooted creatures of the earth, and beasts, and creeping things, and fowls of the air: And I heard also a voice saying to me: Arise, Peter; kill and eat. And I said: Not so, Lord; for nothing common or unclean hath ever entered into my mouth. And the voice answered again from heaven: What God hath made clean, do not thou call common. And this was done three times: and all were taken up again into heaven. And behold, immediately there were three men come to the house wherein I was, sent to me from Caesarea. And the Spirit said to me, that I should go with them, nothing doubting. And these six brethren went with me also: and we entered into the man's house.

And he told us how he had seen an angel in his house, standing, and saying to him: Send to Joppe, and call hither Simon, who is surnamed Peter, who shall speak to thee words, whereby thou shalt be saved, and all thy house. And when I had begun to speak, the Holy Ghost fell upon them, as upon us also in the beginning. And I remembered the word of the Lord, how that he said: "John indeed baptized with water, but you shall be baptized with the Holy Ghost." If then God gave them the same grace, as to us also who have believed in the Lord Jesus Christ; who was I, that could withstand God?

Having heard these things, they held their peace, and glorified God, saying: God then hath also to the Gentiles given repentance unto life (Acts 10:1-48; 11:1-18).

In addition to the disciplinary injunctions, which were not to endure, the Law included the Decalogue, promulgated by Yahweh himself on Sinai. It is a moral and religious code that has been taken over in its entirety and become part of the Christian inheritance and the charter of all civilized peoples.

Since it was both natural and divine law, it could not undergo fundamental modification. The Church has only introduced changes of a secondary nature. They are in connection with the first and third commandments. The third commandment was in the following terms: "Remember to keep holy the Sabbath day. Six days you may labor and do all your work, but the seventh day is the Sabbath of the Lord, your God. . . ."

Why must the Jews sanctify the Sabbath? In order to commemorate the rest that Yahweh took after the six days of creation, according to Exodus (20:11); in order to show gratitude to God for having brought them out of the land of Egypt, according to Deuteronomy (5:12-15). The fact that such dissimilar reasons could be given shows clearly the mixture of fundamental and secondary elements included in this commandment. In view of this the Church could fix Sunday, instead of Saturday, as the day on which Christians must interrupt their usual activities and devote themselves to prayer. Sunday continued, of course, to recall God's creative action, but it also, and especially, commemorated Christ's resurrection, which occurred "in the end of the Sabbath, when it began to dawn towards the first day of the week" (Matt. 28:1; Mark 16:2; Luke 24:1; John 20:1).

To the first commandment, "You shall not have other gods besides me," had been added this prohibition: "You shall not carve idols for yourselves in the shape of anything in the sky above or on the earth below or in the waters beneath the earth" (Exod. 20:4-5; Deut. 5:7-9). There was a reason for this prohibition. The Jews were only too prone to adopt the gods of neighboring nations, even when they were bulls or calves, shapeless stones or sacred poles. When the danger of idol worship seemed past, as was the case some centuries after Christ's preaching, the Church allowed this part of the commandment to fall into abeyance and even condemned iconoclasts.

It was Jesus himself who increased the severity of the sixth commandment. Moses stated it in the following terms: "You shall not commit adultery"; the tenth commandment added: "You shall not covet your neighbor's wife" (Deut. 5:18, 21); in addition, the death penalty was decreed for certain unnatural acts. On the other hand, we know that polygamy was for a long time practiced in Israel and that in certain cases a husband could put away his wife. Christians were bound to hold the sanctity of the marriage union in even greater reverence since Jesus restored the primitive principle of monogamy and proclaimed the indissoluble character of marriage:

> And there came to him the Pharisees tempting him, and saying: Is it lawful for a man to put away his wife for every cause? Who answering, said to them: Have ye not read, that he who made man from the beginning, made them male and female? And he said: For this cause shall a man leave father and mother, and shall cleave to his wife, and they two shall be in one flesh. Therefore now they are not two, but one flesh. What therefore God hath joined together, let no man put asunder. They say to him: Why then did Moses command to give a bill of divorce, and to put away? He saith to them: Because Moses by reason of the hardness of your heart permitted you to put away your wives: but from the beginning it was not so. And I say to you, that whosoever shall put away his wife, except it be for fornication, and shall marry another,

committeth adultery: and he that shall marry her that is
put away, committeth adultery (Matt. 19:3-9).

THE VIRTUES: CHARITY AND JUSTICE

According to Jesus, the two great commandments of the
new Law are love of God and love of one's neighbor:

> The Pharisees, hearing that he had silenced the Saddu-
> cees, came together: And one of them, a doctor of the
> law, asked him, tempting him: Master, which is the great
> commandment in the law. Jesus said to him: "Thou shalt
> love the Lord thy God with thy whole heart, and with
> thy whole soul, and with thy whole mind." This is the
> greatest and the first commandment. And the second is
> like to this: "Thou shalt love thy neighbour as thyself."
> On these two commandments dependeth the whole law
> and the prophets (Matt. 22:34-40).

Once again, therefore, Jesus found the principles and
formulation of his own law in that of Sinai.

In connection with the first of these precepts it is often
asserted that the Law of Moses was a "law of fear," while
that of the Gospels is a "law of love." Of course, it is easier
for us to love God than it was for those before the time of
Christ, since Christ has revealed to the world with the uttermost clarity the Fatherhood of God and since he died a death
that was the supreme expression of love. Nevertheless, even
the old Law required love, and its great commandment was
"You shall love the Lord, your God, with all your heart"
(Deut. 6:5).

It is true that the Old Testament is full of threats that are
exceedingly apt to engender fear, but there are some in the
New Testament as well—eternal fire, the worm that dies not,
the merciless creditor, payment to the uttermost farthing,

and so forth. For the sinner, indeed, fear may well be the
beginning of conversion, and for every truly religious soul
"reverential fear" is in reality nothing else than the virtue of
religion. Fear and love are not mutually exclusive, since
Yahweh required both: "And now, Israel, what does the Lord,
your God, ask of you but to fear the Lord, your God, and
follow his ways exactly, to love and serve the Lord, your
God . . ." (Deut. 10:12).

In the matter of brotherly love it can be said that Jesus
broke new ground and perfected the Law. Indeed, he himself
says so:

> But I say to you, Love your enemies: do good to them
> that hate you: and pray for them that persecute and
> calumniate you: That you may be the children of your
> Father who is in heaven, who maketh his sun to rise upon
> the good, and bad, and raineth upon the just and the un-
> just. For if you love them that love you, what reward
> shall you have? do not even the publicans this? And if you
> salute your brethren only, what do you more? do not also
> the heathens this. Be you therefore perfect, as also your
> heavenly Father is perfect (Matt. 5:44-8).

The Sermon on the Mount perfects the Law of Sinai in
that it extends the love of one's neighbor to all men and for-
bids vengeance.

It must be pointed out that the phrase "you shall hate your
enemy" occurs nowhere in the Old Testament, and that
the word "hate" often means "love less," as, for example,
when it is said that Jacob "hated" Esau (Mal. 1:3) or that our
Saviour required his disciple to "hate his parents" (Luke
14:26). Nevertheless, it is true that the Jew did not regard the
"stranger" as his neighbor, and was able to "love him less"
even if he did not "hate" him.

The Jew was required to apply to his coreligionists the law

of retaliation. This law, which is found also in the Babylonian code of Hammurabi, is formulated as follows in Leviticus: "Whoever takes the life of any human being shall be put to death. . . . A life for a life! Anyone who inflicts an injury on his neighbor shall receive the same in return. Limb for limb, eye for eye, tooth for tooth! . . . I, the Lord, am your God" (Lev. 24:17-22; Exod. 21:23-5; Deut. 19:21).

Although pecuniary sanctions and compensation had already for a long time replaced this law, our Saviour entirely repudiated it and laid down the rule of love of one's enemies:

> You have heard that it hath been said, An eye for an eye, and a tooth for a tooth. But I say to you not to resist evil; but if one strike thee on thy right cheek, turn to him also the other. And if a man will contend with thee in judgment, and take away thy coat, let go thy cloak also unto him. And whosoever will force thee one mile, go with him other two. Give to him that asketh of thee, and from him that would borrow of thee turn not away (Matt. 5: 38-42).

One admirable feature of the Old Testament, and in this it forms a prelude to the New, is the way the prophets stand up in defense of the poor, preaching social justice and condemning that kind of hypocrisy which consists of making outward appearances take the place of kindness and purity of heart.

Let us see in what manner Nathan dared blame David for the injustice, combined with lust and cruelty, that he had perpetrated by his adultery:

> And the Lord sent Nathan to David: and when he was come to him, he said to him: There were two men in one city, the one rich, and the other poor. The rich man had exceeding many sheep and oxen. But the poor man had nothing at all but one little ewe lamb, which he had bought

and nourished up, and which had grown up in his house together with his children, eating of his bread, and drinking of his cup, and sleeping in his bosom: and it became unto him as a daughter. And when a certain stranger was come to the rich man, he spared to take one of his own sheep and oxen, to make a feast for that stranger, who was come to him, but took the poor man's ewe, and dressed it for the man that was come to him.

And David's anger being exceedingly kindled against that man, he said to Nathan: As the Lord liveth, the man that hath done this is a child of death. He shall restore the ewe fourfold, because he did this thing, and had no pity. And Nathan said to David: Thou art the man. Thus saith the Lord the God of Israel: I anointed thee king over Israel, and I delivered thee from the hand of Saul, and gave thee thy master's house and thy master's wives into thy bosom, and gave thee the house of Israel and Juda: and if these things be little, I shall add far greater things unto thee. Why therefore hast thou despised the word of the Lord, to do evil in my sight? Thou hast killed Urias the Hethite with the sword, and hast taken his wife to be thy wife (2 Sam. 12:1-9).

And David then heard the punishments which, as a reward for his sin, were to fall on his house.

Amos, too, foretold misfortunes for the wealthy who derive their riches from the wretchedness of the poor:

> Because you robbed the poor,
>   and took choice prey from him,
>   you shall build houses with square stone,
>   and shall not dwell in them:
>   you shall plant most delightful vineyards,
>   and shall not drink the wine of them.
>   (Amos 5:11)

Micheas warns thieves that their sacrifices will not efface their thefts:

> I will show thee, O man, what is good,
> and what the Lord requireth of thee:
> verily, to do judgment, and to love mercy,
> and to walk solicitous with thy God.
> The voice of the Lord crieth to the city. . . .
> Shall I justify wicked balances,
> and the deceitful weights of the bag?
> [Shall I acquit the man with false scales
> and a bag full of deceitful weight?]
>   (Mic. 6:8-11)

Isaias depicts Yahweh turning his face away from those who seek to put prayer in the place of virtue:

> The new moons, and the sabbaths, and other festivals
> I will not abide, your assemblies are wicked.
> My soul hateth your new moons, and your solemnities:
> they are become troublesome to me, I am weary of
> bearing them.
> And when you stretch forth your hands, I will turn away
> my eyes from you:
> and when you multiply prayer, I will not hear:
> for your hands are full of blood.
>
> Wash yourselves, be clean,
> take away the evil of your devices from my eyes,
> cease to do perversely,
> learn to do well.
>   (Isa. 1:13-17)

One of those who inherit Isaias' way of thought shows which charitable works must accompany fasts and Sabbaths in order for these to be pleasing to God.

Behold in the day of your fast your own will is found [you
                    go about your business],
    and you exact of all your debtors [and oppress all
                    your laborers].
Behold you fast for debates and strife [only to dispute and
                    quarrel]
    and strike with the fist wickedly.

Do not fast as you have done until this day,
    to make your cry to be heard on high. . . .

Is not this rather the fast that I have chosen?
    loose the bands of wickedness,
    undo the bundles that oppress [the bonds of slavery];
    let them that are broken go free,
    and break asunder every burden.

Deal thy bread to the hungry,
    and bring the needy and the harbourless into thy
                    house;
    when thou shalt see one naked, cover him,
    and despise not thy own flesh.
                                (Isa. 58:3-8)

It is clear that love of God and of one's neighbor, justice
and kindness, are virtues that it is impossible to practice without divine grace, and this is obtained only by prayer. Christ
said: "Without me you can do nothing," "With God all things
are possible," "Ask and you shall receive." This teaching of
our Lord is already foreshadowed in the Old Testament:

Why hast thou made us to err, O Lord, from thy ways;
    why hast thou hardened our heart, that we should not
                    fear thee?
Return for the sake of thy servants. . . .

Behold thou art angry, and we have sinned:
    in them we have been always, and we shall be saved.
And we are all become as one unclean,
    and all our justices as the rag of a menstruous woman;
And we have all fallen as a leaf,
    and our iniquities like the wind, have taken us away.
There is none that calleth upon thy name;
    that riseth up and taketh hold of thee:
Thou hast hid thy face from us,
    and hast crushed us in the hand of our iniquity.
And now, O Lord, thou art our Father,
    and we are clay: and thou art our maker,
    and we all are the works of thy hands.
Be not very angry, O Lord,
    and remember no longer our iniquity.

(Isa. 63: 17; 64: 5-9)

THE POOR OF YAHWEH

Astonishing as it may seem, the prophets and the Psalms preach the doctrine of "spiritual poverty" which is taught at the beginning of the Sermon on the Mount: "Blessed are the poor in spirit, for theirs is the kingdom of heaven" (Matt. 5:3; Luke 6:20).

As early as the fifth century it appeared in the Book of Sophonias, together with the expression "the remnant," beloved of the prophets. This "remnant," destined to maintain the name of Israel through all trials and disasters and thus safeguard the hope of a Messias, was seen by Sophonias as made up of a people of poor and lowly state:

In that day . . .
I will take away out of the midst of thee
    thy proud boasters,
    and thou shalt no more be lifted up
    because of [on] my holy mountain.

And I will leave in the midst of thee
  a poor and needy people:
   and they shall hope in the name of the Lord.
The remnant of Israel shall not do iniquity.
                      (Soph. 3:11-12)

What is referred to here is not material poverty, which was despised by those who saw in temporal prosperity a sign of Yahweh's protection, but spiritual poverty, that state which, in contrast to pride, evinces trusting abandonment to the will and mercy of God. The poor of this kind are denoted by the word *'anawim,* a term that includes material want, failure in temporal matters, apparent desertion (on the part of Yahweh), real religious humility, suffering, and gentleness. It is the poverty of Saint Francis of Assisi, who has been called "the perfect imitator of Christ and the most Christian of saints."

The Book of Isaias makes frequent mention of the *'anawim:* "The Lord hath anointed me: he hath sent me to preach to the meek, to heal the contrite of heart [to bind up the broken-hearted]" (61:1); ["I dwell in a lofty, holy place with one who is contrite and lowly" (57:15)]:

Give praise, O ye heavens, and rejoice, O earth!
Ye mountains, give praise with jubilation:
Because the Lord hath comforted his people,
  and will have mercy on his poor ones.
                    (Isa. 49:13)

Nowhere is this exaltation of the poor man given such sublime expression as in the poems of the "Servant of Yahweh." As we have seen, it is because the Servant will have been humbled as no child of man ever was, that his victory will be so great and that he will reign forever.

The books of Jeremias and Job also teach that Yahweh reserves his reward and his salvation, not for the proud and powerful, but for the *'anawim*, the poor and the lowly who look to him for help.

Many are the psalms that show Yahweh's special concern for his poor:

When the afflicted man called out, the Lord heard,
and from all his distress he saved him. . . .
Taste and see how good the Lord is;
happy the man who takes refuge in him. . . .
The Lord is close to the brokenhearted;
and those who are crushed in spirit he saves.
(Ps. 33:7-19)

Leave it to the Lord,
and wait for him; . .
For evildoers shall be cut off,
but those who wait for the Lord [the *'anawim*]
shall possess the Land.
(Ps. 36:7-9)

Deign, O Lord, to rescue me;
O Lord, make haste to help me. . . .
But may all who seek you
exult and be glad in you,
And may those who love your salvation,
say ever, "The Lord be glorified."
Though I am afflicted and poor,
yet the Lord thinks of me.
You are my help and my deliverer;
O my God, hold not back.
(Ps. 39:14, 17-18; Cf. Ps. 69:2, 5-6)

At least some of the verses of Psalm 21 must be quoted,
since it is this psalm that our Lord recited on the Cross:

> My God, my God, why have you forsaken me,
>> far from my prayer, from the words of my cry?
> O my God, I cry out by day and you answer not;
>> by night, and there is no relief for me. . . .
>
> But I am a worm, not a man;
>> the scorn of men, despised by the people.
> All who see me scoff at me;
>> they mock me with parted lips, they wag their heads;
> "He relied on the Lord; let him deliver him
>> let him rescue him, if he loves him,". . .
>
> My throat is dried up like baked clay,
>> my tongue cleaves to my jaws;
>> to the dust of death you have brought me down. . . .
> Indeed, many dogs surround me,
>> a pack of evildoers closes in upon me;
> They have pierced my hands and my feet;
>> I can count all my bones.
> They look on and gloat over me;
>> they divide my garments among them,
>> and for my vesture they cast lots. . . .
>
> The lowly shall eat their fill;
>> they who seek the Lord shall praise him:
> "May your hearts be ever merry!"
>
>> (Ps. 21:2-27)

On the eve of our era this mystical doctrine of poverty
formed the inspiration of the groups of Essenes, which we
have already mentioned. It bursts forth afresh in our Lady's
Magnificat, and we know how it informed the whole life of
our Saviour, the gentlest, the humblest, and the most forsaken
of the poor.

CHAPTER 10

Liturgy and Prayer

PRACTICES DERIVING FROM THE TEMPLE
AND THE SYNAGOGUE

Many Christian liturgical practices are derived
from what was done in the Temple in Jerusalem or in the
synagogues.

For a long time the sanctuary of the Hebrews consisted of
the tent (*tabernaculum*) containing the Ark of the Covenant.
The latter, which traveled with them, was a kind of rectangular casket in which Moses had enclosed the tablets of the
Law. It was David who had it brought to Jerusalem, the capital
of the kingdom. Several psalms refer to this event:

[David] swore to the Lord,
    vowed to the Mighty One of Jacob:
"I will not enter the house I live in,
    nor lie on the couch where I sleep;
I will give my eyes no sleep;
    my eyelids no rest,
Till I find a place for the Lord,
    a dwelling for the Mighty One of Jacob.". . .

Advance, O Lord, to your resting place
    you and the ark of your majesty.
                    (Ps. 131:2-8)

The singers lead, the minstrels follow,
    in their midst the maidens play on timbrels.

In your choirs bless God,
>   bless the Lord, you of Israel's wellspring!
There is Benjamin, the youngest, leading them;
>   the princes of Juda in a body,
>   the princes of Zabulon, the princes of Nephthali.
>   (Ps. 67:26-8)

Lift up, O gates, your lintels;
>   reach up, you ancient portals,
>   that the king of glory may come in!
Who is this king of glory?
>   The Lord, strong and mighty,
>   The Lord, mighty in battle.
Lift up, O gates, your lintels;
>   reach up, you ancient portals,
>   that the king of glory may come in!
Who is this king of glory?
>   The Lord of hosts; he is the king of glory.
>   (Ps. 23:7-10)

After Solomon had built the Temple at Jerusalem, the Ark
of the Covenant was housed in it in the Holy of Holies. The
rites of worship were then performed in the Temple.

The principal rite was sacrifice. Its ministers were priests,
descendants of Aaron, assisted by the Levites. The sacrificial
system was more or less that of the ancient East. In particular,
it comprised the holocaust and communion. The former consisted in the destruction by fire, on the "altar of holocausts,"
of bulls, calves, rams, and birds; in this way man acknowledged that these animals did not belong to him but to God,
the sovereign Master of creation. The "sacrifice of communion" was a sacred meal at which man ate the victim; at
one and the same time the gift of divine generosity and the
symbol of man's devotion and homage, the victim was able,
as it were, to unite man to the giver of all good things. We

have seen how the prophets and psalmists insisted on the religious significance of these sacrifices, which were nothing,
they asserted, if they did not express the homage and intentions
of man's heart. For it is his heart that Yahweh requires of man:

> Not for your sacrifices do I rebuke you,
>> for your holocausts are before me always.
> I take from your house no bullock,
>> no goats out of your fold.
> For mine are all the animals of the forests,
>> beasts by the thousands on my mountains.
> I know all the birds of the air,
>> and whatever stirs in the plains, belongs to me.
> If I were hungry, I should not tell you,
>> for mine are the world and its fullness.
> Do I eat the flesh of strong bulls,
>> or is the blood of goats my drink?
> Offer to God praise as your sacrifice
>> and fulfill your vows to the Most High. . . .
>> (Ps. 49:8-14)

We know how in place of the bloody sacrifices of the old
Law was substituted the sacrifice of bread and wine under the
appearances of which lies hid the presence of the Son of God.

The use of incense, which was employed from time to
time in the offering of sacrifice and which was burned on the
altar of incense, also possessed religious significance; it was
offered only to God. The office of burning incense morning and
evening in the Holy Place was reserved to the priests, and
once a year in the Holy of Holies, to the high priest. It will be
recalled that it was while he was performing this office that
Zachary was informed of the birth of John the Baptist (Luke
1:8-22). The smoke of incense rising up to heaven was regarded as a symbol of prayer: "Let my prayer come like
incense before you," says the Psalmist, "the lifting up of my

hands, like the evening sacrifice" (Ps. 140:2). This symbolism is retained in the Apocalypse, in which the smoke of incense on the golden altar before the throne represents the prayers of the saints (5:8; 8:3-4).

The Jewish use of incense was not at once adopted in the Christian liturgy, for its use in pagan rites had left too many unhappy memories in men's minds. It was introduced only gradually. Tertullian allowed it only for its aromatic properties; it was used at first at funerals in order to purify the atmosphere. After the end of the fourth century incensing was introduced not only as a homage to the divinity according to the idea expressed in Exodus, but also, under the influence of the ceremonial of the imperial court, to honor the heads of the community and the faithful.

Our liturgical use of olive oil is also taken from the Old Testament. A lamp was to burn day and night before Yahweh in the Tabernacle:

> "You shall order the Israelites to bring you clear oil of crushed olives, to be used for the light, so that you may keep lamps burning regularly. From evening to morning Aaron and his sons shall maintain them before the Lord in the Meeting Tent, outside the veil which hangs in front of the Commandments. This shall be a perpetual ordinance for the Israelites throughout their generations" (Exod. 27:20-1).

Mixed with different perfumes, the oil became sacred chrism and was used to anoint persons and objects that were consecrated to God:

> "With this sacred anointing oil you shall anoint the Meeting Tent and the Ark of the Commandments, the table and all its appurtenances, the lampstand and its appurtenances, the altar of incense and the altar of holocausts

with all its appurtenances, and the laver with its base.
When you have consecrated them, they shall be most
sacred; whatever touches them shall be sacred. Aaron and
his sons you shall also anoint and consecrate as my priests"
(Exod. 30:26-33).

The time came when the holy chrism was used by the Jews
to anoint their kings, conferring on them in this way a sacred
character. In this, too, they were imitated by the Christians.

The service of divine praise in the Temple was assured by a
special category of Levites, the singers, whom David had
organized in twenty-four groups. Their group leaders—Asaph,
Heman, Idithun, and Core—are often mentioned in the Psalter.
The Psalter, composed of the psalms that we still sing, was
used as the chant book at the Temple ceremonies. The singing was accompanied by an imposing array of musical instruments. Certain psalms were concluded with the double acclamation, *Amen, Amen* ("So be it"); others began or finished
with *Alleluia* ("Praise the Lord").

In the course of centuries verses inspired by circumstances
were added to several psalms. Thus to David's *Miserere* a
captive in Babylon added the two verses that have since
formed its conclusion:

> Be bountiful, O Lord, to Sion in your kindness
> 　　by rebuilding the walls of Jerusalem;
> Then shall you be pleased with due sacrifices,
> 　　burnt offerings and holocausts;
> 　　then shall they offer up bullocks on your altar.
> 　　　　　　　　　　　(Ps. 50:20-1)

In some cases Christians have assigned to the psalms the
same use they had in the Temple at Jerusalem. On Saturdays
we still sing Psalm 91, which the Jews sang on the Sabbath
day. Psalm 67, *Exsurgat Deus*, which the Jews sang at their

Pentecost, we sing at ours. Psalm 140, which formed the accompaniment to the evening offering of incense, when the
priest renewed the oil of the lamp before the tabernacle, is
still used by the Greeks in its entirety and in the Roman
liturgy in part, in the evening office:

> O Lord, to you I call; hasten to me;
> > hearken to my voice when I call upon you.
> Let my prayer come like incense before you;
> > the lifting up of my hands, like the evening sacrifice.
>
> O Lord, set a watch before my mouth,
> > a guard at the door of my lips.
> Let not my heart incline to the evil
> > of engaging in deeds of wickedness
> With men who are evildoers.
>
> (Ps. 140: 1-4)

The five principal Jewish festivals were the Feast of Tabernacles, the Day of Atonement, the Passover, Pentecost, and
the Feast of Dedication. The last three were retained by the
Christian Church.

The Feast of Tabernacles, or Tents (Exod. 23:16; 34:22;
Lev. 23:33-43), lasted for seven days and took place at the
beginning of autumn. It commemorated the sojourn of the
Hebrews in the desert and celebrated the grape-gathering
and the end of the harvest.

The Day of Atonement occurred five days earlier. It was
the only day in the year on which the high priest went into
the Holy of Holies. On this day he offered a sacrifice of atonement for sins. The Epistle to the Hebrews (9:6-28) shows at
length in what way this sacrifice was imperfect, being merely
a foreshadowing of the sacrifice of Christ, which alone was
really efficacious and definitive.

The Jews celebrated the Passover on the fourteenth day
of the first month of their calendar (March-April) by eating

in the evening the paschal lamb, which had been ritually sacrificed. Then followed the seven days of the Azymes, during which they ate only unleavened bread. The Passover was instituted in commemoration of the exodus from Egypt. It will be recalled that the Hebrews had on that occasion marked their doors with the blood of the lamb in order to ward off the destroying angel, and that in the haste of their departure they had not waited for the bread to rise. Christians have retained this festival but endowed it with new significance. For them, the true paschal Lamb is Jesus, whose resurrection took place on the day after the Jewish Passover.

Pentecost, which fell fifty days after the Passover, was at first a feast on which were offered to God the first fruits of the new harvest; later it commemorated the great revelation on Mount Sinai. Since the Holy Spirit came down upon the Apostles on that day, the Christian community retained the feast, endowing it at the same time with a new meaning, which it has since kept.

The Feast of Dedication was instituted in memory of the re-consecration of the Temple after its profanation by Antiochus Epiphanes. The event is described in the Book of Machabees:

> Machabeus, and they that were with him, by the protection of the Lord, recovered the temple and the city again. But he threw down the altars, which the heathen had set up in the streets, as also the temples of the idols. And having purified the temple, they made another altar: and taking fire out of the fiery stones, they offered sacrifices after two years, and set forth incense, and lamps, and the loaves of proposition. And when they had done these things, they besought the Lord, lying prostrate on the ground, that they might no more fall into such evil; but if they should at any time sin, that they might be chastised

by him more gently, and not be delivered up to barbarians and blasphemous men.

Now upon the same day that the temple had been polluted by the strangers, on the very same day it was cleansed again, to wit, on the five and twentieth day of the month of Casleu. And they kept eight days with joy, after the manner of the feast of the tabernacles, remembering that not long before they had kept the feast of the tabernacles when they were in the mountains, and in dens like wild beasts. Therefore they now carried boughs, and green branches, and palms for Him that had given them good success in cleansing his place. And they ordained by a common statute, and decree, that all the nation of the Jews should keep those days every year (2 Mac. 10: 1-8).

The Feast of Dedication was celebrated on the twenty-fifth day of the ninth month (about in the middle of December). It was on this feast that Jesus declared that he was the Son of God as well as the Good Shepherd of mankind:

And it was the feast of the dedication at Jerusalem: and it was winter. And Jesus walked in the temple, in Solomon's porch. The Jews therefore came round about him, and said to him: How long dost thou hold our souls in suspense? If thou be the Christ, tell us plainly. Jesus answered them: I speak to you, and you believe not: the works that I do in the name of my Father, they give testimony of me. But you do not believe, because you are not of my sheep. My sheep hear my voice: and I know them, and they follow me. And I give them life everlasting: and they shall not perish for ever, and no man shall pluck them out of my hand. That which my Father hath given me, is greater than all: and no man can snatch them out of the hand of my Father. I and the Father are one (John 10:22-30).

The Jewish Feast of Dedication became for Christians the feast on which they keep the anniversary of the consecration of their churches.

The usages of the synagogue formed the inspiration of Christian public worship even more than the rites of the Temple. We have seen that the synagogue originated during the Babylonian exile. It continued and became widespread so that wherever there were Jews, a synagogue was to be found. At the Council of Jerusalem, Saint James asserted that "Moses of old time hath in every city them that preach him in the synagogues, where he is read every sabbath" (Acts 15:21).

Synagogue meetings took place once a week. The Scriptures were read, a homily was preached on what had been read, prayers were recited, psalms were sung, though without that marvelous orchestral accompaniment that was the glory of the Temple of Jerusalem.

To what extent did the chant used in the synagogues influence the formation of Christian liturgical chant? The Hebrew "cantillations" available are too fragmentary and too recent to provide an answer to the question. We know, however, that a system of conventional signs placed above or below the text indicated the rhythmical accents and inflexions. According to the philosopher Philo (d. A.D. 42), who was sometimes present at the synagogue services in Alexandria, the psalms were sung by choirs of men and women who sang sometimes alone and sometimes alternately with the congregation. Eusebius, writing three centuries later, quotes Philo's remarks and adds, "In what he relates we find very accurately depicted what we still observe . . . and the hymns that we are accustomed to chant." It is certain that at least in the beginning the religious chants of the Christians were in great part those used by the Jews.

It is particularly the structure of the liturgy itself which owes something to the Israel of old. As among the Jews the

day began on the previous evening, so with us all the feasts
of the Breviary and Missal begin on the eve.

Among the Jews the office of the vigil began with Psalm
94, *Venite exultemus Domino*. It is still this wonderful hymn
that forms the beginning of Matins in the Roman liturgy:

> Come, let us sing joyfully to the Lord;
>> let us acclaim the Rock of our salvation.
> Let us greet him with thanksgiving;
>> let us joyfully sing psalms to him.
> For the Lord is a great God,
>> and a great king above all gods;
> In his hands are the depths of the earth,
>> and the tops of the mountains are his.
> His is the sea, for he has made it,
>> and the dry land, which his hands have formed.
>
> Come, let us bow down in worship;
>> let us kneel before the Lord who made us.
> For he is our God,
>> and we are the people he shepherds, the flock he guides.
>
>   (Ps. 94: 1-7)

The prayers of the Temple at the third, sixth, and ninth
hours have become our Hours of Terce, Sext, and None.

The function of the "readings" in our fore-Mass, or Mass
of the Catechumens, is similar to that of the "readings" in the
Sabbath liturgy of the synagogue. In this liturgy, as in our
Missals, passages from Scripture were appointed to be read
on specific days. Our Epistle has taken the place of the ex-
tracts from the Law that used to be read. Our Gospel comes
instead of passages chosen from the Prophets. There follows,
in both liturgies, the homily or the exhortation and then
prayers concluding with the threefold acclamation of the
Sanctus. But at this point there begins in Christian liturgy an

essential part which transcends anything that took place in
the synagogue: the Eucharistic sacrifice that Christ instituted
for the glory of God and the food of our souls.

As with the Mass, the sacraments of the New Law constitute an entirely new phenomenon, and there can be no comparison between them and the rites that were celebrated under
the Old Law. There is only a remote similarity, for example,
between baptism and circumcision. The latter indicated the
admission of him who was circumcised into the Jewish community, just as baptism indicates the entrance of him who is
baptized into the Christian community. But circumcision did
not bestow divine grace on its recipient, it did not efface
original sin; whereas baptism and our other sacraments effect
in us, by the merits of Christ and the power of the Holy Spirit,
those graces of regeneration and spiritual life of which they
are the signs.

PRAYER

With the exception of the Lord's Prayer, the especial prayer
of the Christian Church is still that which Israel addressed to
Yahweh, and which is contained in the Psalter. It comprises
the four forms of praise, supplication, repentance, and the desire for God.

The Psalmist praises God as the sovereign Lord of the
whole world:

The Lord is king: let the earth rejoice;
    let the many isles be glad.
Clouds and darkness are round about him,
    justice and judgment are the foundation of his throne.
Fire goes before him
    and consumes his foes round about.
His lightnings illumine the world;
    the earth sees and trembles.

The mountains melt like wax before the Lord,
  before the Lord of all the earth.
The heavens proclaim his justice,
  and all peoples see his glory.
                              (Ps. 96: 1-6)

The power of God shines forth when he comes to the help
of his servant who is "overwhelmed in the destroying floods"
and "enmeshed by the cords of the nether world [Sheol]."

In my distress I called upon the Lord
  and cried out to my God;
From his temple he heard my voice,
  and my cry to him reached his ears.

The earth swayed and quaked;
  the foundations of the mountains trembled
  and shook when his wrath flared up.
Smoke rose from his nostrils,
  and a devouring fire from his mouth
  that kindled coals into flame.
And he inclined the heavens and came down,
  with dark clouds under his feet.
He mounted a cherub and flew,
  borne on the wings of the wind.
And he made darkness the cloak about him;
  dark, misty rain-clouds his wrap.
From the brightness of his presence
  coals were kindled to flame.
And the Lord thundered from heaven,
  The Most High gave forth his voice;
He sent forth his arrows to put them to flight,
  with frequent arrows he routed them.
Then the bed of the sea appeared,
  and the foundations of the world were laid bare,

At the rebuke of the Lord,
   at the blast of the wind of his wrath.
He reached out from on high and grasped me;
   he drew me out of the deep waters.

(Ps. 17:7-17)

Other psalms praise God for his gracious mercy and call
on the religious soul to "taste and see how good" he is:

Merciful and gracious is the Lord,
   slow to anger and abounding in kindness.
He will not always chide,
   nor does he keep his wrath forever.
Not according to our sins does he deal with us,
   nor does he requite us according to our crimes.

For as the heavens are high above the earth,
   so surpassing is his kindness toward those who fear him.
As far as the east is from the west,
   so far has he put our transgressions from us.
As a father has compassion on his children,
   so the Lord has compassion on those who fear him.

(Ps. 102:8-13)

Elsewhere God is depicted as a good shepherd and as a
host full of attentive kindness:

The Lord is my shepherd; I shall not want.
   In verdant pastures he gives me repose;
Beside restful waters he leads me;
   he refreshes my soul.
He guides me in right paths
   for his name's sake.
Even though I walk in the dark valley
   I fear no evil; for you are at my side
With your rod and your staff
   that give me courage.

You spread the table before me
    in the sight of my foes;
You anoint my head with oil;
    my cup overflows.
Only goodness and kindness follow me
    all the days of my life;
And I shall dwell in the house of the Lord
    for years to come.

                      (Ps. 22)

In reciting the *Miserere* the Christian again borrows from
the Psalmist his expression of sorrow:

Have mercy on me, O God, in your goodness;
    in the greatness of your compassion wipe out my
                      offense.
Thoroughly wash me from my guilt
    and of my sin cleanse me.

For I acknowledge my offense,
    and my sin is before me always:
"Against you only have I sinned,
    and done what is evil in your sight"—
That you may be justified in your sentence,
    vindicated when you condemn.
Indeed, in guilt was I born,
    and in sin my mother conceived me;
Behold, you are pleased with sincerity of heart,
    and in my inmost being you teach me wisdom.

Cleanse me of sin with hyssop, that I may be purified;
    wash me, and I shall be whiter than snow.
Let me hear the sounds of joy and gladness;
    the bones you have crushed shall rejoice.
Turn away your face from my sins,
    and blot out all my guilt.

A clean heart create for me, O God,
    and a steadfast spirit renew within me.
Cast me not out from your presence,
    and your holy spirit take not from me.
Give me back the joy of your salvation,
    and a willing spirit sustain in me.

(Ps. 50: 1-14)

The *Miserere* and the *De Profundis*, which we recite for our
dead and for ourselves, are the psalms most frequently heard
in our churches:

Out of the depths I cry to you, O Lord;
    Lord, hear my voice!
Let your ears be attentive
    to my voice in supplication:

If you, O Lord, mark iniquities,
    Lord, who can stand?
But with you there is forgiveness,
    that you may be revered.

I trust in the Lord;
    my soul trusts in his word.
My soul waits for the Lord
    more than sentinels wait for the dawn.

More than sentinels wait for the dawn,
    let Israel wait for the Lord,
For with the Lord is kindness
    and with him is plenteous redemption;
And he will redeem Israel
    from all their iniquities.

(Ps. 129)

In sickness and in trouble we, like the Jews, recite Psalm 30
as our prayer:

In you, O Lord, I take refuge;
    let me never be put to shame.
In your justice rescue me,
      incline your ear to me,
      make haste to deliver me! ...
Into your hands I commend my spirit;
    you will redeem me, O Lord, O faithful God. ...
Have pity on me, O Lord, for I am in distress;
      with sorrow my eye is consumed; my soul also and
                   my body.
For my life is spent with grief
    and my years with sighing;
My strength has failed through affliction,
    and my bones are consumed. ...
But my trust is in you, O Lord;
    I say, "You are my God."
In your hands is my destiny; rescue me
    from the clutches of my enemies and my persecutors.
Let your face shine upon your servant;
    save me in your kindness. ...
Blessed be the Lord whose wondrous kindness
    he has shown me in a fortified city.
Once I said in my anguish,
    "I am cut off from your sight";
Yet you heard the sound of my pleading
    when I cried out to you.
                          (Ps. 30:2-23)

Finally, to express longing for the eternal homeland and for
God, we say again, with the Levite exiled far from the Temple
who composed Psalm 41:

As the hind longs for the running waters,
>so my soul longs for you, O God.
Athirst is my soul for God, the living God.
>When shall I go and behold the face of God?
My tears are my food day and night,
>as they say to me day after day, "Where is your God?"
Those times I recall,
>now that I pour out my soul within me,
When I went with the throng
>and led them in procession to the house of God,
Amid loud cries of joy and thanksgiving,
>with the multitude keeping festival.
>>Why are you so downcast, O my soul?
>>Why do you sigh within me?
>>Hope in God! For I shall again be thanking him,
>>>in the presence of my savior and my God.
>>>>(Ps. 41:2-6)

The synagogue has bequeathed to us no prayer that was especially its own. Among those that were drawn up for use in the synagogue is the *Kaddish* [1] (sanctification):

Magnified and sanctified be his great Name in the world which he hath created according to his will. May he establish his kingdom during your life and during your days, and during the life of all the house of Israel, even speedily and at a near time, and say ye, Amen.

Let his great Name be blessed for ever and to all eternity. Blessed, praised and glorified, exalted, extolled and honoured, magnified and lauded be the Name of the Holy One, blessed be he; though he be high above all the bless-

---

[1] Quoted from *The Authorised Daily Prayer Book*, Revised Edition with Commentary by Dr. J. H. Hertz. Copyright 1942 by the Very Rev. Dr. J. H. Hertz, Chief Rabbi, London, England.

ings and hymns, praises and consolations, which are uttered in the world; and say ye, Amen.

Let the Name of the Lord be blessed from this time forth for evermore.

May there be abundant peace from heaven, and life for us and for all Israel; and say ye, Amen.

My help is from the Lord, who made heaven and earth.

He who maketh peace in his high places, may he make peace for us and for all Israel; and say ye, Amen.

Christians possess something even more glorious than this beautiful prayer—a prayer greater than any that men could compose—since the time when Jesus said:

Thus therefore shall you pray:

> Our Father who art in heaven,
>   hallowed be thy name.
> Thy kingdom come,
>   thy will be done
>   on earth, as it is in heaven.
> Give us this day our daily bread.
> And forgive us our debts,
>   as we also forgive our debtors.
> And lead us not into temptation,
>   but deliver us from evil.
>
> (Matt. 6:9-13)

Conclusion

The closest link unites the New Testament with the Old. For from Genesis to the Apocalypse it is the same Spirit that inspires the divine message, that is embodied in the pages of the Bible and gives them life. To lose sight of this spiritual unity of the Bible is a grave mistake, and hinders our understanding the Scriptures.

It is true that the New Testament throws light on the Old, but it is no less true that the Old is found again and prolonged in the New. There is no discontinuity between them. The same Revelation that begins in the Old Testament is continued, amplified, and completed in the New. One cannot be understood without the other. They are the two panels of the same picture, limned by the same hand; they are the seal and the imprint; they form the same coherent, organic, living body whose different elements mingle and complement one another.

The Old Testament can be compared to a royal avenue leading to the New, to the person and the work of the Messias. But this comparison risks obscuring the profound unity of the two parts of the divine work. The roots of the New Testament lie deep in the Old; and the Old, like the tree of Jesse, bears at its highest point the Chosen One of God, Jesus, our Saviour.

Those who read the Bible regularly will discover the truth of the words of Saint Jerome, who lived in a period as unsettled as our own and devoted his whole life to study and meditation on the Scriptures: "If there is one thing that sustains the wise man and enables him to remain serene amid the troubles and sorrows of this world, it is first and foremost a knowledge of the Scriptures. To frequent them and meditate on the truths they contain, to know and to seek nothing else, means indeed, even here below, to live in the kingdom of heaven."

OUTLINE OF THE HISTORY
OF THE COVENANT

CHRONOLOGICAL TABLE

OUTLINE OF THE HISTORY OF THE HISTORY OF THE COVENANT

Principal Features of This History	Date of Events	Books of the Bible Referring to Them	Corresponding Events in General History
God's Plan			
Creation	Date unknown	Genesis	c.3000, Egyptian pyramids
Original Sin			
I. *The Covenant Prepared*			
Abraham and the Patriarchs	c.1850–c.1150	Genesis	c.1700, Reign of Hammurabi in Babylon
The Hebrews in Egypt			
II. *The Covenant Achieved*			
Moses	The Exodus: c.1240	Exodus	c.1385, the Trojan War
		Leviticus	
		Numbers	
		Deuteronomy	
III. *The Covenant in the Life of the Chosen People*			
1. First Results			
(a) The Covenant in danger: Josue, the Judges	c.1220–c.1025	Josue	1200–1000, Doric invasion of Greece
		Judges	
(b) The Covenant accepted: Saul, David, Solomon	c.1025–931	1 and 2 Samuel	
		1 Paralipomenon	
		3 and 4 Kings	
		2 Paralipomenon	

2. Development

(a) The Covenant explained by the Prophets from Elias to Jeremias	931–587	Isaias Jeremias	
(b) The Covenant merited through tribulation: the Exile	587–538	Ezechiel "Second Isaias" (Isaias 40–65)	The Persian Empire
(c) The Covenant lived in patience: Return from Exile Persecution Awaiting the Messias	538 167	1 and 2 Machabees	5th century, the Parthenon 4th century, Alexander the Great 3rd to 1st centuries, the conquests of Rome

CHRONOLOGICAL TABLE

Biblical History · General History

Biblical History		General History	
Abraham and the patriarchal migrations	c.1850	In Chaldea: Babylonian Empire of Hammurabi	c.1700
Descent of the Hebrews into Egypt	c.1650	In Egypt: reign of the Hyksos	c.1720-1560
		Height of power of Hittites	c.1370
Moses and the Exodus	c.1240	In Egypt: Ramses II	1301-1234
		Merneptah	1234-1225
Josue and the gradual conquest of Chanaan	c.1220-1200		
Period of the Judges	c.1200-1025	In Assyria: Tiglath-pileser I	c.1100
Samuel	c.1040-?		
Saul	c.1030-1010		
David	c.1010-970		
Solomon	c.970-931	In Egypt: 22nd Dynasty	945-725
Schism	c.931		

Kingdom of Israel · Kingdom of Juda

Kingdom of Israel		Kingdom of Juda	
		Roboam	931-913
		Abiam	913-911
Jeroboam I	931-910	Asa	911-870
Nadab	910-909		
Baasa	909-886		
Ela	886-885		
Zimri	885		
Amri	885-874		

Kingdom of Israel		Kingdom of Judah		In Assyria:	
Achab	874-853	Josaphat	870-848	Shalmaneser III	858-824
Prophet Elias					
Ochozias	853-852				
Prophet Eliseus					
Joram	852-841	Joram	848-841		
		Ochozias	841		
Jehu	841-814	Athalia	841-835		
Joachaz	814-798	Joas	835-796		
Joas	798-783	Amasias	796-781		
Jeroboam II	783-743	Ozias	781-740	Tiglath-pileser III (745-727)	
Prophets Amos and Osee		*Prophet Isaias*		seizes Damascus and Galilee	
Zacharias and Shellum	743				
Manahem	743-738	Joatham	740-736		
Phaceia	738-737				
Phacee	737-732				
Osee	732-724	Achaz	736-716	Shalmaneser V	726-722
(Capture of Samaria by Sargon II in 721 and end of the king-dom of Israel)		Ezechias	716-687	Sargon II	721-705
		Prophet Micheas		Sennacherib	704-681
		Manasse	687-642		
		Amon	642-640		
		Josias	640-609	Ashurbanipal	621
		Prophets Jeremias, Sophonias, Nahum, and Habacuc		Capture of Ninive by Nabopolassar, king of Babylon	612

CHRONOLOGICAL TABLE—*Continued*

Biblical History		General History	
Kingdom of Juda			
	Joachaz	609	In Egypt: Nechao II	609-593
	Joakim	609-598		
	Joakin (Jechonias)	598	In Babylon: Nabuchodonosor (Nebuchadnezzar) II (604-562) captures Jerusalem in 587	
	Sedecias	598-587		
The Captivity in Babylon		587-538	Nabonidus, last king of Babylon	555-538
Prophet Ezechiel; the Book of Comfort			Cyrus the Persian (555-529) seizes Babylon in 539	
Cyrus authorizes the Jews to return to Palestine		538	In Persia: Cambyses	529-522
Zorobabel rebuilds the Temple		520-515		
Prophets Aggeus and Zacharias			Darius I	521-486
Dedication of the new Temple		515		
Prophets Malachias and Abdias			Xerxes I	485-465
Nehemias rebuilds the walls of Jerusalem		445-443	Artaxerxes I	465-423
Esdras in Jerusalem		458 or 428 or 398	Darius II	423-404
Prophet Joel				
			Artaxerxes II	404-358
Erection of the Samaritan temple on Mount Garizim		c.330	Alexander the Great	336-323

Judea under domination of the Ptolemies of Egypt	323-197
Judea under domination of the Seleucidae of Syria	197-142
Resistance of the Machabees	166
Jewish independence	142
The Hasmoneans: from Hircanus I to Hircanus II	134-63
Judea passes under the domination of Rome	63
Herod the Great	37-4
Herod Archelaus	4 B.C.-A.D. 6

In Egypt: Ptolemy II	285-246
In Syria: Antiochus III	223-187
Seleucus IV	187-175
Antiochus IV	175-163
Demetrius II	145-138
Pompey invades Palestine	63
In Rome: Caesar	48-44
Augustus	27 B.C.-A.D. 14

Index

Numbers given in italics indicate pages on which places are shown on maps